Teaching the Music
of
Six Different Cultures

Revised and Updated

Teaching the Music
of
Six Different Cultures

Revised and Updated

Luvenia A. George

World Music Press
Multicultural Materials for Educators
Danbury, CT

Lovingly dedicated to my parents,
Reverend and Mrs. F.D. Johnson

First printing July, 1987   5 4 3 2 1
Printed in the United States of America by   BookCrafters

[This is a newly revised, fully updated edition of the original hardcover book *Teaching the Music of Six Different Cultures in the Modern Secondary School* published in 1976 by Parker Publishing, West Nyack, NY]

World Music Press
Multicultural Materials for Educators
PO Box 2565
Danbury, CT 06813   (203) 748-1131

Cover design and Illustration by Phyllis Tarlow

Library of Congress Cataloging-in-Publication Data
George, Luvenia A., 1930-
      Teaching the music of six different cultures.

Rev. ed. of: Teaching the music of six different cultures in the modern
              secondary school. c1976.
Bibliography: p.
Includes index.
          1. School music --Instruction and study--United States.
2.Folk music--Instruction and study--United States
I. George, Luvenia A., 1930-   . Teaching the music of six different cultures
in the modern secondary school.
II. Title.
MT3.U5G46 1987   781-7   87-16060
ISBN 0-937203-06-8 (pbk.)
ISBN 0-937203-07-6 (cassette)

PREFACE

It has been over a decade since *Teaching the Music of Six Different Cultures in the Modern Secondary School* was first written; a period of time that has seen many changes in educational philosophies and methodologies in the United States. One of the trends has been toward awareness and emphasis upon the development and utilization of materials of a multicultural and/or cross-cultural nature. The generation of teachers and students who first welcomed the musics of other cultures through this book are now able to hold wide-open the doors through which a new generation of world music lovers may enter.

The updated version of this book incorporates many new materials while preserving standards of the literature which have proven to be indispensable. It is my hope the book will continue to provide exemplars, prototypes, and stimulants for musical learnings that are meaningful as well as exciting. Take these strategies, suggested materials and cultures as a starting point, and be bold in seeking and trying new resources that might increase your understanding and enjoyment of the multitude of musical expressions in the world. Be resourceful, energetic, and enjoy!

Luvenia A. George

3

131551

FOREWORD

To write a book for teachers on ways of introducing students to some of the minority groups among American citizens—black, Indian, Jewish, and the many cultures represented in Hawaii—is a unique idea successfully achieved by Luvenia George. There are, of course, numerous other comparable groups perhaps for later consideration, enclaves of people who preserve some of the traditions, including music, of their countries of origin: Japan, China, Korea, Greece, Armenia, Russia, and others. Perhaps the most important common factor among all these diverse peoples is the tenacity with which they maintain their cultural identity, musically and otherwise, while at the same time assimilating modes of life and means of artistic expression considered as American as apple pie, a process called acculturation.

As a teacher, I know that one can truly communicate and make a class catch fire only for a subject in which one is oneself immersed. Mrs. George has skillfully arranged this book so that each chapter is an independent entity. The best way for a teacher to use it, in my opinion, is to choose one of these cultures and learn all he or she can about it, using the author's excellent research material and everything else he can lay hands on. All of these cultures are in the news and the public consciousness today. Information about them is available to anyone with an alert and inquiring mind. Just as I opt for presenting music *in its cultural setting* to children who are experiencing it for the first time, so as a teacher I would explore the country first, its history and mores, and then find how the music fits in, is used and constructed. The nearer one is to a big city, the more fortunate for this kind of research; in metropolitan centers concerts of music and dance, art exhibits, lectures, courses in social anthropology and music of non-Western cultures abound, as do groups of people of varying cultures who will come forward when the warmth of invitation is evident. But with public libraries, television, radio, and films, there are oases everywhere.

If Africa, the source of black American music, is my choice, I might begin by comparing a current map of that vast continent with one made fifteen years ago. Today there are very few holdouts of colonialism left. In the past few years Northern Rhodesia, the Congo, Tanganyika, and Zanzibar have disappeared to reemerge as Zambia, Zaire, Congo Brazzaville, and Tanzania. Looking over the map, one must realize that there are vast cultural differences in these many countries. "Africa" is too big a word. There is a particular difference between the Muslim-influenced northern region and the sub-Saharan countries, but each country has its own indentity just as do, say, Louisiana and Massachusetts.

The music of black Americans—blues, soul, spirituals, gospel music, ragtime, and jazz in its various manifestations—is particularly enjoyable to the young, though of course it has deep meaning for people of all ages. Let them tell *us* why it is so meaningful and pleasurable to them. We can point out some technicalities (define a "blue note," explain some kinships with sub-Saharan music), but mostly we can listen to the records and enthusiasm they bring in and *learn*. Mrs. George, as her excellent chapter shows, is both young in her interests and a good listener.

If the American Indian is a teacher's choice, he should visit Indian country and festivals, perhaps especially the Southwest, where so much is available: the immense Navaho reservation, the Hopi mesas it encircles, Mesa Verde, the great pueblo at Taos, the Santa Fe museums, and, above all, the annual festival at Gallup, New Mexico, where tribal dances from all over the United States and from Mexico are performed. The sad history of the Plains Indians ending in the massacre at Wounded Knee is vividly portrayed in the film *Tahtonka,* listed by Mrs. George. Wounded Knee has again been in the news for more than a year, one evidence of the frustration of American Indians. Yet in their ceremonials, sand painting, jewelry making, and other arts, the North American natives keep alive their sense of identity and their great dignity.

The history of Jewish music is, according to Abraham Schwadron, one of "tradition and compromise." Luvenia George describes how through two millenia of persecution and wandering the ability to embrace these two rather opposed principles has helped the Jewish people to retain their beautiful ritual, religious and folk music from the time of the destruction of the Second Temple through the Diaspora, the Spanish Inquisition, Russian and other pogroms, the Nazi holocaust, mass emigration to the United States, and finally Israel, constantly on the front page of the newspapers.

The choice of our fiftieth state, Hawaii, is a happy one in that it provides opportunity for an overview of some of the cultures comprising the enormously varied population: Hawaiian and other Polynesians; Asians, particularly from Japan and the Philippines; and Caucasians. The study might begin with one of the travel films of these beautiful islands listed by the author, continue with the history of the various migrations to the islands, including the advent of the missionaries whose impact was certainly considerable, the growth of industries such as sugar and tourism, the paving of a Honolulu street with petitions for statehood, and on to the hula!

Luvenia George writes for other teachers from her years of successful experimentation in arousing children's interest in musics increasingly more in our mainstream. We are fortunate in this encouragement to share in her adventures.

Elizabeth May, PhD., Ethnomusicologist

What This Book Can Do for You:
A Tested Approach for Music Teachers

The fascinating variety of sounds in the music of other cultures offers an extremely wide spectrum of music for you to explore with your students in your classroom. The cultures chosen in this book are those of our fellow American citizens who are all around us, who are regularly in the news, who share with us the American dream but whose musical roots lie outside the mainstream of Western music. The author's own experiences have shown that this music gives all students many opportunities to make good use of their energies, imaginations, and inherent musicality. You will find that those young people with prior knowledge of music are not "one-up" on the rest of the class, and neither are they bored. The lessons are designed to avoid monotony in the classroom, provide opportunity for experimentation and discovery, and, gratefully, break the "what do we do next?" syndrome.

In this book you will find guidelines for the following:

1. Ways of getting students interested and involved in the music of another culture: using classroom instruments imaginatively for active involvement.
2. Effective strategies for getting across important concepts about a people, their culture, and their music: using recordings, films, songs, and classroom and other instruments at exactly the right time.
3. How to get started with the music of another culture: guided listening activities that pique curiosity, stimulate thought and interest, and challenge the imagination.
4. What materials you will need: where to get them and how to use them.
5. Lists of annotated resources and reference materials for teachers and students.
6. How to point up things in the music that students can use as guides to better understanding of people of a different culture: finding out why the music is important to the people and how and when they use it.
7. Ways of getting students actively involved with the sounds

of another culture: getting them to move, react, listen actively, discover what is happening in the music.

8. Tested lesson plans that guide you step-by-step to attainable goals: tells you exactly what to emphasize and listen for in the music that will deepen understanding of the music of the culture.

The chapters are not designed to be used in sequence and each one is complete in itself with its own background information, resources and lessons with plenty of suggested activities to make your classes aesthetically rewarding. In most cases not more than two divergent cultures should be studied in any one term. This not only gives students a basis for contrast, but also the opportunity to accurately learn and remember important facts. You and your students will find a wealth of material that will not only make each lesson a satisfying experience, but will whet the appetite for further study and lay the foundation for a lifetime of musical curiosity and growth.

Luvenia A. George

The author gratfeully acknowledges the advice and assistance of the following people: Dr. Elizabeth May for patiently reading the entire manuscript and offering valuable suggestions; Ruth Srago Ne whouse and Dr. Abraham Schwadron for reading the chapter on Jewish song and graciously giving insights into Jewish music and history; Dr. Louis Ballard for reading the chapter on American Indian music and offering encouragement and aid; Yona Nahenahe Chock for information and assistance regarding Hawaiian music; Francis Bebey, Cameroonian musician, for valuable perceptions about African peoples and their music; and Ernest Dyson for assistance in the area of black American music. Thanks must also go to the fine staff of the Archive of Folk Culture at the Library of Congress and the Center for Ethnic Music at Howard University for their consistent patience and aid.

Last, but by no means least, the author most gratefully and humbly acknowledges the love, patience, and cheerfulness of her family without whose constant encouragement not one word could have been written. A special thanks to my daughter Karen for the illustrations in this book, to my daughter Adrian for her helpful curiosity, and to my husband, Henry H. George, for providing the loving support that made it all possible. Finally, my profound gratitude goes to my many classroom students (both past and present) whose enthusiasm and curiosity about music inspired me to "attempt the impossible." I feel I will have succeeded if other teachers and students can share in the joys and love of some of the world's music as we have done.

Contents

CHAPTER TWO
Experiences with African Music: Six Tested Lesson Plans–40

CHAPTER THREE
Teaching Black American Music–75

CHAPTER FOUR
Understanding American Indian Music—120

Characteristics of Indian Music—120
Principal Classroom Strategies—122

CHAPTER ONE

Beginning with the Elements Common to All Music

Music has been described as a unique sound phenomenon: a search for the ecstatic. While it is no longer considered a universal language, music *is* universal to the extent that all men have seemed capable of responding to it in some manner in all cultures through the ages. To enhance aesthetic sensitivity, the music classroom should be a laboratory wherein young people discover the means by which this unique sound phenomenon, music, is created.

To respond to music is a form of aesthetic sensitivity; this response is what we seek when we teach music. Reimer (1970:114) notes that . . . "General education in music . . . consists primarily of developing the abilities of every child to have esthetic experiences of music, using strategies appropriate to the child's changing capacities for perception and reaction."* Fifteen-year-old Michael cannot read a note of music, but the day he comes to music class and sees the lead guitar, he grabs it immediately, connects it to the amplifier, turns it on and begins to play. "Who taught you?" "I taught myself," he answers not bothering to look up. His classmates listen admiringly, and the alert teacher immediately puts this talent to use: he lets the class create a composition with themselves as a performing unit and Michael an important member.

Sixteen-year-old Raymond had shown no interest whatever in General Music class activities. One day there is a drum set in the room and he asks to play. To the surprise of the class (and astonishment of the teacher) he performs with a rhythmic drive

---

*Full references to books, articles, recordings, films, and filmstrips can be found in the listings at the end of each chapter. Additional source material is in the Appendix.

that rivals some professionals. Inquiry turns up the fact that he is also self-taught.

Seventeen-year-old Sarah is a severe disciplinary problem, resenting all forms of authority. She has, however, a beautiful voice and is a soloist in her church gospel choir where she shows a remarkable talent for improvisatory singing. Sixteen-year-old Steve has an uncanny ear and plays respectable jazz piano though only on the black keys. He, too, is self-taught. The examples could go on and on, but the important fact is that these young people are typical of many: they have bypassed the educational complex and *discovered* music for themselves.

A cursory survey of every music class will turn up several boys who play guitar by ear while those who don't play usually express a desire to do so. There is also an abundance of would-be drummers, singers of all kinds, dancers, pianists and record collectors by the score. There is probably no other subject area, with the possible exception of sports in physical education, that occupies as much of the nonschool time of the adolescent as does music in some form or other.

USING THE ELEMENTS OF MUSIC TO CAPTIVATE STUDENT INTEREST

What a rich resource of energy and interest waits to be challenged! And equally important, what richly varied musical resources are at our command: the whole spectrum of recorded sound. Today's youth are very much aware of today's popular music. So we start there—where they are—and later explore with them the music of other cultures, other forms of contemporary music, as well as the best of "classical" Western music.

Thus the music of today becomes an avenue of discovery as we set up situations that lead to sound, or sonic encounters, requiring those involvements that lead to perception. Since musical sounds exist in time and space, these sounds have certain elements in common: pitch, rhythm, intensity and timbre. When organized, these elements interact and result in music.

Melody is pitch in horizontal arrangement; it moves in linear, horizontal patterns. Harmony is a vertical, simultaneous listening event. Rhythm is the movement of music; of all the musical elements it is perhaps most important in the immediate identification and recognition of musical types. Dynamics and timbre are expressive musical elements. Dynamics (intensities) have great aesthetic potential, whereas timbre gives music the color available from various sound sources. Music is also, of course, to be considered historically and socially as well as aesthetically. (See *Music Educators Journal* 59, 1973:39.)

PRINCIPAL STRATEGIES FOR
MAXIMUM STUDENT INVOLVEMENT

All of the factors mentioned can be derived from the variety of music listened to in class. Our teaching, therefore, must be somewhat eclectic, almost idiosyncratic in order to meet the basic individual needs of students. Students must be allowed to experiment, perform, and listen to increase their musical sensitivities. This does not mean lessons are helter-skelter. On the contrary, carefully planned lessons with definite, predetermined goals must be developed. Within this framework there is room for the flexibility that is needed.

The strategies for this chapter will provide ideas and stimulants for subject-object involvement, experiences and interactions with music. The possibilities are endless; the author will suggest some that have proved to be of value in her classes.

Out of nearly every experience or encounter with music, the youngsters in your own classes will always react in some manner that will lead to other experiences that will increase their understandings. To respond to the music of another culture or ethnic group, students should first be aware of and sensitive to a variety of musical sounds. Thus, we plan first of all for involvement, since students must have direct encounters with music; they learn when *they* do, not by watching the teacher or by listening passively. They must think and act as musicians by creating, conducting, performing, listening, and on occasion doing research. The activities in the following lessons are not sequentially listed and the lessons themselves need not be followed in any exact order.

Lesson One: Orienting the Listener
to What Music Really Is

Sometimes there is a wide discrepancy in the meaning of the word "music" as understood by students and "music" as meant by the teacher. Youth music has a beat that grabs and rivets the attention toward the sound. To youngsters the beat *is* the music. But there are many beats in many types of music; some are obvious and others are subtle.

Begin Lesson One by asking the class to define the word "music" and write key words from their statements on the chalkboard. Have at least two dictionaries on hand and select volunteers to read aloud definitions of "music." Place key words from these definitions on the chalkboard and compare the two lists for similarities and differences. Make no comments that infer your own preference at this time.

Classroom Strategies and Experiences

Purpose of Activities: To hear and recognize contrasting varieties of sounds as being music.

Clues for Listening

Procedure:

1. Show film: *Science of Musical Sounds.* Afterwards discuss how new musical sounds were created and other points of interest shown in the film.

2. Play examples of music such as the following, each example approximately two minutes long. Sentences in parentheses give clues on what to listen for.
   a. American Indian singing and drumming (Vocal characteristics and drumming techniques)
   b. Ground bass (Ex: Purcell, "Dido's Lament") (Ostinato pattern)
   c. Stockhausen: "Kontra-Punkte" (Use of silence)

d. Ancient Hawaiian chant (Vocal characteristics and sound of accompanying instrument)

e. African drumming and singing (Complexity of drumming; rhythms of voice and instruments)

f. Boogie-woogie (Ex: Meade Lux Lewis) (Driving rhythms)

g. Crumb: *Ancient Voices of Children* (Range and use of voice)

h. Indian *tala* drumming (Complexity of drumming)

i. Javanese gamelan music (Layers of sound)

j. Bulgarian village singing (Shifting rhythms)

k. Jewish liturgical chant (Melismatic vocal qualities)

l. Mozart: *Eine Kleine Nachtmusik* (Balance and precision)

m. Mexican *mariachi* music (Trumpets and violins sounding slightly "out of tune")

n. Chicago: "Introduction" (Rock music) (Strong rhythms)

o. Japanese *kabuki* music (Vocal mannerisms)

p. Serial music (Ex: Berg Violin Concerto) (Absense of tonal center)

q. Electronic music-synthesizer (Ex: Lucier, "North American Time Capsule") (Tone colors and use of silence)

r. Ostinato (Ex: Pachelbel, "Kanon") (Repeated pattern)

s. Jazz riff (Ex: Count Basie) (Repeated pattern)

t. Indian *sitar* music (Complexity of string sounds)

u. Stevie Wonder: "You Are the Sunshine of My Life" (Melody and rhythms)

3. Prior to playing the examples make this request of the class: "Listen carefully and say nothing while the music is playing. Write the number of any example that you like and would care to hear more of." (The teacher should call out the number of each example as it is played.)

4. Afterwards, ask: "Did all of the examples fit all of the definitions of music listed on the chalkboard?" "Is it possible to come up with a definition that would include all of the music we heard?" Give the following homework assignment: Construct a definition of music that would be appropriate for musics of all times, places, and peoples.

5. When students have identified by number the examples they liked and would like to hear more of, play portions of these as

time allows. Discuss questions such as: "What is the difference between music and noise?" "Did the musical examples we heard offer any clues to the people or cultures that produced the music?" "As you listened, did you think the various examples might have been saying something, or have been 'about' something?"

Lesson Two: Ten Ways to Explore Sound in Time

Contemporary composers believe that all sounds are legitimate properties of music. One bridge to student understanding is to explore sound and its companion, silence.

The following lessons are based on a premise stated by Paynter and Aston (1970), "If any one aspect of education today is characteristic of the whole, it is probably the change of emphasis from children being instructed to children being placed in situations where they can learn for themselves." The activities in these lessons are to encourage two important aspects of musical learning: involvement and discovery. Within this framework students are involved in situations wherein they make those personal discoveries that tend to heighten aesthetic sensitivities.

Purpose of Activities: Listening and organizing sounds to "break out of the box" of traditional use of musical elements and to introduce students to the concept of any organized sound being conceived of as a musical composition.

Procedure:

1. Show film: *Discovering Where Sound Travels*

2. Play a tape of environmental sounds such as: lawn mower, automobile starting, etc. Then play a tape of natural sounds such as: birds, dogs barking, people laughing, etc. Next, have class listen quietly for one minute and write down the sounds they hear in the room, in the halls, and outside. Ask: "Do man-made sounds overwhelm natural sounds? Why? What about one hundred years ago? How about one hundred years from now?" Encourage speculation.

3. Have students bring to class discarded articles that have interesting sound potential such as old automobile hub caps, empty oil or paint cans and their lids, leftover party noisemakers, bottles, bottle caps, old stove racks, etc. Experiment with these items to discover the range of sound possibilities for each. Keep a record of their "best" sounds and how they were achieved. Use them to supplement classroom instruments on hand as well as for composition.

4. Show pictures of instruments of the orchestra and let any orchestra members in the class demonstrate their instruments. Classify orchestral instruments horizontally such as high-pitched, medium-high, medium-low and low. Play examples of each as class identifies them accordingly. Next, classify orchestral instruments vertically as strings, brass, woodwinds and percussions and identify the instruments as they hear them.

5. Play a composition such as Stockhausen's "Zyklus." Have the class place bingo markers or small cardboard squares on desks as different sounds are heard.

6. Shake a piece of notebook paper gently and describe the sound. Ask: "What happens to the sound if the paper is shaken vigorously?"

7. Have the students tape record sounds in and near their homes. Play them for the class and let everyone identify them.

8. Listen to compositions in which composers have incorporated environmental sounds. Ask: "Are the sounds authentic? If not, how has the composer altered them?"

9. Ask: "What is the loudest sound you have ever heard? The softest? The loudest sound you can imagine? Most pleasant? Most horrible? Can you duplicate any of them with your voices or the instruments we have in the room?" (See Schafer 1970:2.)

10. Have the class create, perform and tape record a composition that uses environmental sounds.

How You Can Teach the Musical Value of Silence

1. Have the students close their eyes and observe one minute of silence. At the end of a minute, ask them to identify any sounds that interrupted the silence.

2. Compose a piece whose duration is two minutes. Decide how many seconds will be devoted to sound and how many to silence. Select the sounds to be used. Order the periods of sound and silence and determine the dynamics to use during the periods of sound. Decide whether or not the piece will be metered and set a tempo. Use a stopwatch or a watch with a second hand to time the piece and to guide the movement from one part to another. Tape the performance so that the class can review and evaluate it.

3. Listen to John Cage's "Variations II" and Stockhausen's "Kontra-Punkte." Ask: "How is silence used in these works?"

4. "Find the quietest place in your house. Is there any such thing as absolute silence? If you were in a soundproof room, what sounds would you still hear?" (Your body.) "Where is there complete silence?" (In death.)

Lesson Three: Fourteen Strategies for Teaching About Recurring Patterns, an Organizing Factor in Music

Most music has some sort of recurring patterns of sound and/or silence. If approached as a type of code, any music can be "cracked" by listening for recurrence of either rhythm, harmony, or pitch patterns. This concept is true whether or not ethnic music, folk songs, or symphonies are used as illustrations. The following activities are good for developing an understanding of organization in music.

Purpose of Activities: To recognize recurring patterns in music.

Procedure:

1. Show film: *Canon.*

2. Explain to the class that recurring patterns are an organizing

factor in music, one way in which a composer "gets his musical thoughts together." Play examples of music that include ostinato patterns such as jazz riffs, strophic songs (Ex: Schubert's "Ave Maria"), boogie-woogie, rounds, rock accompaniments, sequence forms such as the "Dies Irae" portion in Berlioz' *Symphonie Fantastique,* African bell and dance patterns and Indian talas.

3. When the class thoroughly understands that an ostinato is a repeated musical figure in the rhythm (instrumental or vocal line) the following could be done:

   a. Let the students clap the rhythm below until they know it from memory. Then play an excerpt from Herbie Hancock's "Ostinato" (*Mwandishi:* Warner Brothers 1898). The pattern clapped is the rhythm of the ostinato heard throughout the piece. Have the class clap with the record.

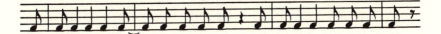

   b. Note the drone of the *gaida* (bagpipe) on the example "Ruchenitsa" *(Village Music of Bulgaria).*

   c. J.S. Bach: Passacaglia and Fugue in C Minor.

   The figure is repeated many times in the fugue; have the class make a mark on a sheet of paper each time they hear it.

   d. Duke Ellington: "Festival Junction" *(Ellington at Newport).* Ask: "How many riffs (ostinati) do you hear in this example? Which instruments are playing them?"

   e. "Pick Up Sticks" (*Time Out:* The Dave Brubeck Quartet). The bass plays an ostinato of six notes on which the entire structure of the piece is built. Let the students find the notes on the piano and resonator bells.

   f. "Chameleon" (*Headhunters* by Herbie Hancock). Let the students find the ostinato notes on piano, bells and guitar.

The rest of the class can improvise an original composition around the ostinato using classroom percussion instruments.

g. "Watermelon Man" (*Headhunters* by Herbie Hancock). Let the class analyze this composition using ABA format. Find ostinato patterns on resonator bells and piano.

h. "Kanon" by Pachelbel. Have the class sing "loo" softly with the eight-note ostinato as they beat time in quadruple meter. If a violinist or other string player is available, have him play the ostinato pattern as the class continues to sing on a neutral syllable. Ask: "How many times is the ostinato played? How does the composer add variety above the pattern?"

i. Organize the class into four or five groups, dividing classroom instruments among them. Each group is to select a leader and create a three-minute composition to be played for the rest of the class. Set a time limit of fifteen minutes in which to work and make two rules: (a) use some sort of recurring pattern; (b) make your composition as interesting as possible. (Always give guidelines for group activities, and let children work together frequently since they learn from each other.) Afterwards, tape each group performance so they may be evaluated by the performers. Play them again the next day for further comment.

j. Have the class sing rounds such as "Dona Nobis Pacem" and "3-Way Canon Blues," listening as they sing for recurring patterns.

k. Encourage the class to sing the song "Jesus Christ Superstar" on "la" and improvise vocally on the ostinato-like melody. They can move into different rhythms if they like, noting that the melody assumes a different rhythmic shape as the song progresses.

l. Play "When I Am Laid in Earth" from *Dido and Aeneas* by Purcell. Have the class count the times the ostinato passage is heard. They should be led to discover that the music reaches its climax as the pitches rise.

m. Show film: *A Bridge in Music*. Discuss the differences between Eastern and Western music as illustrated in the film.

Lesson Four: Ten Activities Involving Rhythm, the Movement of Music

Rhythm has been defined as everything pertaining to the duration of musical sound. In addition, rhythm is perhaps the most easily distinguishable of all the musical elements.

Purpose of Activities: To recognize certain varieties and divisions in rhythmic patterns.

Procedure:

1. Show film: *Music in Motion.*

2. Clap and notate simple patterns in duple, triple and quadruple meter.

3. Teach the class basic conducting patterns in the various meters as they conduct to recordings and songs.

4. Clap the rhythmic pattern of "America" from *West Side Story* with and without the recording.

5. Give the students many opportunities to identify, clap or tap the pulse (basic beat) in recorded examples of music of varied styles and periods.
   a. Pulse 2: "Superstition" by Stevie Wonder (Album: *Talking Book*).
   b. Pulse 3: "Seeking for Jesus" by Sister Rosetta Thorpe (*Sister Rosetta Thorpe* Album).
   c. Pulse 4: "I Want to Be Ready," Negro Spiritual by Tuskegee Institute Choir: *Spirituals.*

Note: Students may be asked to clap or tap a fast pulse with an example, then a slower pulse, then the slowest possible pulse. They may be asked how the rhythmic patterns in the example are grouped, whether they are grouped evenly or unevenly. The teacher should lead the students to discover that meter results when pulses are grouped in patterns and that numerous rhythmic combinations are possible within a fixed metrical design. All regular rhythms can be conceived as moving in twos, threes, or combinations of twos and threes.

6. *Unusual Meters.* Let the class hear the following examples and challenge them to find the combinations of twos and threes by using both hands in smooth, upward motions to capture the shifting meters.
   a. "Everything's All Right" from *Jesus Christ Superstar.* Pulse: 5(3 + 2)
   b. "Blue Rondo à la Turk" by Dave Brubeck (Album: *Time Out*). Pulse: 9 (2+2+2+3)
   c. "Ruchenitsa" (7/16); "Krivo" (11/16) (Album: *Village Music of Bulgaria*).

7. *Multimeters.* (Follow same procedure as suggested for Unusual Meters.)
   a. "Three to Get Ready" (*Time Out:* The Dave Brubeck Quartet). (This example is characterized by two bars in 3/4 meter alternating with two bars of 4/4 meter.)
   b. "Theodora Is Dozing" (Album: *Music of Bulgaria*). The meters could be felt as quick quick quick slow quick quick slow slow, etc.   2   2   2   3   2   2
      3   3

8. Use drums of different sizes to improvise varieties of rhythm; add other percussion instruments plus handclapping. Let volunteers from the class coordinate the improvisations.

9. Play a rock composition such as "Introduction" by Chicago Transit Authority (Album: *Chicago Transit Authority*). Have the class tap palms of hands together on unaccented beats and tap wrists together on heavy beats. Ask: "What is going on above the rhythm? Where does the rhythm change—at the beginning or end of a phrase?" Have the class listen for pitch, dynamics and timbre found in the recording.

10. Select compositions of varying meters and have students identify them as being duple meter, triple meter, or changing meter.

11. *Beginning Rhythmic Dictation.* Have students number from one through eight across a sheet of paper and rule the paper off in columns with each number heading a column. Instruct the students to place an X under numbers on which a sound is heard. (The teacher may count and tap, count and play on a melody or rhythm instrument, or tape the examples to be used.)

Example:

	1	2	3	4	5	6	7	8
1.	X		X		X	X		
2.	X			X			X	
3.		X				X		X
4.	X	X	X		X		X	
5.		X	X			X	X	

After several examples have been given, the students may perform the resulting patterns with recordings whose pulse is 2, 4, or 8. Later, notes may be substituted for the X's and rests for the blank spaces.

Lesson Five: Nine Experiments with Timbre and Texture

Timbre is tone color, the quality that distinguishes identical tones when played on different instruments or sung by different voices. Texture can be considered the "warp and woof" of a composition. Texture is the horizontal and vertical elements, the monophonic, polyphonic, and homophonic characteristics found in music. Contemporary music places a great deal of emphasis on both tone color and texture. The understanding of timbre and texture is vital to an acceptance of all types of music.

Purpose of Activities: To recognize timbre and texture as important elements in music.

Procedure:

Discovering the Effects of Timbre on a Sound Source

1. Show film: *Percussion Sounds.*

2. Give the students many opportunities to experiment with performing techniques to discover how many different timbres can be produced from a single sound source. Catalog them for reference as composition resources.

3. Experiment with dynamics to discover the effect on the timbre of a sound source.

4. Identify and describe the timbres of the sound sources in such recorded examples as the following:
   a. "Day by Day" from *Godspell* (Piano, guitar, solo voice, drums, cymbals, voices, tambourine, handclapping).
   b. "Vetar Vee" (Album: *Village Music of Bulgaria*). (Note that the song is diaphonic, or for two voices. Also note the way the voices are used to produce unusual timbres.)
   c. Olly Wilson: "Piano Piece for Piano and Electronic Sound" (Album: *Music of Black Composers*). Piano textures are changed from their normal timbre by placing such devices on the strings as a lightweight wooden ruler with a metal edge, three 3" diameter metal rings, three metal protractors approximately 3-3/4" in length, striking the keys in clusters, by plucking the strings inside the piano, etc.
   d. George Crumb: "El niño busca su voz" from *Ancient Voices of Children.* Note the use of the voice as a timbral source. Of all "instruments" the human voice is unmatched in agility and variety.

5. Select a volunteer to organize the class into a performing unit utilizing the most contrasting timbres among the musical instruments in the room. Don't let the conductor forget about the voice and body as sources of sound.

6. Have the class perform "Axis" found in *Sound, Beat, and Feeling,* page 56.

7. On the chalkboard write the following:

Sounds of Instruments				
Winds	Drums	Striking or Hitting	Strings	All Together

Play a tape you have prepared or use recordings that feature instruments of the above categories. As they listen, have the students place a mark on a sheet of paper underneath each sound category. A sample tape with each example approximately two minutes long could be similar to the following: African drums, Japanese bamboo flute *(shakuhachi)*, symphony orchestra, Hawaiian nose flute, Indian *sitar*, Javanese *gamelan*, solo jazz instrumentals, Japanese *koto*, African thumb piano *(mbira)*, rock instruments.

Underneath the categories on the board add the following:

Winds	Drums	Striking or Hitting	Strings
Aerophones	Membranophones	Idiophones	Chordophones

Explain that most musical instruments can be placed in one of the categories, and the words you have added are the names given to them by musicians who specialize in the study of world music.

Exploring Textures in Music

1. *Monophonic Texture.* Have the students sing a chant that they used as small children when jumping rope, playing hopscotch or other games, as an example of single-voice texture. Listen to examples from Gregorian chant, Arabic, Japanese, and American Indian music for single-voice texture.

2. *Polyphonic Texture.* Sing a round as an example of simple polyphonic texture. Note that the sound is based on exact repetition. Listen to recognize polyphonic texture in the following recorded examples:

    a. The Modern Jazz Quartet: "Versailles" by John Lewis (Album: *Fontessa*). In the opening section, separate melodies are stated by the piano and the vibraphone, then combined.

b. "Behold the Lamb of God," Chorus from *Messiah* by Handel. Note the entrances of the voices and interweaving of the melodies.

c. Organ Fugue in G Minor, by J.S. Bach. The subject, introduced in the soprano voice, is answered in the alto voice. The next entrance of the subject occurs in the tenor voice and is answered in the bass. Direct the students' attention to the shift of the subject from minor to major and to the conclusion of the work on a major chord. Compare an orchestral version of this fugue with the original.

3. *Homophonic Texture.* Sing a familiar song in parts. Direct the students to listen for a main melody with accompanying harmony in recorded examples such as these:

a. "Adagio for Strings" by Samuel Barber.

b. "Almighty Father" from *Mass* by Leonard Bernstein.

c. "Pilgrim's Chorus" from *Tannhauser* by Richard Wagner. (Describe the vocal and instrumental timbres in this example.)

Lesson Six: Learning About Structure in Music

Every musical composition has some sort of structure that can be thought of in terms similar to the structure of works of visual art and architecture.

Purpose of Activities: Correlating music with visual art.

Procedure:

1. Show film: *The Anatomy of an Orchestra.*

2. Show the class a slide or a picture of a famous building or painting. Look for repetition, contrast, variety, unity, and balance in the work. Direct their eyes to the horizontal, vertical, and curved lines that are evident in the overall shape of the object in question. Reduce the picture to straight and curved lines.

a. Compare and contrast the resulting diagram with comparable musical forms such as AB, ABA, rondo, etc.

b. Use the resulting diagram as a score for an original composition. Divide the class into groups of five or six students and let each group create a composition that follows the "score." Tape record each composition, play them for the class and let the performers determine how well they adhered to the "score."

Some Examples:

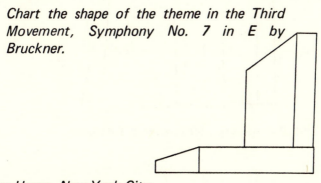

Egyptian pyramids Giza, Egypt

Jagged Lines

Chart the shape of the theme in the Third Movement, Symphony No. 7 in E by Bruckner.

Lever House, New York City

Contrast

AB (Binary) Form: Analyze the structure of "America" by Smith and Carey.

Sacred Heart Basilica (Montmarte), Paris

Repetition and Contrast

> *ABA Form: Listen to and analyze the design of the Third Movement, Symphony No. 7 in E by Bruckner. Listen to and analyze the design of "Will It Go Round in Circles" by Billy Preston from* Music Is My Life.

Shrine of the Immaculate Conception, Washington, D.C.

Unequal Balance

> *Rondo Form: Listen to and analyze "Blue Rondo à la Turk" (*Time Out: *The Dave Brubeck Quartet). Listen to and analyze the last movement of Beethoven's Sonata in C minor, Op. 13.*

ADDITIONAL IDEAS TO CONSIDER

Knieter (1971) believes that . . . "It is significant for students to learn that the desire to express feeling is natural: this is a high potential for motivating student involvement." Motivation, still the most potent term in learning, will come when we plan first for the involvement of each child in order to stimulate and nourish his aesthetic potential.

There are, of course, many ways to plan relevant experiences: around musical elements, around principles of organization surrounding these elements, or taking an extra-musical idea and relating it to music. Musical experiences can be gainfully related to the other arts. The relationship of a poem or a work of art to a musical concept can sometimes result in deeper meaning and understanding of both the work of art and the musical concept. Above all, select music worthy of use and incorporate the music of all peoples and times.

The use of contemporary and ethnic music goes well with now-oriented students. This music has an advantage because it does not require the ability to read notes to be performed or understood. This is especially true of most ethnic musics and in certain types of contemporary music. Students with note-reading ability and prior training can always be challenged to perform more difficult tasks. Art music and ethnic music co-exist; this is a fact that students accept and affords us the opportunity to use any music at our command.

Equally important is the role of the teacher who not only represents authority and maturity but becomes a resource guide to the class. This means a continual search for a diversity of knowledge as a result of the many types of music presented.

Students must function as practicing musicians who perform, conduct, compose and sometimes teach their peers. In order for students to think and act musically, the teacher must structure the environment. For example, as an introduction to serial music, give students the notes of the tone row used in Berg's Violin Concerto. Let different students hold a resonator bell for each note in the row and everyone plays his tone with as much contrast as possible from the tone that precedes his. Do this several times.

Then ask: "Would you like to hear what another composer has done with those very same notes?" and play a portion (or all) of the Berg Violin Concerto. The environment described was structured to stimulate the student's aesthetic capabilities and provided a more complete musical experience. The students were involved and as a result discovered; their perception of what serial music is was increased. Most important of all, perhaps, is the clarity of the goal, which was to teach a sensitivity to serial music.

Train young people to start musical activities and share responsibilities, in other words, to function independently and make value judgments based on knowledge and experience. Western culture has crossed the bridge to the sciences; we stand now at the threshold.of the humanities. Our students must be "turned on" to their musical potential with the music of all peoples, all styles, and all times as a bridge to understanding.

SELECTED BIBLIOGRAPHY
Books

Becoming Human Through Music. Reston, VA., Music Educators National Conference, 1985. Collection of papers by ethnomusicologists and music educators presented at the Wesleyan Symposium on the Perspectives of Social Anthropology in the Teaching and Learning of Music. Topics include how music is learned in various cultures.

Cage, John. *Silence*. Cambridge, MA.: The M.I.T. Press, 1961.

Documentary Report of the Tanglewood Symposium. Ed. by Robert Choate. Reston, VA: Music Educators National Conference, 1968. An in-depth look at music and the arts in American society and education.

Moore, Janet S.L. *Understanding Music through Exploration and Experiments*. Lanham, Md.: University Press of America, 1986. Challenging activities for the music class.

Motycka, Arthur, ed. *Music Education for Tomorrow's Society: Selected Topics*. Jamestown, R.I.: GAMT Music Press, 1976. Eight thought-provoking essays concerning music education in the next century.

Paynter, John and Peter Aston. *Sound and Silence*. Cambridge:The University Press, 1970. Describes many provocative and creative projects used in certain British schools.

Reck, David. *Music of the Whole Earth*. New York: Charles Scribner's Sons, 1977. A marvelous world view of music.

Reimer, Bennett. *A Philosophy of Music Education*. Englewood Cliffs, N.J.: Prentice-Hall, Inc., 1970.Chapters four and five are concerned with aesthetics; supplementary readings listed at ends of chapters.

Russcol, Herbert. *The Liberation of Sound*. Englewood Cliffs, N.J.: Prentice-Hall, Inc.,1972. Absorbing account of developments in contemporary music, particularly electronics.Exc.

Sawyer, David. Vibrations: *Making Unorthodox Musical Instruments*. Cambridge: Cambridge University Press, 1977.

Schafer, R. Murray. *Creative Music Education*. New York: Schirmer Books, 1976. Filled with refreshingly different approaches to music learning.

Self, George. *New Sounds in Class*. London: University Edition, 1967. 24 short percussion compositions by the author. Good introduction to contemporary notation.

Vulliamy, Grahan and Ed Lee. *Pop, Rock and Ethnic Music in School.* Cambridge: University Press, 1982. Good source of ways and means to utilize a wide variety of musics.

Articles

Artsploration Magazine. A publication of the John F. Kennedy Center for the Performing Arts through its Education Program in cooperation with the College of Fine Arts, University of Texas at Austin. A very fine arts magazine for elementary and junior high, it includes the musics of other cultures within its format.

"Comprehensive Musicianship," *Music Educators Journal* 59 (May 1973).

Regelski, Thomas A., "A Sound Approach to Sound Composition," *Music Educators Journal* 72 (May 1986).

Reimer, Bennett. "Putting Aesthetic Education to Work," *Music Educators Journal* 59 (September 1972).

AUDIO-VISUAL MATERIALS

Films

The Anatomy of An Orchestra. B & W, 52 min., Bell Telephone Co. Part of the Leonard Bernstein Concert Series.

A Bridge in Music. B & W, 20 min., McGraw-Hill. Yehudi Menuhin and Ayana Angadi illustrate differences between Eastern and Western music.

Canon. Color, 10 min., McGraw-Hill. Demonstrates how a canon is constructed using both live action and animation.

Discovering Where Sound Travels. Color, 11 min., Academy Films, 1965. Good for scientific basis of musical sound.

Music in Motion. Color, 18 min., Bell Telephone Co. "Film combines the story of visible sound in telephone research with . . . music performed by a famous orchestra and a world-renowned violinist."

New Sounds in Music. Color, 22 min., Churchill Films, 1968. Shows classical instruments altered and original instruments constructed to achieve new and different sounds. Good; holds student interest.

Percussion Sounds. Color, 16 min., Churchill Films, 1969. Children are shown using both standard and unusual instruments plus an interesting variety of sound sources. Good.

Science of Musical Sounds. Color, 11 min., 1964. Depicts basic principles of sound production.

Recordings

Bernstein, Leonard, *Mass* (2-CBS M231008). Scribner and
    Bershire Boys' Chorus.
Brubeck, Dave, *Time Out* (Columbia CS 8192). Cool jazz with
    varying and shifting meters.
Chicago Transit Authority (Columbia CP8).
Crumb, George, *Ancient Voices of Children* (Nonesuch 71255).
    Prize-winning work contains stunning musical images.
Ellington, Duke, *Ellington at Newport* (Col. PC 8648).
Ensembles for Synthesizer (Finnadar 9010). Compositions by
    Babbitt, Ussachevsky, Davidovsky and Arel.
Gilberto, Joao, Caetano Veloso and Gilberto Gil, *Brasil - Samba
    and Bossa Nova Collection* (Philips 6328382 PSI).
Godspell (Arista ALB6 - 8337).
Hancock, Herbie, *Headhunters* (Columbia CK 32731).
_____. *Mwandishi* (Warner Brothers 1898).
Jesus Christ Superstar (2-MCA 11000). The classic rock opera.
The Modern Jazz Quartet, *Fontessa* (SD 1231).
Music by Black Composers (Desto Records DC 7102-3).
Music of Bulgaria (Nonesuch H-72011). Fine singing with
    shifting meters and interesting instrumentals.
New Jazz Poets (Folkways 9751).
Best of Billy Preston (A & M SP-3205).
Sister Rosetta Thorpe (Crown Records CST 243). Outstanding
    Black gospel singer in traditional style.
Stockhausen, Karlheinz, *Zyklus, for Percussion* (Wergo 60010).
    Approximately fourteen percussion instruments of vary-
    ing types.
Switched-On Bach., Wendy Carlos, Moog (CBS MS-7194).
Treasures- Koto, Shamisen, Shakuhachi (LYR 7228).
Tuskegee Institute Choir, *Spirituals* (Westminster WST 14989).
    Authentic Black spirituals done with grace and fervor.
Village Music of Bulgaria (Nonesuch H-72034).
Wonder, Stevie, *Talking Book* (TAMLA TAM 3191). A classic;
    driving rhythms, fine melodies, poetic lyrics.
_____. *Innervisions* (TAMLA T3261).

CHAPTER TWO

Experiences with African Music:
Six Tested Lesson Plans

African music holds the possibilities of great fascination for young people because of the exciting uses of that most basic of musical elements: rhythm. The sounds and rhythmic interplay of the drums, bells, xylophones, *mbiras,* rattles, and handclaps capture interest immediately and students are usually quite eager to try their skill at duplicating them.

African music performed today can be generally divided into two broad categories: traditional and modern. Nketia (1963:5) identifies the two types of musical events in Ghana as: (1) "Those wherein the combination of music and nonmusical events is traditional, and (2) those in which such combinations are spontaneous." These types could be safely said to be indicative of most of black Africa.

Traditional music is performed at ceremonies involving royalty, cults, religions, certain festivals, and the life cycle: birth, puberty, marriage, and death. Without traditional music these events could not be sanctioned by society, since the music is an important prearranged part of the occasion. Spontaneous music is heard at any time: while grinding millet; as lullabies; on the appearance or loss of a child's first tooth; while tending cattle; in games and storytellings of both children and adults, and in other everyday occurrences.

CHARACTERISTICS OF THE MUSIC

As would be expected on the world's second largest continent with a population of around 360,000,000 people, musical styles vary from one area to another. There are distinctive characteristics from the Savannah regions down through the Virgin Forest areas on to South Africa. There are, however, many stylistic similarities in music throughout black Africa. Jones (1959:203) cites the homogeneity in African music and details many examples. The following musical characteristics are found in many areas throughout Africa:

- The functional uses of music.
- The use of polyrhythms; the recurrence of certain rhythmic patterns; the two-against-three rhythmic concept.
- Certain musical instruments and the manner in which they are constructed and played.
- Use of the gong (or bell) as a time-line: particularly widespread throughout West and Central Africa.
- Call-and-response pattern of singing: sometimes found in instrumental and instrumental/vocal performances.
- Group singing in tones usually a fourth or fifth apart. (Traditionally, Africans do not think in terms of harmony; rather, it is singing a duplication of the melody a fourth or fifth lower.)
- The "buzz" effect in the voice and in some musical instruments.
- Repetition in musical patterns both vocal and instrumental; particularly the use of short, repeated phrases.

African music must be studied in terms of its culture and the African frame of reference in order to avoid common misconceptions. Also, the music cannot be separated from its setting. Most of the transmission of African culture is in the oral tradition, typical of nonliterate societies. Music is used as an important device through which the history and mores of the people (those concepts and behaviors deemed acceptable and valuable) are handed down from one generation to another.

African music, even when performed spontaneously, is often highly organized. What may seem to be improvisation is done within a preselected structure with basic standards of performance. In some areas there are professional musicians whose livelihood comes entirely from performance, but the average member of an African society participates in musical activities to a much greater degree than is done in Western culture. In Africa the distinction between the audience and the performer is not nearly so rigid.

CLASSROOM STRATEGIES

The basic classroom strategies in the study of African music will be: (1) listening experiences that include a wide variety of musical sounds to aid in recognition of those elements and characteristics that make the music *sound* uniquely African; (2) activities that emphasize the polyrhythmic characteristics of the music; and (3) singing, dance improvisations, body use and games to further the understanding of African music within the framework of the culture. Three of the characteristics that most distinguish African music are the emphasis on polyrhythms; the sound and use of the voice, melodically and harmonically; and the use of the bell as a time-line in West and Central Africa.

Authentic songs are few in the current song series, but there are other books available from which delightful songs can be chosen. Good recordings of African music are plentiful, and where the words are given on the record jackets (found on some of the newer albums) we have another source for songs.

INSTRUMENTS YOU'LL NEED

Basic musical instruments needed will be: one set of bongos; one large conga drum; one medium-sized drum; one small drum; a double bell or two cowbells of different pitches; one pair of maracas; one pair of claves; one set of resonator bells; several pairs of rhythm sticks (or use ordinary dowels found in hardware stores, cut to twelve inches and painted bright colors). Purchase the best quality musical instruments that you can afford, have a designated place to keep them, and caution the children to use them carefully. This they will do readily; the fun is gone when the instruments are broken.

A guide to organizing the lessons will be based on recognition of the sounds of the musical instruments in the four established categories: membranophones, idiophones, aerophones, and chordophones, with emphasis on their functional usage in the context of

African culture and life. One of the delightful things about African music is that a careful selection of materials can give students quite a few things to participate in actively without too much practice. This does not necessarily designate specific pieces to be played in their entirety, but the use of different musical ideas that can be easily performed or understood by a class or group. In African culture many musical activities are performed by groups who are members of the community, *not* professional musicians. There, it is necessary for the audience to be a part of the performance.

Lesson One: Orienting the Listener to the Variety of Sounds in African Music

African musical instruments can be divided into four groups: membranophones, idiophones, chordophones, and aerophones. Membranophones are drums with heads of animal hides; idiophones are those instruments struck or shaken such as gongs, xylophones, rattles, logs, and mbiras (thumb pianos); chordophones are stringed instruments; and aerophones are wind instruments such as horns, trumpets, flutes, and oboe-type instruments. Within these classifications wide varieties of musical instruments are found, producing an astounding quantity and quality of sounds.

Purpose of Activities: Listening to recognize the wide varieties of musical instruments, vocal styles, and rhythms found in African music; performing rhythmic patterns.

Clues for Listening

Procedure:

1. Show map of Africa. (Use map throughout the study to identify origins of music examples.)

2. Show films: *Discovering the Music of Africa* and *Rhythm of Africa.*

3. Play a prepared tape (or use recordings) of African music,

selecting examples that give as much variety in sound as possible. A sample tape, each example approximately two minutes long, could be the following:

a. "Bagandou Music" (Album: *Musique Centrafricaine*). An *mbira* and a xylophone with calabash resonators have fascinating rhythmic interplay.

b. "Bronto Music" (Album: *Musique Centrafricaine*). Four small animal horns and eight large wooden trumpets sound like incredibly orchestrated automobile horns.

c. "Chant pour les Forgerons" (Album: *Niger: La Musique des Griots*). Singer accompanying himself with virtuosity on a single-stringed instrument.

d. "Musique pour la danse" (Album: *Niger: La Musique des Griots*). Excellent example of *alghaita* (an oboe-like instrument) combined with fast, precise drumming.

e. "Msitso" Movement (Album: *African Dances of the Witwatersrand Gold Mines,* Part I). Intriguing sound of fourteen xylophones playing in five different pitches.

f. "Guabi, guabi" (Album: *Guitars: 2,* by Hugh Tracey). A delightful game song accompanied by guitar.

g. "Ashanti Ntumpani" (Album: *Mustapha Tettey Addy—Master Drummer from Ghana*). Excellent example of drumming on the *atumpan,* the talking drums of Ghana.

h. "Akonodey" (Album: *Folk Music of Ghana*). Ghanaian women singing, playing instruments; male drummer punctuates to indicate changing dance steps.

i. "Royal Drums of the Emir of Zaria" (Album: *The Music of Nigeria: Hausa Music I*). Four large kettle-shaped drums emit steady, deep resonant sounds with near hypnotic effect.

j. "Elephant-Hunting Song" (Album: *Music of the Ituri Forest*). Pygmies using their unique hocket technique in singing. Very interesting.

k. "Shekere Orchestra" (Album: *Egbe Omo Nago*). A Nigerian orchestra composed entirely of two different types of rattles with soft drum pulsations in the background.

l. "Soul Makossa" by Manu Dibango (Album: *Soul Makossa*). Electric guitar, saxophone, drum set, and African drums combine to give an exciting sound of contemporary Africa, called Afro-Soul. Be prepared to play all of this one—youngsters love it!

Specific Suggestions for Activities

1. Have the students number from one through twelve on a sheet of paper. As each selection is heard, have them identify what *sounded most interesting to them:* instruments, voices, rhythms, or combinations of the three. It might be good to let them use letters, such as "I" for instruments, "V" for voices, "R" for rhythms, in order to allow more time to concentrate on the music.

2. During a second playing of the tape the class could listen to identify the instruments heard on each example, using "M," "I," "C," or "A" for membranophones, idiophones, chordophones, and aerophones.

3. Performance is a vital part of understanding African music. Begin by having students clap different meters to acquaint them with a basic concept of African music, the two-against-three rhythmic patterns. Handclapping is widely used throughout Africa as accompaniment to songs and dances, so to be able to clap precisely and rhythmically against other patterns is a skill that can be used repeatedly in performing.
   - Divide the class into two groups. Let one half clap a duple meter and the other half a triple meter. Allow this to continue until a steady, consistent, precise rhythm is obtained.
   - It is important that a "metronome-like" precision be achieved, since this is what African musicians are able to maintain. Use a metronome and set it for varying speeds to see if the class can keep in time, not getting any faster or slower.
   - Alternate to give each side of the class a chance to clap a triple and a duple rhythm.
   - Vary the patterns. Use any combinations of duple and triple meters such as 2+2+3; 3+2+2; 3+3+2; 2+3+3; etc.
   - Sing songs such as "Everybody Loves Saturday Night" (a Liberian song) using handclapping, maracas and drums for accompaniment.
   - Show film: *The Hunters.*

Lesson Two: Getting Involved with African Drumming

Ask any class: "What musical instrument do you think about

first when you think of Africa?" Invariably the answer will be: "Drums!" Among certain people on the continent drums are the most often used instruments. African drums come in a large variety of shapes and sizes. They are played in many ways, from ensembles (or drum batteries) such as the *bata* batteries of Nigeria; in pairs like Ghana's *atumpan* (*ah*-toom-pahn) talking drums, as well as played singly. Most frequently they are played in ensemble with other instruments. Some are played by hand, some with sticks, or with a combination stick-and-hand technique, while others are pressure drums such as Nigeria's *dundun*. Many West African drums can be tuned, and all are carefully constructed for a desired sonority.

Unlike many other instruments, certain types of drums are rarely owned or used by individuals for their private use, but are owned corporately and used in social dances, or belong to a chief. Some drums are, in fact, directly associated with royalty in Africa. The status of a chief determines the types of drums he may own; drums are symbols of power and authority. The *atumpan* drums of Ghana are owned by the Principal Paramount Chief, the *Ashantihene*, and are used primarily on state and other important occasions.

Many drums are beautiful works of art, typical of the African tendency to beautify musical instruments as well as other objects of common use. Nketia (1963:17) identifies three modes of drumming: signal, speech, and dance, all of which are heard at various times in many musical events connected with African life.

Classroom Strategies and Experiences:
Strategies for Performing and Listening

Purpose of Activities: Listening and performing to develop aural acuity in distinguishing sounds and techniques in traditional African drumming.

Procedure:

1. Show films: *Africa Dances* and *Atumpan.*

2. Show pictures of African drums (*Musical Instruments of Africa*, pp.25-39).

3. Recording: "Royal Drums of the Onwami of Ruanda" (Album: *Musical Instruments 3: Drums*, Side 1, Bands 6 and 7). This is an example of the royal drum tattoos, played as the chief goes from one place to another. A functional use of music, this is a type of signal drumming.

• Have the class listen closely to this excellent example of polyrhythms and see, first, if some parts of each drum's pattern can be memorized; if not, notate in some manner to aid memory.

• Have the class make a score for entry patterns of drums.

• Challenge any four students to attempt to reproduce the royal tattoos played by the four different drums, each of a different pitch. Let several groups of fours try it, with the class listening to hear which groups come closest to the recording. (They might not be able to do it exactly, but it will be quite a challenge!)

4. Recording: "Nyanza" (Album: *Music from Rwanda*, Side 1, Band 1). This battery of seven drums of the *Mwami* are royal drums played only by the hereditary nobility. The function of this music is to praise the ruler, as the words of the song are laudatory.

• Challenge the class to listen to the layers of rhythms and to analyze this recording for recognition of the polyrhythms played by the seven drums.

• Have a student come to the chalkboard and write his analysis as the record plays, while the class writes and listens with him.

• An analysis might look like this:
A   (first drum pattern heard)
A¹ (second drum pattern sounds)
A² (third drum enters, etc.)
B   (voices enter), etc.

• Listen several times to hear if any of the original patterns are repeated and, if so, indicate this.

• Challenge students to try to notate some of the rhythms, for example:

(Music notes are not necessary for notation; any symbols the class decides on will suffice.)

5. Recording: *Africa East and West*, Side 1, Selection 3. Features a drummer playing a poem on the principal talking drum of Ghana, the *atumpan*, while a voice translates it into English.
  • Listen to hear if the phrases of the poem can be recognized in the drums.

6. Recording: "Ewe Atsimivu" (Album: *Mustapha Tettey Addy-Master Drummer from Ghana*, Side 1, Band 3). This is dance music from the Ewe people of Ghana. Here the master drummer controls the dance movements. The bell pattern provides the time-line around which the organizing idea is based, which is typical of West African music.
  • Have the class clap the bell pattern and keep it going.
  • Next, ask them to keep pattern going with their hands and with right or left foot.
  • Ask feet to stomp alone.
  • Ask hands to start and bring feet in.
  • Have one student play the pattern on double bell or cowbells while the rest of the class keeps the pattern going with hands and feet. It's also a good idea to make a tape loop of the bell pattern to be used.
  • With and without the recording, have class members perform the following score:

	1	2	3	4	5	6	7	8	9	10	11	12
Bell	X		X		X	X		X		X		X
High Drum	X		X		X			X				
Medium Drum	X	X	X	X	X	X	X	X	X	X	X	X
Low Drum	X		X		X			X				♫

7. Recording: "Religious Song" (Album: *Music of the Ituri Forest*, Side 1, Band 4). Drums are used here to accompany a ritual song

characterized by short, gruntlike sounds of the chorus in response to the leader. A thunderstorm brewing in the background adds an interesting touch.

- Have the class make an analysis of this recording.

8. Recording: "Dundun Drums" (Album: *Drums of the Yoruba of Nigeria,* Side II, Band 1). A very good illustration of the talking pressure drum. The drummer speaks, then plays what he has said on the drums. Remind the class that the drums do not speak English, but reflect the tonal variations of the language used. Here, the drummer is calling out greetings as he moves through town.

- Listen closely to the spoken phrases and compare the drum sounds with the rise and fall of the vocal tones.

9. Recording: "Dundun Drums" (Album: *Drums of the Yoruba of Nigeria,* Side II, Band 2). A five-drum set of *dunduns* play singly, then in ensemble.

- Listen as each drum plays separately. Describe the sound of each one.
- When drums play together, describe the color and texture of the ensemble.

10. Recording: "Bata Drums" (Album: *Drums of the Yoruba of Nigeria,* Side II, Band 7). A three-drum set plays with rapid, interlocking patterns. The *bata* battery is used only for religious purposes.

- Analyze this recording using ABA or other method. Each drum is clearly heard and the rhythmic changes are distinct.
- Let students use three drums of different sizes and duplicate some of the rhythms.

11. Recording: "Royal Drums of the Emir of Zaria" (Album: *The Music of Nigeria: Hausa Music I,* Side I, Band 6). The drums and music heard are played only for the installation of royalty.

- Ask class to raise hands when they hear the entrances of each of the four *tambura* (kettle-shaped) drums.
- Encourage descriptions of the sound of the drums: tone color, rhythm, mood evoked, texture.

Lesson Three: Learning How Idiophones Are Used in African Music

Idiophones of all types are probably the second most important and commonly found groups of instruments used in traditional African music. Nketia (1974:70) observes: "From the musical point of view, two major categories of idiophones need to be distinguished: those used mainly as rhythm instruments, and those played independently as melodic instruments." Instruments used mainly for rhythm are rattles, single and double bells (or gongs), clappers, slit-log drums, scrapers, sticks and tubes.

The melodic idiophones are *mbiras* (frequently called thumb pianos) and xylophones. Both types of tuned instruments come in many sizes and forms and range from simple to complex in their construction. Some of the xylophones have as few as four and as many as twenty-five wooden slabs often with a gourd resonator attached to each slab. Xylophones are played singly or in large ensembles, the latter producing a fantastic interplay of rhythmic sonorities. Although the popular *mbira* is unique to the African continent, it (as well as the xylophone) is not found everywhere in Africa.

On occasion, dancers make interesting uses of idiophones. They use bells on their ankles, waists, and wrists, which add exciting rhythmic and tonal dimensions to the music of the dance. Clapping hands and stomping feet serve the same rhythmic purposes as instruments and are used in place of drums in some societies. Idiophones are used for many purposes and occasions. Some uses are purely functional such as keeping birds from eating freshly planted seeds, while other uses are ceremonial and ritualistic often in connection with dance music.

Classroom Strategies and Experiences: Dealing with Sounds That Are Struck and Shaken

Purpose of Activities: Listening and performing to distinguish some of the characteristic sounds and usages of idiophones in African music.

Procedure:

1. Show film: *Chopi Africa.*

2. Show pictures of idiophones (*Musical Instruments of Africa*, pp. 42-47).

3. Recording: "Shekere Orchestra" (Album: *Egbe Omo Nago*, Side 1, Band 3). The *shekere* rattles of Nigeria are grouped and played in families as drums are, as they come in many shapes and sizes. The music heard here is used on festival and religious occasions, with the *shekere* and *agbe* rattles combining with drums for an intriguing sound.
   - Have the class clap rattle and drum patterns for a portion of the recording to feel the polyrhythmic effect.
   - Use maracas, drums, and handclaps with and without the record until the rhythm is secure and steady.

4. Recording: "Bariba Music" (Album: *Musique Dahomeennes,* Side 2, Band 6). On this record a xylophone made of four pieces of wood is placed on the thigh of a player where it resonates as he hits it with a stone held in each hand. This music has a functional usage: to keep animals and birds away from the crops.
   - Using resonator bells, encourage students to attempt a fast, ostinato-like pattern on four black keys.
   - Challenge the class to notate the rhythms of the repeated patterns heard.

5. Recording: *African Dances of the Witwatersrand Gold Mines,* Side 1. This side contains the ultimate in xylophone virtuosity: the music of the *Ngodo* orchestral dance of the Chopi (shō-pee) people in Portuguese East Africa. Not only do we hear fourteen xylophones playing in five different pitches, we also hear the dancing feet, the songs, and the dancers'shields striking the ground. Tracey (1948:10) gives a complete and fascinating description of the *Ngodo* dance.
   - List on the chalkboard the four movements of the *Ngodo* played on the recording. (They are listed on the record jacket.)

a. *Msitso* movement: orchestral introduction.
b. *Chibudu* movement: sound of shields striking the ground can be clearly heard.
c. *Mzeno* movement: a little quieter; the words of the song are important.
d. *Ngeniso* movement: four xylophones and three drums accompany dancers.
- Have the class raise hands as the different movements begin.
- Ask: "Can you *hear* any differences in the movements?"
- Let them describe the way the music sounds to them.

6. Recording: "Congo: the Bambala" (Album: *African and Afro-American Drums*). The slit-log drum is another type of talking drum used widely throughout West Africa. Here the drum is clearly signaling.
- Ask: "What makes the drum *sound* as if it is signaling or talking?"
- "How does the sound differ from a dance accompaniment?"

7. Recording: "Chemutengure" (Album: *Mbira Music of Rhodesia*, Side 1, Band 1). The *mbira* is considered to be one of the most popular instruments in Africa. In this charming song about a wagon driver the music follows the form and structure of *nyunga nyunga* songs, an outline of which is given in the excellent notes that accompany this album.
- Place the structure of *nyunga nyunga mbira* songs on the chalkboard, as given in the album notes: preparation, beginning, basic pattern, development, etc. (There are twelve sequences to be listened for.)
- Ask the class to raise hands as they hear the various sections enter. Or, on a sheet of paper, have them write the names of the sequences as they enter. Several hearings may be needed.
- Perform the rhythmic example on page 173 of *Sound, Beat, and Feeling.*
- Assign students to create a rhythmic pattern involving the entire class; tape and evaluate the performance.

8. Recording: "Bariba Music" (Album: *Musique Dahomeennes*, Side B, Band 5). The *teke bora* sticks are heard while men are singing and dancing at a royal celebration.

- Have the class analyze the recording, listening closely for the rhythmic interplay of the instruments.
- Count the beats that elapse between the sounding of the *teke boras.*
- Use claves, sticks, and hands to clap the rhythmic pattern of the *teke boras* with and without the recording.
- Use two drums, one low and one medium-pitched, to duplicate the steady, persistent rhythms.

9. Recording: "Dance of a Witch Doctor" (Album: *Anthology of Music of Black Africa,* Music of the Baoule, Record 2, Band 6).
- Listen for the sounds of the dancer's metal ankle bells.

10. Recording: "Idina Mariana" ("Song in Praise of Iron Workers") (Album: *Niger: La Musique des Griots,* Side A, Band 7).
- Listen as four men, each striking two iron rings (one large and one small) achieve a fascinating polyrhythmic sound.

11. Recording: "Adaawe" (Women's Play Songs) (Album: *Folk Music of Ghana,* Side 1, Band 2). Women are singing in call-and-response manner.
- Listen for a good example of steady handclapping "against the beat."
- Clap along with the singers.

12. Recording: "Dance Music" (Album: *Music of the Ituri Forest,* Side 1, Band 6). Clappers, song, drum and voices combine in this pygmy music.
- Have class use sticks to reproduce the steady "machine gun" precision of the clappers.

13. Recording: "Festival Music" (Album: *Anthology of Music of Black Africa:* Music of the Malinke, Record 2, Band 1). Classes find this sound to be very interesting: three xylophone players with tinkling bells on their wrists accompanying singing women.
- Analyze using ABA or other pattern.

14. Recording: "Gong Signalling" (Album: *Music of the Ituri Forest,* Side 1, Band 7). An important announcement is being made.

• Challenge the class to listen for the recognizable signals heard in the gongs.

15. Recording: "Kpanlogo" (Album: *Talking Drums*, Side 2, Band 1). Gongs introduce this traditional Ghanaian recreational dance music.

16. Teach class a Ghanaian folk song found in *Let Your Voice Be Heard!* Add any suggested instrumental accompaniment; use the recording that accompanies the text.

Lesson Four: Finding Out About African Aerophones

Flutes, whistles, trumpets, horns and reed pipes are types of aerophones used in Africa, although not all types are found in all areas. These instruments are made from a wide variety of materials: elephant tusks, bamboo, clay, wood, and, in some places, metal tubing.

Flutes play an important melodic part in instrumental ensembles. They are played as solo instruments and in flute orchestras. Whistles can be necessary to initiation rites in certain societies played singly or (like flutes) in groups. Aerophones are often played in groups using a hocketing, or interlocking, technique.

In many parts of Africa horns and trumpets are directly associated with royalty. They are used on state and other important occasions to announce important persons and can "talk" in a tonal language. The horns and tusks of animals are commonly employed and many of them are beautifully and intricately decorated. Horns and trumpets come in many sizes from very small to extremely long and slender.

Reed instruments are not as widespread on the continent as are the other types. Reeds are found most often in those areas with Moslem, or Islamic heritages. Here again there is much variety with double- as well as single-reed instruments in use. The wind instruments serve to remind us of the importance of melody in African music. The rhythmic element is so pervasive that the melodic tends to receive less emphasis, but melody is very much an important aspect of African music.

Classroom Strategies and Experiences:
Listening for Flutes, Whistles, Horns and Trumpets

Purpose of Activities: Listening and analyzing to recognize sounds and usages of certain African aerophones.

Procedure:

1. Show film: *The Congo*

2. Show pictures of Aerophones (*Musical Instruments of Africa*, pp. 61-69).

3. Recording: "Battle Signals, War Horn" (Album: *African Music*, Side 2, Band 3). In this recording of the Nigerian Kru tribe, horns play, a native interprets the horn message, and another person translates the action into English. One can hear the agitation in both words and music as the battle nears.
   - Tell the class to listen closely to hear changes in the horn signals.
   - Ask: "Could drums have served the same function as the horns?"

4. Recording: "Dompago Music" (Album: *Musique Dahomeennes*, Side B, Band 1). This music is connected with a circumcision ceremony, an important life cycle event where music is required. Three transverse flutes and two small bells are heard.
   - Analyze: "How often are repeated patterns played?"
   - "Can you hear the polyrhythms?"
   - Clap the steady bell pattern; combine clapping with cowbells.

5. Recording: "Trumpet Fanfare for the Emir of Zaria" (Album: *The Music of Nigeria: Hausa Music I*). The Sultan's musicians praise him with a fascinating, stately sound befitting royalty. The following instruments are used: three long trumpets, *kakai*; three single-reed oboes, *algaitas*: five medium horns, *farai*; and two medium drums with snares. The royal musicians play with great virtuosity.
   - Listen to recognize the difference in sound of trumpets, reeds and horns.

6. Recording: "Broto Music" (Album: Musique Centrafricaine, Side A, Band 4). An engrossing series of sounds are produced here by an orchestra of four small animal horns and eight large wooden trumpets of varying sizes. Two pieces are played using the same

general outline: the smallest horn begins, entire orchestra sounds, and each instrument enters in succession from the highest to the lowest. A "vertical" sound effect is achieved.
- Have the class make a listening chart indicating the instruments as they enter and devising a means of approximating time elapsing between sounds.

7. Recording: "Trumpet Orchestra" (Album: *The Music of the Senufo*, Side 1, Band 7). Seven cross-blown trumpets play one or two notes each; the melody results from the instruments blowing alternately, giving a hocketing effect. (Hocketing is a fast alternation of notes or groups of notes between instruments.)
- Have the class analyze this recording: "When does the melodic pattern change?"
- "How many times do you hear repeated phrases or patterns?"
- Notate and clap the steady two-drum accompaniment.

8. Recording: "Dance of the Poro Initiates" (Album: *The Music of the Senufo*, Side 2, Band 4). This ensemble consists of one wooden whistle with three fingerholes, one xylophone, and two drums. (The Senufo people live in parts of the Ivory Coast and Mali.) Listen for the following:
- The independent melodic patterns of the whistle and xylophone as both instruments follow the rhythm of the drum.
- The ensemble begins in triple meter, but gradually quickens to duple.

9. Recording: "Duet for Flutes" (Album: *Anthology of Music of Black Africa*: Music of the Baoule, Record 2, Side B, Band 2).
- Beautiful playing by two perfectly tuned flutes.
- Challenge the class to analyze this selection.

10. Recording: "Extrait de Sara, par la Musique du Chef" (Album: *Niger: La Musique des Griots*, Side B, Band 3). "Sara" is a composition in honor of dead chiefs. The tempo is majestic and steady; the music is in call-and-response pattern. The ensemble consists of seven drums; one *algahaita* (reed instrument); two *kakaki*, long tubes made of tin that can only produce two sounds; one *kouque*, made of two metal tubes welded together and struck with an animal horn.

• Listen to identify sounds of the aerophones, the *algahaita* and *kakaki.*

11. Recording: "Bamileke-Bandjoun Music" (Album: *Musiques du Cameroun,* Side B, Band 5). Fourteen instruments are heard in this recording: two drums, three rattles, and nine whistles of varying sizes each blowing only one tone.
  • Analyze this selection indicating the following: (1) when each group of instruments enters; (2) at what points the drums change rhythm patterns; (3) the places where the large drum is heard striking in heavily punctuated accents.
  • "Describe the texture of the total composition. What mood is evoked: gaiety, sadness, etc.?" (The music is used on gala occasions.)

12. Recording: "Devitukui" (Album: *Talking Drums,* Side B, Band 4).Traditional Ewe atenteben (bamboo flute) tune.

13. Show film: *The Bend in the Niger.*

Lesson Five: Becoming Acquainted with Chordophones in African Music

There are many varieties of stringed instruments in use in Africa that range from the simplicity of the musical bow to many-stringed, complex instruments. These instruments have many different tunings, sizes, and shapes; yet even one-string fiddles can be played with virtuosity and finesse. Among the varieties are plucked instruments such as zithers, harps, and lutes, all of which have many subdivisions. Musical bows are usually struck, but there are also types that are bowed.

As is the case with other classifications of instruments, not all types of chordophones are found in the same areas. On a continent of such immense size, the diversity in cultures, histories and traditions is great. All of this has a direct bearing on the musical instruments in use. In East Africa, for example, chordophones are much more common than in West Africa and there are many areas of the continent where no stringed instruments are found at all.

Nketia (1974:107) observes: "Chordophones are particularly

suitable for use as solo instruments (and) may accompany solo singing or   recitations of poetry, praise singing, and narrative songs." Guitars (a type of lute) are the most important instrument in Africa today. This is not surprising when one considers that guitars were introduced in Africa by the Portuguese before Columbus discovered America.

Classroom Strategies and Experiences:
Learning About Harps, Lutes, Musical Bows and Fiddles

Purpose of Activities: Listening to become familiar with the sounds of African chordophones.

Procedure:

1. Show films: *The Slave Coast* and *Africa's Gift*.

2. Show pictures of chordophones in *Musical Instruments of Africa,*

3. Recording: "Sambalga" (Album: *La Musique des Griots*, Side A, Band 1). The *godjie*, a single-stringed instrument with a half-calabash resonator, accompanies a high-pitched voice. The singer is praising a famous *Griot*. (The *Griots* are wandering musicians considered to be recorders of history.)
   • Listen closely for the sound of the *godjie* as it does three different things: follows the contours of the vocal part; plays alone; punctuates and accents the vocal part.
   • Challenge the class to make a sequential listening chart of the musical events.

4. Recording: "Bako" (Album: *La Musique des Griots,* Side B, Band 2). On this recording we hear six *garaya* (two-stringed lutes with calabash resonators) played by singers who celebrate hunters exclusively. Some of the lutes are the size of a man and possess a deep, rich resonance. Five gravel-filled calabashes accompany lutes and singers.
   • Analyze this recording. Ask: "Do you hear three distinct musical events taking place, each rhythmically indepent? How shall we indicate this?"

5. Recording: "Nahawandi" (Album: *The Music of Africa Series: Guitars 2*, Side 2, Band 6). The *ud* is an Arabian guitar, or lute, which produces a sound that shows, perhaps, North African influence. Here, the singer is singing for his individual pleasure, with at least one person listening.
- Listen closely for the regular pauses between phrases.
- "Can the elapsed beats be counted?" (Analysis)
- Listen for the word *"Hawadi"* at the end, which a listener says to show appreciation.

6. Recording: "Babinga Music" (Album: *Musique Centrafricaine*, Side B, Band 3). A harp-zither, called a *bogongo*, is heard as two men sing after a hunt.
- Clap the rhythmic pattern of the hand claps.
- "Listen for the sounds of nature in the forest background. What do you hear?"

7. Recording: "Solo for Musical Bow" (Album: *Anthology of Music of Black Africa:* Music of the Baoule, Record 2, Side B, Band 3). A player uses a wooden bow with a grass string placed between his lips.
- "Count the times the musical pattern is repeated in this music."
- "Can you describe the sound?"

8. Recording: "Solo for the Seron" (Album: *Anthology of Music of Black Africa:* Music of the Malinke (People of Mali), Record 2, Side A, Band 2). The *seron* is a very large instrument with nineteen strings. It is a plucked instrument. This selection has a contemporary western sound and "flavor."
- Analyze this recording using ABA or other pattern.
- Challenge members of the class to compose a repeated pattern on the strings of a guitar or autoharp.

9. Recording: "Chorus of Men's Voices with Harp" (Album: *Anthology of Music of Black Africa:* Music of the Baoule, Record 2, Side B, Band 5). The harp heard here is made of a branch and has five strings.
- Listen for the repeated pattern played by the harp.
- Observe the cross rhythms created by the men singing an

independent rhythm in parallel thirds against the music of the harp.
• Analyze this recording.

10. Recording: "Masengu" (Album: *Guitars 2: The Music of Africa Series #36*, Side 2, Band 5). Two guitars and a bottle accompany this song.
• Listen for brief rhythmic changes that add delightful variety.
• Analyze: indicate where player hits the body of the guitar.
• Call-and-response singing.

11. Recording: "Etoile des Neiges" (Album: *Egbe Omo Nago*, Side 1, Band 1). A combination of traditional instruments and folk guitar combine to produce a uniquely African sound.
• Have students clap basic meter; they love the Western sounds they recognize in this song.
• Identify instruments: drum, bell rattles, guitar.

12. Teach song "Ne Nkansu" on page 177 of *Sound, Beat, and Feeling.*

Lesson Six: Discovering Contemporary African Music

Many African musicians who have studied Western music place importance not only on preservation of their traditional music, but on the inclusion of modern trends in music within this tradition. They feel that the music is viable and vigorous enough to absorb new ideas and materials and still retain its integrity. Western music has done this, why not African?

The Highlife was among the first examples of contemporary music to come out of Africa. It is still the most popular dance in West Africa, having originated in Ghana around World War II and literally swept the continent. Essentially, it is a synthesis of African music and American jazz with South American rhythmic qualities. The Highlife is played with Western instruments. An interesting analogy can be made here. Whereas black Americans created jazz when they came into possession of Western instruments, black Africans created Highlife.

Today a combination of American jazz, rhythm and blues and

soul music is synthesized with African rhythms and instruments to produce an infectious sound called "Afro-Soul." Many recordings of this music are now very popular in Europe and the United States as well as in Africa. The popular music in African cities has definite South American rhythms. The South American influence reached the African continent at the end of the nineteenth century when many former slaves returned home. West Africa immediately adopted certain aspects of the music the expatriates brought with them. One thing seems certain as to the future of contemporary music in Africa: there will continue to be diversity through individuals who are free to express themselves as they like.

Classroom Strategies and Experiences:
Working with Highlife and Afro-Soul

Purpose of Activities: Listening to absorb the sounds of contemporary African music.

Procedure:

1. Recording: "Drum Rhythms of the High Life" (Album: *African Dances and Games*, Side B, Band 5).
   • Have the class clap rhythms to the score below.

	1	2	3	4	5	6	7	8
Bells		X	X		X		X	X
Low Drum	X				X			
High Drum	X	♫		X	X			

   • Use the recording with bells, drums and handclapping.
   • Encourage class members to learn Highlife dance steps and dance to recording and other Highlife records. (See page 11 of *Manual of African Dances and Games.*)

2. Recording: "Srotoi Ye Mli" (Album: *Stars of Ghana*, Side 1, Band 1). A Highlife selection.

- Clap along with the recording; add maracas, rhythm sticks.
- Encourage dancing, since the music has a Latin/African sound. Some of the latest teen dance steps will fit this music.

3. Recording: "Dibate La Nalolo" ("The Loin Cloth of My Love") (Album: *African Queen: Lydia Ewande and Her Family,* Side 1, Band 4).
- Listen for interplay of percussion instruments, some of which are made from kitchenware.

4. Recording: "Ikwunmokon–Okoitiho" ("To Live Is to Hope") (Album: *Ray Stephen Oche and his Matumbo,* Side A, Band 3). This Nigerian musician achieves an exciting blend of jazz and traditional African music.
- Analyze recording using ABA patterns.
- Listen for trumpet improvisations over an infectious and persistent percussion rhythm.
- Identify those elements in the music that make it sound African.

5. Recordings: "Soul Makossa" and "O Bosso" (Album: *Soul Makossa*). Manu Dibango, born in the Cameroons, is a shining light in current Afro-Soul music. An expert saxophonist, pianist, bassist, composer, and arranger, he is well known over most of black Africa and Europe, and his fame has spread to America as well. Students love his music!
- While listening to the above recordings, ask:
  "Can you name the instruments used?"
  "Can your ears discern the African instruments?"
  "What sounds African about the music?"
  "What sounds like American soul music?"
- Students can easily analyze these recordings using ABA patterns.
- Use rhythm instruments and "keep the beat" with the records.

6. Recording: *Missa Luba.* A mass sung by young Congolese, taught by a Belgian priest.
- Listen for changes in sound as portions of the mass are heard.
- Compare this with any mass by a Western composer.

7. Recording : "Black Tears" (Album: *Compositions for Solo Guitar*). Cameroonian musician Francis Bebey playing guitar in a highly original manner.
  • Listen for the variety of rhythms, range of sounds, and how and when the guitar is used as a percussion instrument.
8. Recording: *Aura*. "King"Sunny Ade and his African Beats. (Mango 90171-1)
  • Listen for African characteristics in a contemporary setting.
9. Recording: "Diamonds on the Soles of Her Shoes" and "Homeless" (Album: *Graceland*). Paul Simon and the South African acapella group Ladysmith Black Mambazo. This is the *mbube* style of men's choral music extremely popular in South Africa used with-in an American ethnic-rock framework.
  • Listen to discern Western, Afro-American and African influences in this astonishing musical hybrid.

ADDITIONAL THINGS TO DO AND DISCUSS

This chapter has outlined one approach to a difficult musical complex. Music in black Africa is interwoven with religion, art, history, and philosophy. It is highly studded with sociological implications and is in many cases socially controlled. The social context of the music can hardly be divorced from the music itself. This is because African music is so closely connected with African life and the way the people live. The music is not just an art of combining sounds, but a combination of sounds to express death, puberty, and other life events.

This importance of the music to the people should be stressed to students; it will be of invaluable aid to their understanding of the music. Not only is music in Africa used in ceremonials of many different types, but on all occasions as one passes from one stage of life to another, ending, finally, with funeral dirges. (Funeral music is very important in Africa.) There are various kinds of African music, and there is variety within that music in certain communities. In traditional Africa, in the villages where three-fourths of the people live, music is not an art in itself but is connected with other aspects of art.

Rapid change has brought sharp and vivid contrasts between the new and the old on the African continent. Nowhere is this more evident than in the music. In the large cities, and the urban areas that surround them, the Western influence is very strong. American jazz and soul musicians are extremely popular and well known and have many imitators. Traditional, or folkloric, music is alive and well in the rural villages, which is where the vast majority of the people live.

Music is used in games: for boys and for girls, for men and for women, and for combinations of the sexes. There is special music for cults and secret societies; for associations such as those of warriors, hunters, and the like. Music is used in healing services, in litigation, as a means of praise or censure of individuals, as a teaching-learning device, and for political reasons. Much music is associated with occupations that we might consider mundane: sowing, plowing, harvesting, rowing, and even grinding grain.

Since a considerable amount of the music is functional, it is therefore quite varied. In addition to the many functional uses of music, however, Africans also make music for individual pleasure—for their own enjoyment. This aesthetic use of music is by no means true of all nonliterate cultures. Music is, in short, thoroughly integrated with African life, with emphasis on group participation. Buildings are not built to "house" music: the music is where the people are.

There are, of course, certain regional differences. Ethnomusicologists have noted differences in West, Central, East, and South African music. Central Africa has, perhaps, the widest variety of musical instruments and styles, with a fifty-mile belt along the Congo that uses slit-drums to send messages. Yodeling and hocketing is a distinctive feature of certain areas in Central Africa.

West Africa, which has so greatly influenced American music (Negro spirituals in the call-and-response pattern; "hot" rhythms that eventually evolved into jazz), uses highly intricate polyrhythms and talking drums because of the tone languages spoken. East African music also uses the hocket technique, but the music is not as rhythmically complex. African musical scales seem to range from pentatonic to heptatonic, with singing done in thirds, fourths, fifths, and octaves, depending upon the area. Both sexes engage in singing, dancing, and playing instruments. Women, however, generally do not play drums. (The Venda women in South Africa are a notable exception.)

SOME MORE SPECIFIC SUGGESTIONS

Decide in advance exactly what and how much you want the students to learn and remember about African music. It is far better for them to know a few things accurately and in some detail than to have inaccurate concepts and fragmented information. Study African history; its past is very interesting and there have been historic changes since 1960.

Thus, keep a library of books, magazines, and African artifacts on hand while the culture is being studied. Show pictures and slides of African art, which has had a tremendous influence on Western art. Encourage reports and reading by the students on both Africa and African music. Rely heavily on audio-visual aids; good recordings and films are invaluable. Take museum trips and see live performances where possible.

Use children's games and songs in classroom activities. African children play rhythmic games that include polyrhythmic handclapping, striking the body, passing rocks, pounding sticks and even stomping as in many African dances. (See Selected Bibliography-- Adzinyah, Beal and Serwadda, and Recordings--*African Songs and Rhythms for Children* by Amoaku and *African Dances and Games* by Blum.)

Always encourage the students to let their bodies move when listening and performing scores; in African music, rhythm and movement are used almost as one. Emphasize instrumental improvisations: use cowbells or double bell to indicate the timeline; select a master drummer; let the other instruments improvise. One good, basic rhythm can be used as a basis for classroom study. The ability to recognize specific sounds that are characteristic of African music would be a basis for evaluation.

Developing a sensitivity to *treat the music with respect,* as if it's our own, should be a desired outcome of the study. As citizens of the world, the music *is,* in a very real sense, our own. We are not telling our students "this is how it's done in Africa," but rather, "here is how these people see themselves in their music." Since African music shows us how Africans express and view themselves, they show us an important part of their humanity. And music is, after all, an expressive way of being human.

Books

Africa: A list of Printed Materials for Children. New York: Information Center on Children's Cultures; U.S. Committee for
UNICEF; 1968, 76 pp. Every African country is represented.

African Music. Paris: La Revue Musicale, 7 Place Saint-Sulpice,
1972. Thirteen monographs by outstanding African musicians read at a meeting organized by UNESCO in Cameroon

African Short Stories. NY: Heinemann Edition Books. Twenty
stories by contemporary writers across the continent.

Akpabot, Samuel Ekpe. *Ibibio Music in Nigerian Culture.* Lansing,
MI: Michigan State University Press, 1975. A discussion of
music within a socio-cultural context.

Bascom, William R. and Melville J. Herskovits. *Continuity and
Change in African Cultures.* Chicago: The University of
Chicago Press, 1959. Monographs dealing with Africa. In-
cludes "African Music" by Alan P. Merriam.

Beal, Newton. *Pygmies Are People.* Far Rockaway, N.Y.: Carl Van
Roy, 1964. Pygmy songs, games and dances for youngsters.

Bebey, Francis. *African Music: A People's Art.* Westport, CT: Law
rence Hill and Co., 1975. Interesting and accessible over
view of African music by the renowned Cameroonian musi
cian. Excellent photographs, comprehensive discography.

Berliner, Paul F. *The Soul of Mbira: Music and Traditions of the
Shona People of Zimbabwe.* Berkeley: Univ. of Calif. Press,
1981. Detailed discussion of the music, history, performance practices and construction of the popular mbira (some
times referred to as the "thumb piano").

Blacking, John. *Venda Children's Songs.* Johannesburg: Witwatersrand University Press, 1967. Fascinating. Filled with
insights into the philosophies, mores and social values of the
Venda people as illustrated by the children's songs. Most
valuable are the fifty-six songs with music, original language, and English translations, suitable for classroom use.

Carrington, J.F. *Talking Drums of Africa.* New York: Negro Uni-
versities Press, 1969. Drum messages, how to beat them;
discussion of African languages on which talking of drums
is based.

Chernoff, John Miller. *African Rhythm and African Sensibility.* Chicago: Univ. of Chicago Press, 1981. Highly readable, intensely personal account of studying West African traditional percussion and learning about West African society as a result.

Courlander, Harold. *A Treasury of African Folklore.* New York: Crown, 1975. Stories, legends, riddles and proverbs.

Dietz, Betty, and Michael Olatunji. *Musical Instruments of Africa.* New York: John Day Co., 1965 (includes recording). Good for school use; most valuable are the many excellent photos of musical instruments and musicians. Chapter on ways to use the body in African music is good for class activities.

Historical Atlas of Africa. Ajay, J.F. Ade and Michael Crowder, editors. Cambridge: Cambridge Univ. Press, 1985. Full-color maps and text. African history to 1980.

Jessup, Lynne. *The Mandinka Balafon: An Introduction with Notation for Teaching.* St. Louis: MMB, Inc., 1983.(Xylo Publications)Good teaching tool for an exploration of the xylophone tradition of Gambia, West Africa.(2 tapes/book)

Jones, A.M. *Studies in African Music* (2 vol.). London: Oxford Univ. Press, 1959. Excellent reference work for teachers. Thorough examination and analysis of Ghanaian music.

Kaufman, Fredrick and John P.Guckin. *The African Roots of Jazz.* Alfred Publishing Co., 1979. Personalized account of two jazz musicians' sojourn in Africa. LP recording available.

Kirby, Percival R. *The Musical Instruments of the Native Races of South Africa.* Johannesburg: Witwatersrand Univ. Press, 1953. Reprint of 1934 edition, marvelous photos and descriptive prose.

Mazrui, Ali A. *The Africans: A Triple Heritage.* New York: Little, Brown, 1986.Profusely illustrated companion to TV series.

Nketia, J.H. Kwabena. *African Music in Ghana.* Evanston: North western Univ. Press, 1963. Good reference for teachers. 18 songs in native language, with music, included in appendix.

_____.*The Music of Africa.* New York: Norton, 1974. Overview with numerous illustrations, musical examples, information on music in daily life.

_____.*Our Drums and Drummers.* Accra: P.O. Box 4348, State Publishing Corporation, 1968. Good for school use; written for Ghanaian children in easily understandable prose.Excellent photos of variety of "drums and drummers."

Oliver, Roland, and J.D. Fage. *A Short History of Africa.* Baltimore: Penguin Books, 1962. Concise and factual.

Standifer, James A. and Barbara Reeder. *Source Book of African and Afro-American Materials for Music Educators.* Reston, VA: MENC, 1972.Part I, "African Music,"contains extensive bibliographies, discographies, and materials useful for teaching about African music.

Tracey, Hugh. *Chopi Musicians.* London: Oxford Univ. Press, 1970.Details of the music of the incredibly talented Chopi people are engrossingly described in this standard work.

Wachsman, Klaus and Peter Cooke, "Africa,"in *The New Grove Dictionary of Music and Musicians,* Vol. 1 (1980), 144-153. Comprehensive overview of music on the continent.

Warren, Fred, with Lee Warren. *The Music of Africa.* Englewood Cliffs, NJ: Prentice-Hall, 1970. Simply written introduction to various musical concepts as well as the idea of the integration of music into African life.

Warren, Lee. *The Dance of Africa.* Englewood Cliffs, NJ: Prentice-Hall, 1972. Background material on integration of dance in African life. Includes dance and game instructions and photographs.

Willett, Frank. *African Art.* New York: Oxford University Press, 1971. Concise, uncluttered text; profusely illustrated.

Article

George, Luvenia A., "African Music Through the Eyes of a Child." Music Educators Journal 69 (May, 1983), pp. 47-49. Description of an experiment with middle school-junior high students with African music.

Song Collections

Adzinyah, Abraham Kobena, Dumisani Maraire and Judith Cook Tucker. *Let Your Voice Be Heard! Songs from Ghana and Zimbabwe.* Danbury, CT: World Music Press, 1986. Fine collection of game, story and multipart songs arranged and annotated with in depth information on cultural background and performance practice. For use with K-12. (Companion tape available.)Photos; glossary.

Amoaku, W. Komla. *African Songs and Rhythms for Children.* W. Germany: Schott, 1971. Ed. 6376. Orff-Schulwerk in the African Tradition. Best for grades 3+.(Companion LP-Folkways:FC 7844).Good variety, clear, useful.

Edet, Edna Smith. *The Griot Sings: Songs from the Black World.*
New York: Medgar Evers College Press, 1978. Children's
songs, games and dances including several from various
parts of Africa.
Lowe, Mona. *Singing Games from Ghana.* Cerritos, CA: MM
Publishing, 1970. (Avail. from 19603 Jacob, Cerritos, CA) Almost every song and game here can be used. LP available.
Makeba, Miriam. *The World of African Song.* Chicago: Quad-
rangle Books, 1971. Many of the songs have been recorded by Makeba on her various albums. Twenty-four
songs divided into "traditional, recent folk songs, popular
songs by African song writers." Good background notes.
McLaughlin, Roberta, editor. *Folk Songs of Africa.* Hollywood:
Highland Music Co., 1963. Sixteen songs accompanied
by notes and instructions for performance.
Nketia, J.H. Kwabena. *Folk Songs of Ghana.* Legon: University
of Ghana, 1963. A good classroom resource. The fifty-six
songs are in native language with English translation.
Forty-three preparatory rhythmic exercises are included.
Serwadda, W. Moses. *Songs and Stories from Uganda.* Danbury,
CT: World Music Press, 1987. Thirteen story songs with
narrative, work and game songs and lullabies from East
Africa. Beautifully illustrated by Leo and Diane Dillon.
Companion tape.

AUDIO-VISUAL MATERIALS
Films
Africa Dances. Color, 28 min., Contemporary, McGraw-Hill
Films. A vivid, exciting presentation of the Ballets Afri-
caines performing at the United Nations. Good, holds stu-
dents' interest.
African Musicians. B&W, 15 min., Macmillan Audio, Brandon
Films. Excellent film about Congolese music and musi-
cians. Instruments are shown being played, narrator gives
pertinent, detailed information. Good photography.
African Village. Color, 17 min. NYU. A tribe in Guinea is
shown. Includes music.
An African Community: the Masai. Color, 16 min. BFA. Music
is shown as part of ordinary functions.
Atumpan. Color, 42 min., Institute of Ethnomusicology, UCLA.
Shows construction of *atumpan* drums from selection of
tree to the completed drum. Engrossing film.

Bitter Melon. Color, 30 min., JM. Life on the Kalahari desert. Interestingly depicted; good scenes of children singing and playing games.

Black African Heritage. Color, 4 films, each 60 min.,WFD,UCLA.

1. *The Congo*; narrated by Julian Bond.
2. *The Bend in the Niger*; narrated by Ossie Davis.
3. *The Slave Coast;* narrated by Maya Angelou.
4. *Africa's Gift*; narrated by Gordon Parks. A fine series; highly recommended.

Chopi Africa. Color, 53 min. MMP. A xylophone orchestra, for which the Chopi are famous, is shown, and several rituals involving music. Good.

Dance Like a River :Odadaa! Drumming and Dancing in the U.S. Color, 45 min., Oboade Institute c/o Barry Dornfeld, 294 Huron Ave., Cambridge, MA 02138. Portrait of a traditional drumming and dance ensemble from Ghana in residence in the U.S. Well made, interesting.

Discovering the Music of Africa. Color, 22 min. BFA Film Assoc. The music of Ghana, featuring a master drummer, singing, dancing. Good; holds students' interest.

First World Festival of Negro Arts. Color, 18 min., McGraw-Hill. Excellent for correlation of African music and art; emphasis is on visual arts, however.

The Hunters. Color, 76 min., Contemporary Films, University of Indiana. Very interesting; shows the Bushmen of the Kalahari Desert in Southwest Africa in daily pursuits that include music, in their culture.

Rhythm of Africa. B& W., 20 min., Radim Films. Poetic and moving; Jean Cocteau's beautiful script evokes haunting images of African life. Music, dance, culture of Chad. Excellent photography, fine narration.

Filmstrips

Africa: Musical Instruments; Percussion, Strings, Wind. Warren Schloat, 1969. Each section of this three-part filmstrip is approx. 15 min. long and in color. Good for school library

Folk Songs of Africa. Bowmar. Includes songs suitable for classroom.

Recordings

A. Traditional African Music

Africa East and West, edited by Mantle Hood (African Studies Center, Univ. of CA at Los Angeles). Side I is about music in Ghana, includes narration. Side II covers other African areas. Good for classroom use. Kit with filmstrip, maps and articles available.

Addy, Mustapha Tettey, *Master Drummer from Ghana* (Tangent TGS 113). Wide variety of drum rhythms and techniques, all brilliantly done. Side 1, Band 7, "Ga Gongs," has Addy playing drum rhythms on a pair of gongs for an exciting sound.

African and Afro-American Drums, edited by Harold Courlander (Folkways FE 4502). Good survey recording of African drumming from different areas of the continent; informative notes. Records 3 and 4 contain examples of African drumming techniques that are still heard in the Americas.

African Dances and Games, the Ladzekpo brothers, compiled by Odette Blum (S&R #2000). Manual accompanies the recording (at extra cost) which includes dance steps, game patterns, basic rhythm parts. Excellent for encouraging participation in African dance. Ewe music from Ghana.

African Music, recorded by Laura C. Bolton (Folkways FW 8852). Important album. "Secret Society Drums" are played individually before they are heard in combination. "Battle Signals, War Horn" has interpreters. Interesting for students.

African Story Songs, Abraham Dumisani Maraire (Univ. of WA Press). Eight stories from Zimbabwe told with songs interspersed. Stories narrated in English, songs sung in Shona with English translation, suggestions for use, notes on back.

An Anthology of African Music (UNESCO Collection). Includes separate albums of music from various countries. Examples used in this chapter: *Music from Rwanda* (BM 30L 2302); *The Music of Nigeria: Hausa Music I* (BM 30L 2306); *The Music of the Senufo* (BM 30L 2308). Excellent notes and photographs.

Anthology of Music of Black Africa (Everest 3254/3). Contains "Music of the Princes of Dahomey," "Music of the Malinke," and "Music of the Baoule." Many excellent examples.

Bantu Choral Folk Songs   (Folkways FW 6912).   Detailed notes
   and transcriptions of South African songs, most quite sing-
   able by junior high and older. Good teaching tool.
Dance Suites from West Africa (Zadonu ZAD 901 Avail. World
   Music Press). Agbi and Kobla Ladzekpo perform four tradi-
   tional dance, drumming and singing ensembles with the
   CalArts African Ensemble. Informative notes.
Drums of the Yoruba of Nigeria (Ethnic Folkways FE 4441). Fan-
   tastic drumming, good notes and photographs.
Music of Golden Africa   Egbe Omo Nago Folkloric Ensemble,
   (Universal Stereo DC-6485, Desto). Many good examples
   of traditional and neo-traditional African music. Words of
   some songs are on the record jacket.
Folk Music of Ghana (Folkways FW 8859). Bands one and two on
   Side I contain good rhythmic patterns for classes to notate
   and duplicate.
Mbira Music of Rhodesia, performed by Abraham Dumisani Maraire (Univ. of WA Press UWP-1001). Delightful recording
   that contains a valuable booklet about the history and performance practices surrounding the *nyunga nyunga mbira* of
   the Shona people of Zimbabwe.
The Music of Africa Series, recorded by Hugh Tracey. Examples
   used in this chapter are from the following albums: *Guitars:*
   Two (GALP 1503, Series No. 36);   *Musical Instruments*
   Three: Drums (SGALP 1324, Series No. 29);   *African*
   Dances of the Witwatersrand Gold Mines,   Part I   (Decca
   GALP 1032, Series No. 12).   A very valuable series filled
   with excellent musical examples.
Musiques du Cameroun (Ocora OCR 25). Good variety.
Music of the Ituri Forest, recorded by Colin M. Turnbull. (Folkways
   FE 4483). Fine example of the highly sophisticated and
   complex music of the Pygmy people. "The Elephant Hunt-
   ing Song," which demonstrates the hocketing and yodeling
   technique, is quite fascinating to classes.
Musique Centrafricaine (OCORA 43). Excellent album that contains an astonishingly wide variety of music. (If only one
   album could be purchased, this would be the one.) Very good
   for classroom use; excellent notes and photographs.
Musique Dahomeennes (OCORA OCR17). Rich variety of musical
   examples. Good notes and photographs.
Niger: la Musique des Griots (OCORA OCR 20). Fine musical
   examples, good pictures. Notes are in French.

Olatunji: Drums of Passion, Michael Babatunde Olatunji (Columbia CS 8210). Nigerian drumming and singing group; exciting music for group movement, percussion practice, call-and-response singing.

Soul of Mbira (Nonesuch H-72054). Traditions of the Shona people of Zimbabwe. Recorded by Paul Berliner. Variety of players, with singing; notes on back.

Watamba Tamba , Ephat Mujuru (Lyrichord LLST7398). A range of traditional *mbira* ("hand-piano") pieces played with virtuosity by a master player.

B. Contemporary African Music

Acquaye, Saka, *Voices of Africa: Highlife and Other Popular Music* (Nonesuch Records H-72026). A very good Ghanaian ensemble. Classes like this recording.

Ade, "King" Sunny and the African Beats, *Aura,* (Mango 90171-1) Nigerian pop that blends traditional and urban influences.

_____.*Juju Music*, (Mango 9712). Wonderful introduction to juju that covers a spectrum of rhythms.

Africa Dances (Authentic Records ARM 601 order from Original Music). Anthology of modern African dance music from 11 Black African nations, including Ghana, Nigeria, South Africa, Kenya, Tanzania, Zaire. (vintage sound)

African Queen: Lydia Ewande and Her Family (Barclay 920 120) Contemporary sounds by a popular Cameroonian singer.

Bameli Soy (Shanachie SH 43025). M'Bilia Bel sings with soaring bird-like vocals and irresistible high energy Congolese rhythms. One of the few prominent women in African pop.

Bebey, Francis, *Akwaaba* (Original Music 105). Finger-piano, African flute, percussion and bass guitar create a range of African musical moods.

_____,*Compositions for Solo Guitar* (OCORA OCR27). Cameroonian composer- guitarist- author Bebey gives interesting rhythms and sonorities to the guitar.

Dibango, Manu, *Soul Makossa* (Atlantic SD 7267). Dibango's music is a hot blend of soul, rock and African rhythms. Students love his Afro-Soul music.

Ladysmith Black Mambazo, *Induku Zethu* (Shanachie SH43021). *Mbube* style acapella singing group - the most popular in South Africa.Featured on Paul Simon's *Graceland* album.

_____, *Ulwande Olungwele* (Shanachie SH43030).

Makeba Sings! (RC LSP 3321). In her inimitable way, Miriam Makeba represents modern Africa to many people.Though the songs are in her native language, the meaning seems to come through very well.

Missa Luba (Philips PCC 606). Considered a standard. Enthusiastic voices of young Congolese singers in a good example of the synthesis of African music in a Western context.

Ray Stephen Oche and His Matumbo (Discodis Paris ESP 155501). Blend of African melodies, rhythms, instruments with Western instruments and jazz elements. Good.

Paul Simon, *Graceland* (Warner Bros. 25447-1). Co-operative composing by Simon and various musicians including Ladysmith Black Mambazo and others from African, Cajun and Latino backgrounds. Exciting fusion results.

Stars of Ghana (WAP 21 Decca). An example of Highlife music. Also contains an example of African blues.

Talking Drums (Avail. from World Music Press). Traditional and Highlife music from Abraham Kobena Adzinyah, Maxwell Amoh and ensemble. Includes bamboo flutes, keyboard, brasses, guitar, traditional drums and vocals. Varied.

The Indestructible Beat of Soweto (Shanachie SH 43033). Various artists play " Zulu Jive," the infectious, jumpy amalgam of South African street music influenced by reggae, American R & B and traditional South African styles.

CHAPTER THREE

Teaching Black American Music

Today's students are interested in the "here and now"; they are very knowledgeable about the leading popular musicians, the latest hits, the most popular radio stations and disc jockeys. Of the current "top ten" songs played daily quite a few are black music. Even the white music hits, with the sole exception of most country-western, are usually black-derived, especially rhythmically. The origins of black music in this country will thus be of interest to students for they will be able to better understand the roots of much of the popular music of today.

Most black music has been born and nurtured outside the mainstream of Western art music due to its origins in a segregated society with its own culture and mores. Black music is a vital part of the black experience in America and should be approached and studied in its own terms within its own context, as the music of any culture should be.

DEFINING BLACK MUSIC

Exactly what *is* black music? Musicians and laymen alike have been groping for a precise definition for some time now with varying degrees of success. The reasons for this uncertainty are varied, but the process of acculturation with the music beside which it has coexisted for so long is one important factor. Leroi Jones (1968:13) states that: "Negro music is essentially the expression of an attitude, or a collection of attitudes, about the world, and only secondarily an attitude about the way music is made." Certainly one definition could be: music written and performed by blacks primarily for the entertainment and understanding of other blacks. Even in the popular music of today, the words of many black songs have real meaning only for other blacks, while the rhythms, melodies, and harmonies can be understood and enjoyed by everyone.

Not to be overlooked is the fact that music can become black in performance; that is, compositions written by whites sound black when performed by blacks. An awareness of the historical past of Negroes in America will aid in understanding the accompanying development of black music in this country.

CORRELATING BLACK HISTORY WITH BLACK MUSIC

Black Americans, numbering over 22,000,000 persons, constitute the largest racial minority in the United States. Their impact upon American life and history has been considerable. Nowhere has the black influence been more strongly felt than in the culture and particularly in the music. Blacks were brought to this country from West Africa as early as 1619. Coming at first as indentured servants, in the latter part of the seventeenth century they were brought in as slaves. By the year 1700 slavery was a firmly established institution throughout the American colonies.

The most pressing problem facing the Europeans who colonized the New World was the securing of labor to exploit the resources of the land. The apparently inexhaustible supply of African slaves became the solution to a major economic problem.

The vast majority of slaves were concentrated in the South. States such as South Carolina, Louisiana, Mississippi and Alabama contained large plantations on which sugar cane, cotton and tobacco were among the major crops. The average slave worked fourteen or fifteen hours per day, lived in a one-room cabin, slept on the dirt floor, ate meager rations of corn and a little meat, wore only the barest necessities for clothing, and was in constant fear of the lash. Still the slaves sang of heaven, over "yonder," deliverance, and of better times to come. This music reflected a deep and abiding faith of almost incredible durability. The black spirituals expressed in music those hopes and feelings that dared not be said.

The Civil War saw many blacks serving in the Union Army, quite a few with distinction. The issuance of the Emancipation Proclamation on January 1, 1863, caused rejoicing among nearly

4,000,000 former slaves throughout the land. But in a few years the rejoicing turned into a nightmare of despair. The Reconstruction era was followed by a wave of segregation laws that turned the South into a place of severe oppression for blacks. But out of this period came America's only original contribution to Western music: jazz and its companion, the blues. "The music went back to the slave cabins and further. (The music) went back to the polyrhythmic complexity of the forgotten land—West Africa. It was a melding of African, European, and American elements; of the 'devil songs' and shouts and stomps; of slow drags, marches, funeral dirges, and hymns. It was a blend and yet it was new" (Bennett 1966:240). The Great Depression saw blacks being "the last hired .. the first fired," but a joyous music came out of the period called "swing."

Today, blacks in America are still struggling for total assimilation in the mainstream of society. Their religion and their music have sustained them for over three hundred years in a land that is theirs by right of birth and the labor of their forebears.

PRINCIPAL CLASSROOM STRATEGIES

The principal classroom strategies in the study of black music will be the following: rhythmic activities that will result in the feel of the beats; listening experiences that will aid in the recognition of musical styles and their distinctions while developing aural acuity; placing the development of black music in historical perspective; and singing for reinforcement of these aims and for fun! As a lead-in to the study of black music, it is a good idea to start with the popular soul music of today. The following sample lessons are given as idea-stimulators for classroom strategies.

Lesson One: Orienting the Listener to Distinctive Characteristics in Black Music

Purpose of Activities: Listening for discernible musical traits in black music.

Clues for Listening

Procedure:
1. Show film: *Black Music in America: From Then Until Now.*

2. Play a prepared tape (or use recordings) of black singers, each selection approximately two minutes long. A sample tape could be:
   a. "Sign O' the Times" by Prince
   b. "Move On Up a Little Higher" by Mahalia Jackson
   c. "Lost Your Head Blues" by Bessie Smith
   d. "It's Tricky" by Run-D.M.C.
   e. "I Couldn't Hear Nobody Pray" by the Fisk Jubilee Singers
   f. "Beat It" by Michael Jackson
   g. "All of Me" by Billie Holiday
   h. "Give Me the Reason" by Luther Vandross
   i. "What Have You Done for Me Lately" by Janet Jackson
   j. "Amazing Love" by Joe Williams

3. Students are to listen for: characteristics of black speech in song; use of falsetto; groans; grunts and moans; distinctive phrasing and use of rubato; words with meanings relevant to blacks.

4. Play a prepared tape (or use recordings) of black instrumentalists. A sample tape could be the following:
   a. "Ole Miss" by Louis Armstrong
   b. "Najee's Theme" by Najee
   c. "Boplicity" by Miles Davis
   d. "Body and Soul" by Coleman Hawkins
   e. "Charleston Rag" by Eubie Blake
   f. "Koko" by Charlie Parker
   g. "Lester Leaps In" by Count Basie with Lester Young
   h. "Blue Serge" by Duke Ellington
   i. "The In Crowd" by Ramsey Lewis
   j. "Chameleon" by Herbie Hancock
   k. "Honky Tonk Train" by Meade Lux Lewis

5. Students are to listen for: use of instruments as in imitation of the voice; syncopation; rubato; the variety of rhythms.

6. Give the following assignment to interested students for the next class meeting: bring in your favorite record by a black performer and be able to point out to us the things in the music that make it sound distinctly black to you.

7. Select a song of Negro origin from a song series and teach it to the class. Songs such as "Children, Go Where I Send Thee," or "Amen" are good to begin with.

Lesson Two: Black Popular Music

Black popular music is a synthesis, or blend, of all the histori-cally dominant elements of Afro-American music, such as: jazz, blues, gospel, spirituals, and including minstrelsy and ragtime. Through use of electronic media, contemporary sounds solidify the biracial character of "crossover" music. With stars such as Lionel Richie, Tina Turner, Prince, Michael Jackson, Whitney Houston, Dionne Warwick, Patti LaBelle and Janet Jackson, this crossover tendency underscores the tremendous strength of the black influ-ence on American popular music today.

Until the emergence of rock and roll, black popular music in America was defined by stars such as Ethel Waters, Louis Arm-strong and Billie Holiday who were outstanding blues and jazz performers in the thirties and beyond (Shaw 1986:272). In the fifties, rock and roll, as performed by white musicians, was the white counterpart of black rhythm and blues. Today, however, such distinctions are blurred and disappearing, due to the crossover trend wherein black and white artists are heard on radio stations that cater to either race.

Black popular music today has many categories and styles: soul, r & b (rhythm and blues), disco, go-go, street, dance, etc. The teen market in certain urban areas relies upon disk jockeys to provide music at private parties, proms and in clubs. This use, along with music played by radio and TV stations focused on a young au-dience, creates a segment of the industry that values and promotes fast dance music more than ballads.

Professional DJ organizations are able to advance aspiring groups by giving their music air time and playing time in clubs. The special genre of dance music used has certain characteristics that relate it to the break dancing and rapping that became popular in the late 1970's and '80's (Shaw 1986:292-296). The music usually has a heavy, fast beat and incorporates strong vocals that utilize several tracks; individual cuts tend to be longer than radio time allows. Grace Jones' "Slave to the Rhythm" and Shannon's "Do You Want to Get Away" are good examples of this dance beat. It is perfect crossover music, which makes it highly prized by the recording industry.

Classroom Strategies and Experiences

Purpose of Activities: Identifying and responding to varying layers of rhythmic events occurring in black popular music.

Procedure:

1. Show film: *Aretha Franklin, Soul Singer*

2. Continuing the previous lesson, allow the students who brought records by black performers to play them and point out what makes the music sound black to them.

3. Explain to the class that even experts have had difficulty in defining black music, but that you will give them some generally accepted definitions and let them hear examples.

    a. Basically, black music is music by black composers and performed by blacks. (Example "It's Wrong [Apartheid]" by Stevie Wonder.)

    b. Music stemming from the black experience and reflecting that culture in any of its forms. (Example: "It's Tricky" by Run-D.M.C.)

    c. Music with vocal inflections akin to black speech. (Example: "I'd Still Say Yes" by Klymaxx).

    d. Use of the falsetto technique among black male vocalists. (Example: "Sign O' the Times" by Prince).

4. Play a Shannon recording, "Do You Want to Get Away" and have the class tap out the rhythm on desks with pencils. Next, use rhythm instruments with the same recording such as maracas, claves, sticks, tambourine, drums, etc. Let the class decide on instrumentation: whether or not they need all the instruments playing at once. Have a class member come forward and indicate when certain instruments are to play.

5. Let the class improvise rhythmically with and without records, encouraging them to feel and accent the beats as they play.

Analyzing the Music

Purpose of Activities: Encourage students to listen for musical changes in black popular music by analyzing compositions.

Procedure:

1. Show film: *Roberta Flack.*

2. Select a recording and analyze it in advance using only ABA, etc., as symbols for changing musical patterns. Have several of the latest hits available. Example: "Billie Jean" by Michael Jackson can be analyzed thus:

    Introduction (instrumental)

    A ("She was more like a beauty, etc.")

    B ("People always told me, etc.")

    C ("Billie Jean is not my, etc.")

3. Have the class write down what you are putting on the board; make the ABC changes in "Billie Jean" as they occur *in the music*. (Do not use the words of the song as you analyze; the music moves too fast.)

4. Ask a student to come to the chalkboard and analyze another record. Tell him to listen closely in order to analyze the music, not the words. If there is disagreement from any student about the accuracy of an analysis, playing the record again will show them not only that careful listening is a priority, but that there are often different ways to analyze any one recording. Youngsters are very quick to catch on to this type of analysis, and it is a valuable aid in developing aural acuity.

Becoming Physically Involved

Purpose of Activities: More active, physical involvement with rhythms by using hand and body "jibes" while listening to recordings.

Procedure: Now is a good time to let the class see you "in motion."

1. Select a fast, rhythmic number such as "Who Is It?" by Mantronix. Tell the class to do exactly what you do, *if they can*. (Of course they can; this challenge always puts them on the alert and adds suspense.) Start the recording; as the music moves along in measures of either four or eight, do the following:

a. Clap hands   b. Tap thighs
c. Alternate hand and thigh claps   d. Roll hands in air
e. Point rhythmically over right shoulder; repeat over left
f. Alternate between right and left shoulders with each point
g. Place hands on his and move head from side to side, etc.

In other words, do anything you like, but keep it moving rhythmically and enjoy it! It *is* fun, and the kids love it.

2. Select another record and ask for a student volunteer to lead the class; follow along while they keep up with their classmate. (They'll be looking anyway to see if you can do it!) Anything goes as long as the students can do it in their seats.

3. On another day, if space and class size allow, have the class stand as a volunteer leads body movements to a recording. Some students will include a few of the latest dance steps; maintain careful control. Not everyone will be extroverted enough to want to participate in this; do not insist. Those who do will thoroughly enjoy it; those on the sidelines can keep the beat with their hands or instruments.

Lesson Three: Identifying Certain
Characteristics of Spirituals

The Negro spirituals originated with the slaves who sang to relieve the monotony of their labors and to enliven their religious services. It was the music of the "christianized" slave. Jones (1968: 13) observes that: "One of the very reasons Christianity proved so popular was that it was the religion, according to older Biblical tradition, of an oppressed people. The struggles of the Jews and their long-sought 'Promised Land' proved a strong analogy for the black slaves." The spirituals were often about biblical stories with the words portraying vivid pictorial images.

Some of the spirituals undoubtedly had hidden or double meanings and served as signals for escape attempts. "Steal Away to Jesus" is a classic example. It is widely believed that these songs appeared in a religious setting first and were later put to other uses. The spirituals had certain distinctive features: the strikingly syncopated rhythms; the call-and-response (or leader and chorus) technique, and rich harmonies. In the syncopated patterns handclapping accented the weaker, or "off" beats, while the foot would pat the meter accents. This is a common practice in many black churches today.

There is great dignity in all of the spirituals and they are all intrinsically sad. They served to "lighten the load" of an oppressed people and thereby left a musical literature unsurpassed in aesthetic beauty.

Classroom Strategies and Experiences:
Emphasizing Distinctive Features in Spirituals

Purpose of Activities: Recognition of unique characteristics in Negro spirituals.

Procedure:

1. Show film: *Helen Tamiris in Her Negro Spirituals.*

2. Have a recording of a spiritual such as "I'm A-Rolling Through an Unfriendly World" by the Fisk Jubilee Singers playing as class enters. Ask: "What kind of music are you hearing?" Have on the board a few sentences about spirituals to be read and discussed.
   • Teach songs such as "Rock-A-My-Soul" and "Michael, Row the Boat Ashore." Use accompanying recordings if available.
   • Encourage harmonizing by ear.
   • Since both songs are very rhythmic, let the class tap their feet on the meter accents and clap on the weak beats.

- Jazz the piano accompaniment—let it swing! After the songs are well learned , let the class sing them unaccompanied and add a few percussion instruments–especially tambourines.
- Tape record a class performance of the songs; evaluate it for improvements. Ask: "Do you think the slaves might have sounded the way we do? Why, or why not?"
- Teach the class "I Couldn't Hear Nobody Pray." Listen to the accompanying record.
- Listen to an African recording such as "Song of Praise of Nigeria" and see if the class can hear the similarities between the call-and-response technique of Africans and that found in the spirituals.
- Show filmstrip: *Black Songs of Slavery*.
- Songs with secret meanings are especially interesting. Correlate these with students' knowledge of American history as much as possible. "Michael, Row the Boat Ashore" expressed a longing to leave this country and go to another where slaves would be free. Subsequent verses asked for a helping hand from white abolitionists or others willing to aid.

3. Show film: *Buckdancers*.

Lesson Four: Learning About Ragtime

Ragtime has been described as: "The application of systematic syncopation to piano playing and composition. More precisely, it consists basically of a syncopated melody played over a regularly accented beat (2/4 time) in the bass" (Chase 1966: 434). Ragtime is a black art form that originated in black communities for the entertainment of its residents. Ragtime was the first black music to have a significant impact upon American culture, having been taken from the ghettos to become the rage of both the United States and Europe.

It is difficult today to realize how great an impact ragtime music had on the public during 1890-1915. The piano was the major instrument found in many homes and served as the focal point of family gatherings and entertainment, much as television does today. The popularity of piano rolls and sheet music played a large part in the music's widespread popularity.

Ragtime was the precursor of jazz in being the "first black instrumental music in America" (Walton 1972:40). It was also the first music of black men in America to be notated by them, thus making the re-creation of their music as consistent with their intent as possible.

The black composer Scott Joplin (1869-1917) wrote the most famous of all rags, "The Maple Leaf Rag." There has been a recent revival in the interest of both ragtime music and Joplin, who is considered ragtime's greatest composer. On the East Coast there was a style of ragtime piano that developed somewhat independently of the Midwestern branch of Joplin and his followers. James Hubert ("Eubie") Blake (1883-1983), born in Baltimore, Maryland, was a leading exponent of the style which flourished along the eastern seaboard, including New Jersey, Maryland, New York and Washington, DC. This music was fast, difficult to play, improvisatory, and rarely published in a form approaching its complexity in performance. The ragtime piano of Eubie Blake was a direct influence on future jazz piano styles. *Class activity*: Listen to Eubie play his piano rags on the album, *The Eighty-Six Years of Eubie Blake*.

Classroom Strategies and Experiences:
Activities Designed to Focus on Distinctive
Characteristics in Ragtime Music

Purpose of Activities: Recognition of distinct characteristics found in ragtime music: syncopation, conventional harmonies and melodies that combine to create a unique piano-playing style.

Procedure: Have the class clap the following patterns while counting *aloud*:

Divide the class; let half clap "A" and other half "B" and then combine.

Divide the class again; combine A, B, and C patterns.

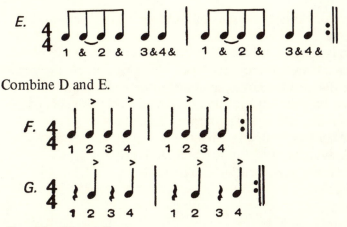

Combine D and E.

Combine F and G.
- Next, use a percussion instrument and repeat the patterns.
- Let the students improvise. After they understand that syncopation is the accentuation of beats not regularly stressed, many of them will be able to lead the class in interesting patterns.
- Have a Guided Listening Lesson using a ragtime record, Scott Joplin's "Original Rags," for example. Material should be duplicated with everyone following their own copy. Below is an example of a Guided Listening Lesson to be followed as the recording is being played.

Original Rags by Scott Joplin

Introduction: Piano plays in octaves for two measures; V7 leads into A.

A–First melody is lyrical; left hand accented in "scoop-like" manner. Bass walks at certain intervals.
B–Right hand melody begins alone in thirds; a little softer, more syncopated and jazzy at cadences; a little echo pattern is heard.
C–Right hand melody seems to "ripple" along in single-note melodies; cadences end in a high register, as if asking a question; ending is soft.

Introductory material is heard; V7 patterns of two measures lead again into A.

A–First melody is heard again, left hand accents in "scoop-like" fashion.

D–Tempo is faster; "walking" bass in left hand is heavily accented; music swings and gets "hotter."Right hand plays syncopated patterns in chords; left hand more prominent.

E–Interplay between left hand and right hand is highly syncopated. Descending right hand patterns end section.

More heavy syncopation in left hand; interplay between hands even more rhythmic and infectious.

Accents are prominent in both hands.

John Malachi at 219 Restaurant, Alexandria, VA (1982) [Photo by L. George]

• Upon hearing this composition the second time, the class could do the following:
(1) Raise hands when a new theme is heard.
(2) Raise hands to identify the walking bass patterns.
(3) Raise hands to identify the V7 patterns that lead into A.

Lesson Five: Introducing the Blues

There is considerable evidence to support the theory that the blues may well have been sung by the slaves in some form or other many years before the songs were actually given the name "blues." Certain field hollers, cries, and work songs bear striking resemblances to some blues forms. The Northern cities to which blacks poured in the early part of the century produced the ghetto life that was conducive to this music. No less conducive was the situation in the South that stimulated the gigantic exodus.

Courlander (1963:128) states: "The blues is a genre utilized to express personal dissatisfaction, remorse, or regret; to tell the world about your misfortunes and the way you feel about it; to air a scandal; and perhaps to point the finger of accusation at someone who has caused an injury or misery." The lyrics of blues songs are always directly stated in a matter-of-fact fashion and on occasion filled with double entendres. No aspect of life has been untouched by a blues verse.

Southern (1971:333) lists the following general characteristics of the blues: they are vocal and mournful in style, usually stating the singer's personal feelings about situations that affect him, most often the rejection or disappointment of a lover; blues melodies use scales in which the third, fifth and seventh tones tend to be flatted, resulting in "blue" notes; the blues has syncopation and duple rhythms with an AAB form for the text; the phrases are four measures each, with a complete blues song consisting of twelve measures. (The latter is not a hard-and-fast rule; there are

blues of as many as sixteen measures and of as few as eight.)
Harmonically, the chord progressions move in a I IV I V I pattern.

The best-known early blues singers were women such as Ma
Rainey, the powerful Bessie Smith, Ethel Waters, Clara Smith, Ida
Cox and Mamie Smith. Huddie "Leadbelly" Ledbetter, Robert
Johnson, Blind Lemon Jefferson, Joe Williams (who sang with
Count Basie), Joe Turner and B.B. King are blues singers with
highly individualized styles.

Classroom Strategies and Experiences:
Recognizing Specifics in the Blues Idiom

Purpose of Activities: Recognition of "blue notes," chord progressions, form, and vocal individuality in the blues tradition.

Procedure:

1. Show films: *The Blues*; *Sam "Lightnin'" Hopkins.*

2. Have the class sing blues songs such as "Joe Turner's Blues" and
"Easy Rider," noting the AAB form and blue notes used.
   • Play a major diatonic scale, and then flat the third, fifth, and
     seventh tones to produce "blue" notes.
   • Listen to blues recordings by Ma Rainey such as "Hear Me
     Talkin' to You"; Bessie Smith's "Any Woman's Blues" and
     "Nobody Knows You When You're Down and Out"; Joe
     Turner's "Chains of Love"; and Joe Williams's "Amazing
     Love."
   • Encourage students to state their reactions to the highly
     individual manner in which the different singers plead, moan,
     shout, etc., in his/her expression of the blues. (These are vocal
     characteristics of black singers found not only in blues.)
   • While listening to early blues recordings such as those by
     Rainey and Smith, have the class do the following:
   (1) Raise hands when they hear (a) blue notes; (b) the B section
       of a blues song.
   (2) Lift one finger when they recognize a tonic harmony; two
       fingers for subdominant; three fingers for dominant.
   • Prepare a Guided Listening Lesson for W.C. Handy's "St.
     Louis Blues."
   • Have students analyze blues recordings at the chalkboard using
     ABA, etc. to indicate harmonic and rhythmic changes.

- Show filmstrip: *Black Songs After the Civil War.*
- Compare recordings of current blues singers such as B.B. King and Ray Charles to hear differences in instrumentation and vocal styles. Ask: "Are the basic characteristics of blues still evident in contemporary blues?" and "What changes, or differences, do you hear?"
- Encourage class members to give reports about the lives of any of the blues musicians mentioned in the study or any others they may become interested in.

Lesson Six: Discovering the Uniqueness of Jazz

Jazz is considered America's only original contribution to Western music. Its world-wide impact has been, and continues to be, phenomenal, yet only relatively recently has it been accorded serious treatment in scholarly circles. In fact, there are still many histories of music that make no mention of jazz. Jazz originated in black communities, notably New Orleans, in the years following the Civil War when band instruments became accessible to the former slaves and their descendants.

Brass bands were very popular and the music they played evolved into early jazz. In New Orleans, the bands often played for funerals. They would accompany the body to the cemetery playing a slow, traditional hymn. On the way back they would play a lively, syncopated tune to "cheer up" the mourners. Onlookers would clap their hands and sometimes form a line and dance as the band made their way back to the city. This custom is still practiced on occasion in New Orleans today.

Southern (1971:374) observes: "The fusion of blues and ragtime with brass band and syncopated dance music resulted in the music called jazz, a music that developed its own characteristics." There are many ways of defining jazz, but most experts seem to agree on the following characteristics: improvisation, which makes jazz a performer's art, producing intimate communication between performer and listener; rhythmic accentuation, with the best musicians having an extraordinary time sense akin to that of African musicians; imaginative use of instruments whereby the inflections and innuendoes of the human voice are attained; the antiphonal, or call-and-response, performance between individual

instruments or a solo instrument and the entire ensemble; and the
use of "blue" notes.

Early Jazzmen

The early jazz bands were small ensembles. The clarinet, tuba,
cornet, trombone, violin and guitar or banjo made up an average
group. Syncopation combined with group improvisation gave the
music a completely different and excitingly "hot" sound. In 1917
the U.S. Navy closed Storyville, a section of New Orleans that
employed most of the jazzmen. The musicians then moved up the
Mississippi River to cities such as Memphis, St. Louis, Kansas City
and Chicago.

Since jazz is primarily a performer's art, the jazz firmament is
studded with stellar performers. In consideration of space limita-
tions and clarity of classroom presentation, this chapter will focus
on selected musicians who are generally considered to be highly
innovative and *influential* in their genres. In early jazz, Ferdinand
(Jelly Roll) Morton and Louis Armstrong are clearly outstanding.

Morton (1885-1941) is considered "the first great master of
form in jazz" (Williams 1970:19). An outstanding pianist, he
played in New Orleans's Storyville section and from there followed the trail of other musicians to cities up the Mississippi.
From 1926 to 1930 he made a series of recordings as Morton's
Red Hot Peppers that made him famous. He recorded for the
archives of the Library of Congress in 1938 and became the most
written-about jazz musician of his time. Morton's compositions
lifted jazz from the restrictions of mere ragtime music to a much
broader concept of what jazz could be.

Louis Armstrong (1900-1970) was the first great jazz soloist
who "when on June 28, 1928 unleashed the spectacular cascading
phrases of the introduction to 'West End Blues,' he established
the general stylistic direction of jazz for several decades to come"
(Schuller 1968:89). Armstrong's style of trumpet playing was so
spectacularly different that he and thousands of imitators changed
the way the trumpet was to be played in this country for all time.
His contributions were so extensive that he was as pre-eminent in
the Swing Era and beyond as he had been during the formative
jazz years.

Some Stars of Swing

By the early thirties jazz had entered the Swing Era, which was characterized by the big band sound. Hodeir (1956:30) calls swing "the crystallization and logical termination of tendencies that had struggled to find expression during the earlier periods." The swing bands had the following characteristics: larger numbers of instruments playing in sections; short phrases that were repeated over changing chords, called "riffs"; use of call and response; the steady drive of duple meter that resulted in perfect dance music.

The Swing Era produced many fine musicians who developed the form to near perfection. The following were among the outstanding innovators of the era. Fletcher Henderson (1898-1952) "had a prominent role in the development of swing" (Chase 1966:477). By 1927 he was famous for leading the largest and most star-studded band then playing jazz. Henderson was also a great arranger whose work was used extensively by Benny Goodman. He was the first jazzman to create written arrangements that still sounded like jazz (Keepnews 1966:103). Henderson's written arrangements included the instruments playing in sections, which was one of the foundations on which swing was built.

Duke Ellington (1899-1974) "became the great composer-orchestrator of jazz and the great leader of a large ensemble, the master of form in jazz and the great synthesizer of its elements; he radically expanded the jazz orchestral language" (Williams 1970:92). Ellington was one of the most influential and outstanding musicians of all time. A gifted and prolific composer, his arrangements included passages that showed the talents of his sidemen to best advantage to the enhancement of the entire band's total sound. His orchestrations were brilliantly conceived and his arrangements included controlled improvisations that resulted in a distinctively collaborative sound.

In Kansas City in the early twenties, Bennie Moten (1894-1935) led an outstanding jazz band that played with definite blues feeling and driving rhythms accented by bassist Walter Page (1900-1957). After Moten's death, pianist Count Basie (1904-1984) formed a band that included some of Moten's musicians. The Basie band developed a rhythmic character and sound that was highly individualized. Basie's piano playing was unique and subtle, covering a wide range of styles all of which he used with taste and wit. "The Basie Orchestra played with a surging, joyous momentum and a new rhythmic flexibility . . . (which) fundamentally and permanently affected the most basic jazz idiom—the twelve-bar blues" (Williams 1970:92).

Lester Young (1909-1959) was a member of Basie's band who "created a new esthetic, not only for the tenor saxophone but for all jazz" (Williams 1970:114). Young's light, clear tone and sense of phrasing was a predecessor of cool jazz. His style was the complete opposite of the lush, round tones of the then-popular Coleman Hawkins.

"Coleman Hawkins's (b. 1904) contribution has been so comprehensive that it is impossible for any tenor saxophonist to avoid some reflection of his influence" (Williams 1970:71). The man was a supreme melodist and improvisor with an innate sense of rhythm. Hawkins, the first great tenor saxophonist, influenced a generation of performers with his full, warm tones and sensuous vibrato.

Among the jazz singers of the Swing Era, none have had more imitators than Billie Holiday (1915-1959) and Ella Fitzgerald (b. 1918). Both women had that indefinable quality termed "presence" and were masters of phrasing and improvisation. Fitzgerald is a great "scat" singer. Her voice had, according to Feather (1966:215), a "bell-like clarity of tone, flexibility of range and rhythmic brilliance of style." Holiday's voice had a timbre and quality that was startling upon first hearing but produced an emotional impact on her listeners that made her a legend in her lifetime.

The Bebop Innovators

In the early forties the Bebop Era hit the music world like a thunderbolt. The music was a reaction against what some musicians considered the commercialism of swing. Stearns (1956:219) noted that "The advent of bop was not only sudden but also highly threatening to many established musicians." This was true because bebop, or bop, was characterized by "complex polyrhythms; steady but light and subtle beats; exciting dissonant harmonies; new tone color and irregular phrases" (Southern

1971:494). The technical demands on bop instrumentalists were great.

Three who met all technical demands but also set new standards of performance were Charlie Parker (1920- 55), the legendary saxophonist; Dizzy Gillespie (b.1917), trumpeter; and Thelonius Monk (1920- 82), pianist. Undoubtedly the most influential was the incredibly gifted Parker. A fantastic improvisor with a command of his instrument and a rhythmic sense that was phenomenal, Williams (1970:127) considered him to be "perhaps the greatest inventor of melodies jazz has seen." The man was truly a creative genius.

Bop differed greatly from swing not only rhythmically, but in total concept: here was jazz to be listened to. The smaller ensembles encouraged longer solos and freedom for improvisation unknown in swing. Singer Billy Eckstine formed the first big Bop band, which included Parker, drummer Art Blakey, trumpeters Miles Davis and Dizzy Gillespie, singer Sarah Vaughan and pianist John Malachi (1919-1987), a highly talented and eminently qualified bop-influenced player. Malachi taught at Howard University in Washington, D.C. where he served as inspiration and link to one of jazz's most innovative periods.

Two Styles and Stylists of the Piano

Boogie-woogie, popular in the thirties and forties, is a form of piano blues. According to Chase (1966:463) boogie-woogie "transfers to the piano the twelve-bar pattern of the blues with its basic harmonic structure and is characterized by a persistent percussive rhythmic figure in the left hand which continues unchanged." The right hand, meanwhile, plays a series of riffs. Meade Lux Lewis was one of the better boogie-woogie pianists.

Art Tatum was a blind jazz pianist whose "appearance on the scene in the early thirties upset all the standards for jazz pianists" (Feather 1966:436). He was a marvelous technician who "embroidered" melodies with astounding proficiency.

Cool Jazz and Soul Jazz: A Contrast in Style

The appearance of "cool jazz" in the late forties and early fifties did not have as startling an effect on the music world as bebop had. For one thing, it was not nearly as sudden a sound since the playing of Lester Young. The cool musicians played in a relaxed manner and stayed much closer to the stated melody than bop musicians did. Their concept of jazz was, among other things, one of a different sonority. Hodeir (1956:127) described it as a "chamber orchestra by virtue of both (the band's) composition and the style imposed on it."

Trumpeter Miles Davis (b. 1926) was in the vanguard of the cool jazz style, creating some of the most representative music of the genre. Davis is one of the great jazz composers and performers of all time. Thoroughly rooted in the bop tradition (he played with Charlie Parker) his inventiveness is seemingly endless, and he exerts a great influence on many jazz trumpeters.

Cool jazz was followed in popularity by soul or hardbop jazz, which stripped the music of artificialities and returned to a basic blues format. This was combined with a conscious effort to recapture the basic harmonies and rhythms of an earlier era and was somewhat reminiscent of rhythm and blues. Saxophonist Julian "Cannonball" Adderley (1928-1975) and pianist Ramsey Lewis (b. 1935) were well-known exponents of soul jazz.

Modern Jazz and Beyond

The trend from the fifties has been the ascension of many college-trained jazz musicians who take a serious and somewhat intellectual view of their art. This has resulted in a considerable amount of jazz that is as atonal, polyrhythmic, complex, eclectic, and individual as any contemporary music in the classical tradition. As a matter of fact, the careful listener will find many facets of classical music in the new jazz.

The Modern Jazz Quartet was a tightly knit ensemble in the forefront of the modern jazz movement. Under the leadership of the brilliant pianist John Lewis (b. 1920), the vibraphone, bass and drums of this group produced some very balanced and exciting jazz. Another shining light, saxophonist Ornette Coleman (b. 1930), launched innovations that were astonishing in 1959. His playing has been called as musically abstract as an abstract painting.

The late, great saxophonist John Coltrane (1926-1967) has had a profound effect on the development of jazz. Williams (1970:200) made the following observation about Coltrane: "Coltrane could superimpose a complex of passing chords, substitute chords, and harmonic extensions upon a harmonic structure that was perhaps already complex. And at times he seemed prepared to gush out every possible note, career through every scale, and go even beyond that prolixity by groping for impossible notes and sounds on a tenor saxophone that seemed ready to shatter under the strain." Listening to Coltrane is a moving experience; one can hear the presence of genius. Coltrane was one of the first to use traditional African instruments in his jazz arrangements.

The use of folkloric, or traditional, instruments of Africa and other areas is a continuing trend of contemporary, or free, jazz. Saxophonist Pharoah Sanders (who played with Coltrane) continues in the tradition by reaching over to North Africa for some of his inspiration as evidenced in the titles of certain compositions. His uses of complex melodies, harmonies and rhythms are in the tradition of Coltrane: free form and exciting sonorities.

Archie Shepp (b. 1937), tenor saxophonist, has an interesting approach to both his instrument and his concept of jazz. His music is a synthesis of the abstract and concrete. Joseph Zawinul (b. 1932), the Austrian pianist, played with Miles Davis. A brilliant innovator, his group Weather Report combines synthesizers, folkloric instruments and contemporary jazz forms for very satisfying effects. Pianist Herbie Hancock (b. 1940), who also utilizes electronics and folkloric instruments, is another pacesetter in the "new wave" jazz. Both Weather Report and Hancock are masters of electronic jazz.

Jones (1968:175) observes that this is the music of contemporary black culture: "The people who make this music are intellectuals or mystics or both. The black rhythm energy blues feeling (sensibility) is projected into the area of reflection." Jones goes even further. He assigns characteristics to the music such as "Projection over sustained periods (more time given), and time proposes a history for expression, hence it becomes reflective projection. Arbitrariness of form (variety in nature). Intention of performance as a learning experience."

The vitality inherent in jazz is nothing short of incredible. It is an elastic, flexible form that can accommodate and challenge the best expressions of the most brilliant and sophisticated musical minds. The influence of black music on Western classical music has been great. Debussy, Stravinsky, Gottschalk, Dvorak, Brecht and others were all influenced by black music from spirituals to ragtime to jazz.

The jazz musicians of the seventies were consciously reaching back for Egyptian, even pre-Roman sounds and inspirations. The search was on for the very *roots* of blackness: the African elephant tusk tones, the talking drums, the xylophones of music of the ancestors. The conversion of some jazzmen to Islam (sometimes to escape from white religious racism) was reflected in their music. This music on occasion screams, chants, pleads, prophesies and sometimes dissolves into a sea of mysticism and dissonance. The music must not only be listened to with respect, but must be contemplated as another facet of black culture. The eighties finds jazz in a period of assimilation, synthesis, and fusion...attempting to absorb and combine those techniques that might logically fuse jazz with rock and roll, pop music and electronic break-throughs. All of the traditional areas of the past are still very much alive, but the emphasis now is not on authenticity of form, but on a somewhat "synthetic" type of music where roots and traditions are blurred. Will jazz survive? Of course! The lines of succession remain with us, for instance, with trumpeters from Buddy Bolden to King Oliver to Louis Armstrong to Dizzy Gillespie, Miles Davis and Wynton Marsalis. Jazz musicians give us the music of their era, born of the environment, the socio-cultural context in which they live. We can ask no more of any music, or of any musician.

Classroom Experiences Designed to Identify
Unique Characteristics in Jazz

Purpose of Activities: To differentiate among the many types of jazz by developing aural acuity and rhythmic response.

A. Early Jazz

Procedure:

1. Show films: *Discovering Jazz* and *American Music: from Folk to Jazz and Pop.*

2. Have the class clap while singing "When the Saints Go Marching In." (Often played by early jazz bands returning from the cemetery.)

3. Recording: "West End Blues" by Louis Armstrong and His Hot Five (Album:*Smithsonian Collection of Classic Jazz*, Side 2, band 9). Williams (1970:54) notes that "Armstrong's contributions to 'West End Blues' represent a beautiful balance of brilliant virtuosity and eloquent simplicity."

•Class should listen for: brilliant, free-flowing trumpet cadenza, revolutionary at that time; the band's easy double-time rhythm; the trombone solo; Armstrong and clarinet in call-and-response pattern

(Armstrong on vocals); piano solo by Earl Hines; trumpet holding high B flat; piano descending to entire group ending.
• Analyze other Armstrong recordings such as "Hotter Than That" and "I Got a Right to Sing the Blues."

4. Recording: "Dead Man's Blues" by Jelly Roll Morton (Album: *Smithsonian Collection,* Side 1, Band 8). This recording is a good example of Morton's concept of a jazz composition. All of the melodies are logical and orderly while following an infectiously rhythmic progression from beginning to end.
• Listen for: introduction with trombone prominent in short phrase from Chopin's "Funeral March"; trumpet and clarinet interplay of melody; clarinet solo followed by trumpet solo; trio of clarinets playing in harmony; heavy drum accents; trombone, trumpet, and clarinet "swinging" together; clarinet trio ending the selection.
• Encourage the class to clap the syncopated rhythms of the music as the record plays.
• Listen to and analyze other Morton selections such as "Black Bottom Stomp."
• While listening to early jazz, have the class lift one finger when a muted instrument is heard, as use of mutes produced previously unheard-of sounds.
• Have the class lift two fingers when an instrument sounds as if it might be imitating the human voice. (These sounds are made with a plunger, or cup mute, and is very obvious in "Ole Miss" by Louis Armstrong.)
• Listen to an early white Dixieland jazz recording such as "Ostrich Walk" by Bix Beiderbecke, and compare the sound to the black jazz records. Tell the class that Dixieland is a type of early jazz played by white musicians.

B. Swing

Procedure:

1. Show film: *Body and Soul.*

2. Recording: "Wrappin' It Up" by Fletcher Henderson and His

Orchestra (Album: *The Smithsonian Collection,* Side 3, Band 7). This selection is an example of Henderson's innovations, which came to be widely imitated in the Swing Era.
  • Have the class listen for: the call-and-response patterns; instruments playing in sections; rhythmic momentum.

3. Recording: "Blue Serge" by Duke Ellington and His Orchestra (Album: *The Smithsonian Collection,* Side 7, Band 3). An illustration of the types of sonorities that characterize much of Ellington's music. A short Guided Lesson could be the following:

> Introduction: clarinet dominant; trumpets provide bridge to . . .
> A   Trumpet introduces theme accompanied by trombones.
> A^1 Muted trumpets, trombones and cornets with saxophones give marvelous color to a variation on the theme.
> B   Trombone solo.
> C   Muted brasses.
> A^2 Piano solo with variation on theme.
> D   Saxophone solo accompanied by muted brass.
> A^3 Entire ensemble in thematic variation; ends quietly.

  • Listen to other Ellington standards such as "Mood Indigo," "Sophisticated Lady" and "Do Nothing Till You Hear from Me."
  • Analyze the recordings listening for those characteristics that give Ellington arrangements their distinctive sound.

4. Recording: "Kid from Red Bank" by Count Basie (Album: *Kid from Red Bank,* Side 1, Band 1). One can hear the joyous, carefree sound and infectious rhythm of the Basie Band.
  • Listen for driving rhythms propelled by the bass and the piano.
  • Note tremolo and riffs in the brass section.

5. Recording: "Lester Leaps In" by Count Basie (Album: *The Smithsonian Collection,* Side 6, Band 1). The light, clear sound of Lester Young's saxophone is a standout along with Basie's fine piano playing. Young used vibrato sparingly and was an excellent improvisor.
  • Have class analyze this composition.

6. Recording: "Body and Soul" by Coleman Hawkins (Album: *The Smithsonian Collection*, Side 4, Band 4). Williams (1973:24) observes: "Hawkins's 'Body and Soul' was that rare exception, a recording that was both an artistic success and influence among musicians."
  • Listen for fully rounded, lush saxophone sound.

7. Recording: "Willow Weep for Me" by Art Tatum (Album: *Art Tatum Solo Piano*, Side B, Band 1). An example of Tatum's incredible virtuosity and formidable technique.
  • Listen for Tatum's numerous melodic embellishments.

8. Recording: "All of Me" by Billie Holiday (Album: *The Smithsonian Collection*, Side 4, Band 7). "One of the incomparable voices that jazz produced in the thirties" (Feather 1966:258) is heard here.
  • Listen for Holiday's phrasing technique and use of rubato.

9. Recording: "You'd Be So Nice to Come Home To" by Ella Fitzgerald (Album: *The Smithsonian Collection*, Side 4, Band 8). Fitzgerald's voice is a great instrument, as demonstrated by this recording.
  • Listen for the security with which the singer attacks pitches during her improvisations.

C. Bebop

Procedure:

1. Show film: *Jammin' the Blues.*

2. Recording: "Koko" by Charlie Parker (Album: *The Smithsonian Collection*, Side 7, Band 7). A demonstration of Parker's brilliance as a melodist, technician and supreme improvisor. Trumpeter Dizzy Gillespie and Max Roach, a fine bop drummer, are also featured. Roach (b. 1925) pioneered in the use of the cymbals as accompaniment in jazz drumming.
  • Have the class graph the contours of the melodies on a plain sheet of paper, drawing lines indicating the directions of the melodies played by the solo instruments.

3. Recording: "Embraceable You" by Charlie Parker (Album: *The Smithsonian Collection*, Side 7, Bands 8 and 9). Two versions of the same song, each different. Parker refers only briefly to the title song, a bop characteristic, in each case letting his inexhaustible store of melodic ideas combine into beautifully conceived phrases.
- Identify differences in Parker's approaches to the same song.
- Listen to selections such as "Confirmation" and "A Night in Tunisia" for further examples of Parker's originality.

4. Recording: "Shaw 'Nuff" by Dizzy Gillespie (Album: *The Smithsonian Collection*, Side 7, Band 6). A fine example of Gillespie's virtuosity.
- Listen for the precision with which Gillespie and Parker perform their duet sequences.
- Use a metronome. Can a steady pulse be found?

5. Recording: "Misterioso" by Thelonious Monk Quartet (Album: *The Smithsonian Collection*, Side 9, Band 4). Monk's concept of jazz piano, the development of ideas within a clearly outlined form, is brilliantly demonstrated in this classic. A short Guided Listening Lesson for this recording could be:

A   Theme stated by piano and vibraphone.
B   Vibraphone improvisation.
C   Piano improvisation.
A[1]   Vibraphone states theme, piano plays countermelody, joining vibes at final measures.

D. Boogie-Woogie

Procedure:

1. Teach selected students to play the following boogie-woogie patterns:

- Ask: "Can you hear the chord changes I IV V?" and "Can you hear the blue notes?" If any uncertainty exists, review what was learned in the *Blues* section regarding chord changes and blue notes.

2. Recording: "Honky Tonk Train" by Meade Lux Lewis (Album: *Folkways FP73*). A very good example of the power and momentum of boogie-woogie.
  • Listen for I IV V chord changes.

E. Cool Jazz

Procedure:

1. Recording: "Boplicity" by Miles Davis (Album: *The Smithsonian Collection,* Side 9, Band 1). A performance that illustrates the best of cool jazz.
  • Listen for the understatements of the solos and the transparent sonorities that allow each instrument to be clearly heard when playing in ensemble.

F. Hardbop or Soul Jazz

Procedure:

1. Show film: *Afro-American Music: Its Heritage.*

2. Recording: "The 'In' Crowd" by Ramsey Lewis (Album: *The In Crowd,* Side 1, Band 1). A return to traditional jazz sources can be heard in this rendition.
  • Use hand and body jibes while listening.
  • Use rhythm instruments to softly accent the basic meter.

G. Modern Jazz and Beyond

Procedure:

1. Recording: "Kulu Se Mama" by John Coltrane (Album: *Kulu Se Mama,* Side 1, Band 1). A classic of early "new wave," or free, jazz this composition features chantlike singing. African drums, bells, and a conch shell are used with the traditional instruments, which frequently sound anything but conventional.
  • Have the class place a mark on a sheet of paper for every different sound they hear.

2. Recording: "My Favorite Things" by John Coltrane (Album:

My Favorite Things, Side 1, Band 1). Coltrane's magic with a melodic line and his great ability to improvise interestingly make this selection a standout.
- Teach the class the song "My Favorite Things."
- Instruct them to raise their hands whenever they recognize portions of the melody during Coltrane's improvisations.

3. Recording: "Lonely Woman" by Ornette Coleman (Album: *The Shape of Jazz to Come,* Side 1, Band 1). Coleman's interesting concepts of jazz are evident here.
- Listen for the counter-rhythms of the bass and drums against the starkness of the melodic line.
- Listen for the interplay of the trumpet and saxophone.

4. Recording: "God Rest Ye Merry, Gentlemen" by The Modern Jazz Quartet (Album: *The Modern Jazz Quartet at Music Inn*). A crisp, very "together" rendition gives this old Christmas carol an entirely new dimension.
- Have the class analyze this using ABA pattern.

5. Recording: *Romeo and Juliet* by Hubert Laws.
- A fascinating lesson: compare Tchaikovsky's *Romeo and Juliet* with Laws' version.

6. Recording: "Boogie Woogie Waltz" by Weather Report (Album: *Sweetnighter*, Side 1, Band 1). An excellent blend of electronic instruments and jazz.
- The class could keep the rhythm by softly playing sticks, drums and tambourine.

7. Recording: "Chameleon" by Herbie Hancock (Album: *Headhunters*, Side 1, Band 1). An infectious riff prevails throughout this recording with rhythmic interplay by the other instruments, which include folkloric and electronic ones.
- Encourage dancing with this recording.

8. Recording: "The Revolution Will Not Be Televised" by Gil Scott-Heron (Album: *The Revolution Will Not Be Televised*).
  • Interpret the meaning behind the words of this contemporary black poem with music.
  • Encourage students to write poems with music background for class participation.

Lesson Seven: Examining Rhythm and Blues

Rhythm and blues was the designation for the records made for the black communities in the forties and early fifties. Many singers became popular and influenced a generation of white performers, among them Elvis Presley and The Beatles. Garland (1969:55) notes that: "Rhythm and blues singing groups of the fifties helped set the scene for the Soul Era." Among the many exponents of this music were Ruth Brown, Joe Turner, The Coasters and The Platters.

Classroom Strategies and Experiences

Purpose of Activities: To locate the roots of soul and rock music in rhythm and blues.

Procedure:

1. Recording: "Five, Ten, Fifteen Hours" by Ruth Brown (Album: *History of Rhythm and Blues*).
  • Have the class listen for chord changes of I IV I V I.
  • Correlate with music forms studied previously such as blues and boogie-woogie.
  • Clap as the record plays; encourage body movements.
  • Listen to "Sgt. Pepper's Lonely Hearts Club Band" by The Beatles for basic rhythm and blues rhythms and the sound of singer Paul McCartney's voice. "Is the black influence obvious in this selection? Why?" (The Beatles, who started the tremen-

dous rock effect on the music industry, freely admit their indebtedness to black musicians.)

Lesson Eight: Becoming Aware of Black Gospel Music

Nowhere are the feelings and emotions of black Americans more vividly expressed than in their gospel songs. The black church has nurtured this music since its inception and it is still the principal music of most black worshippers. It is joyous music that utilizes "contemporary harmonies over embellished melodic lines with syncopated polyrhythms" (Williams-Jones 1970:202). But it is much more than that to the people who perform, write, listen and respond to it. To them it is the essence of life.

Some Differences Between Spirituals and Gospel Songs

Black gospel music has seemingly replaced the Negro spiritual as a traditional vocal expression. This is true even though spirituals are still being sung; in many cases they are given the "gospel treatment" or rearranged in contemporary form. The traditional spiritual is vastly different in sound and mood from gospel songs. Many gospel songs are composed. Interestingly enough, the songs are rarely, if ever, performed as written. Even the composers do not play or sing them as they have written the notes down. They simply cannot put the embellishments on paper, and the songs are hardly ever done exactly the same way twice.

Playing from the score of a gospel song is akin to realizing a figured bass. The piano, organ, and other instruments are essential in the performance of gospel music, whereas the spirituals were sung unaccompanied. (Gospel quartets, however, sometimes sing unaccompanied.) The rhythmic drive, harmonies and melodies of gospel music are complex, unlike the relative simplicity of spirituals.

There are other differences between gospel songs and spirituals. In nearly all the spirituals there is an element of sadness. There is also a great dignity in the spirituals that is not found in the happiness and abandon of much gospel music. Upon first hearing, most contemporary gospel songs sound exactly like secular popular music. Historically, however, much popular music evolved from black church music.

Since all black American music has the same roots this is not sur-prising or unusual. Williams-Jones (1970:210) observes: "The distinction between sacred and secular, in some instances, depends upon the words which are used." The male quartet was always a favorite gospel ensemble whose leaders were often gifted soloists with a flair for narrative in the preaching style, startingly similar in some ways to male vocal groups in Africa throughout this century. An early group in the twenties was The Invincible Four, a quartet out of Conroe College, Conroe Texas. They were followed by outstanding foursomes such as the Dixie Humming-birds and the Soul Stirrers. The influence of this tradition can be seen today in groups such as The Temptations, the Jacksons, and others.

Influences of Gospel Music

Thomas Dorsey, the Chicago-based composer, has written many gos-pel songs and is considered the "father" of gospel music. Chicago is the "home" of urban gospel music, which started in the early thirties. Mahalia Jackson became perhaps the best-known gospel singer of her time. Roberta Martin was a Chicago singer and pianist who set the standard for gospel pianists in the late thirties and forties. James Cleveland, the Hawkins family and Andre Crouch are extremely popular today. The influence of gospel on popular music has been great; many black perform-ers such as Aretha Franklin, Sam Cooke and Wilson Pickett began their careers as gospel singers. Even the current freedom movement in popular dance is an outgrowth of the shouting done in black churches, which is stimulated as much by gospel singing as by preaching. Lucie E. Campbell (1885-1963), a Memphis, Tennessee school teacher, was the first black woman composer in the development of gospel music. As Music Director of the National Baptist Convention, the largest black organization in the world with over 7,000,000 members, Campbell was a major force in the dissemination of religious music composed by Afro-Americans. Her first song, "Something Within" was published in 1919. Gospel music is also influenced by the current generation of college-trained musicians such as Richard Smallwood of Washington, DC, who incorporates contemporary techniques into the gospel sound.

Heilbut (1971:10) observed: "For forty years America has nurtured unacknowledged a cultural form as imposing as jazz, and a life style (that is) peculiarly native...." Gospel music is as distinctively American as it is black, a music with its own literature, stars and traditions.

Classroom Strategies and Experiences

Purpose of Activities: To recognize characteristics in gospel music that make it unique.

Procedure:

1. Show films: *Ephesus*; *Got to Tell It...A Tribute to Mahalia Jackson*.

2. Recording: "Down Here, Lord, Waiting on You" (Album: *The Gospel Sound*, Side 1, Band 2).
   - Listen for the sounds of moaning, one of the most distinctive aspects of black singing, done by both Rev. Gates and the congregation.

3. Recording: "I'll Live Again" by the Dixie Hummingbirds (Album: *The Gospel Sound*, Side 4, Band 3).
   - Listen for the lead singer whose style is reminiscent of the black "singing preacher" tradition.
   - Analyze the selection using ABA pattern; the quartet makes several subtly effective rhythmic changes.

4. Recording: "Move On Up a Little Higher" by Mahalia Jackson (Album: *The Gospel Sound*, Side 3, Band 2). Vintage Mahalia at the top of her form.
   - Listen for her phrasing techniques and the lilt, fervor and rhythmic drive that propels the song to an emotional peak.

5. Recording: "I'll Do His Will" by James Cleveland (Album: *James Cleveland and the Southern California Community Choir*, Side B, Band 1).
   - Listen for Cleveland's use of rubato and the interplay between soloist and choir.

6. Recordings: a) "I'm Goin' Away" by Edwin and Walter Hawkins and the Love Center Choir (Album: *Love Alive II*, Side 2, Band 2). b) "I Wish You Love" by the Richard Smallwood Singers (Album: Richard Smallwood Singers, Side 2, Band 3.
   - Listen for the contemporary harmonies and expressive dynamics by one of the innovative young gospel groups.

7. Recording: "Jesus is Love" by Lionel Richie (Album: *Heroes* Motown MOTC 5353).
   - Listen closely to the words as the singer relates in an intimate way to Jesus. This is frequently done by gospel solo-ists.(Have the class compare this with the slaves' use of imagery in spirituals.)

AMEN

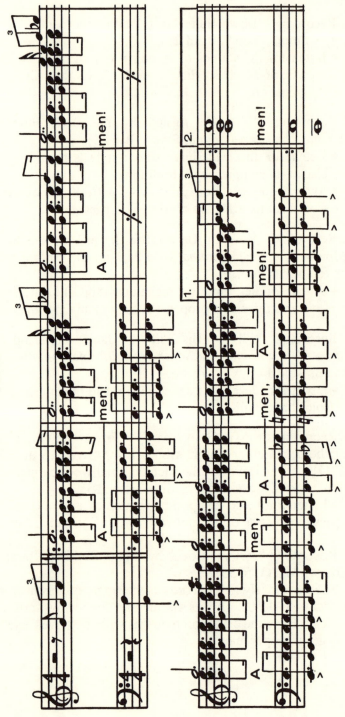

108

- Listen to Donny Hathaway's and Roberta Flack's performance of "You've Got a Friend" (Album: *Roberta Flack and Donny Hathaway*, Side 2, Band 2).
- Next, listen to Aretha Franklin's "You've Got a Friend" (which is combined with an arrangement of Thomas Dorsey's "Precious Lord, Take My Hand").
- Listen for the vocal melisma, the embellishments, rubato, and fervor that make Franklin's arrangement an effective gospel song. (This is also an example of a song becoming black in performance; "You've Got a Friend" was written by a white composer.)

9. Teach the class "Amen" and swing it in the joyous manner of a gospel song. The music shown (pg. 108) is one example of a gospel-style accompaniment to the song.

10. Album: *The Gospel at Colonus* (Warner Bros 25182-1). Listen to this album for good examples of the gospel style in a Broadway musical format.

Discovering The Georgia Sea Islands

The Georgia Sea Islands are lush former plantation lands directly off the coast of Georgia and the Carolinas. Here, large numbers of blacks lived and worked in relative isolation, with only minimal contact with whites until quite recently. As a result, the Sea Islands have musical and cultural traditions very similar to West Central Africa. The language spoken, particularly by older residents, is an English dialect referred to as Gullah, based on West African speech patterns. The traditional music includes spirituals, blues, call-and-response songs, work chants and field hollers, singing games and "plays," stories with songs and narrative interwoven, and dance songs. Techniques include the use of "blue" notes, slurs, slides and vocal percussive elements as well as body slaps, foot stamps, tambourine and polyrhythmic clapping. Harmonies are most often improvised. The best-known and widely respected singer was Bessie Jones (1902-1984), who was born in Dawson, Georgia but spent most of her adult years on St. Simons Island. She joined Willis Proctor, John Davis and the other Georgia Sea Island Singers and sang with them on tour for many years as they shared their musical heritage with enthusiastic audiences. The power of their singing can be heard on several recordings and films.

Procedure:

1. Show films: *Georgia Sea Island Singers* (Available from Radim Films) and *Yonder Come Day* (McGraw Hill Films).

2. Recording: "Sheep, Sheep, Don't You Know the Road" (Album: *Georgia Sea Island Songs*, New World 278, Side 1, Band 3). Point out this is a call-and-response spiritual, and have the class join in on the response. Encourage improvised harmony parts, clapping, moving.

3. Recording: "Raggy Levy" (*Georgia Sea Island Songs*, Side 2, Band 2) A black stevedore's song. Have the students imagine they are lifting heavy weights. The cue for lifting or pulling comes at the end of every pair of lines.

4. Teach the class "Hambone" and "Juba" (clapping games with exciting rhythms and chants) found in *Step It Down* .

A BRIEF INTRODUCTION TO REGGAE

The vital and increasingly popular music from Jamaica called *Reggae* appeared to be a fad in the late seventies and early eighties, but has shown great staying power, and with good reason. Reggae's roots are African traditional and contemporary music, heavily influenced by American blues, rock and roll, and even topical/ political folk music of the 1960's-70's. Messages about love, Rastafarianism, world peace and Jamaican social, political and religious upheaval abound. It features a heavily syncopated sound, mesmerizing rhythms, instrumentation emphasizing the electric bass, keyboards, guitar and percussion and wonderful vocal nuances caused in part by use of the Jamaican dialect and fresh harmonies. Reggae was introduced to the US with the movie *The Harder They Come* and concert tours by Jamaican musicians such as Bob Marley and the Wailers, Rita Marley, Jimmy Cliff, Judy Mowat, and others. The continued presence of the sound and its assimilation into the rhythm, instrumentation and phrasing in selected songs of almost any contemporary pop or rock group (black or white) attests to its good health and importance.

1. Recordings: "We and Dem" and "Coming In From the Cold" by Bob Marley and the Wailers (Album:*Uprising*, Island ILPS 9596). Note the Jamaican-isms and political/religious focus as well as the instrumental accompaniment.

2. Recordings: "Shanty Town" and "Rivers of Babylon" (Album: *The Harder They Come*, Mango MLPS-9202). Note the call-and-response form and dialect of "Shanty Town"; ask if anyone recognizes "Rivers of Babylon" (it is a hymn), and how this version is rhythmically and grammatically distinctive.

ADDITIONAL THINGS TO DO AND DISCUSS

The key to understanding black American music lies in grasping both the rhythmic manifestations from the West African heritage and the sociological implications of the experiences of blacks in the United States. From slavery to the present time, black men and women have expressed their hopes, fears, joys, frustrations and sadness in their music. When drums were forbidden, they used their voices and bodies to make music. Many times the music was all they had.

When Western instruments became obtainable, they took them and made revolutionary innovations both in the way the instruments were played and the music that was played on them. Black music that was written and performed first for the rigidly segregated black audiences invariably made its way into the white communities and beyond, influencing everything it touched.

SOME MORE SPECIFIC SUGGESTIONS

In general, always briefly review selections from the previous class session with emphasis on the recognition of musical styles. Analyzing, hand and body jibes, playing rhythm patterns and improvising with instruments, singing, etc., are to be continued throughout the study of black music, and can be used at any time to keep up interest, reinforce a concept and do away with the "what do we do next?" dilemma.

Films can sometimes be used as an entire lesson. *Discovering Jazz*, for example, has teacher notes with questions to guide the viewing. Preview all films and give students specific things to look for. Use films throughout the study.

For evaluation, place a greater emphasis on the students' abilities to recognize the musical types upon hearing them than on dates, spelling of names, etc. A sample quiz could be the following:

Place these words on the chalkboard:

Spirituals	Swing	Hardbop Ragtime	
Blues	Avant Garde	Soul	Gospel
Boogie-Woogie	Cool Jazz	Bebop	Early Jazz
Rhythm and Blues		Jazz Fusion	

Play examples of each of the styles in varying order (it would be convenient to prepare a tape), and have the students write the correct words as they listen.

Encourage interested students to give brief oral reports on black musicians and the various types of music they will be hearing. Many articles are found in Sunday newspaper supplements and other periodicals. Keep a library of books and magazines in the room for student use and watch for appearances of black musicians in concert and on TV.

Use comparisons between white and black singers to emphasize the use of rubato, falsetto, and other distinctively black vocal traits. Compare Isaac Hayes's style, for example, in "By the Time I Get to Phoenix" to Glen Campbell's rendition; Al Green's use of his voice in "Let's Stay Together"; Curtis Mayfield's voice in "Superfly" in contrast to white male vocalists. Ask the class: "How does the black experience in America affect Sweet Honey in the Rock's choice and performance style of political songs in contrast to Holly Near and Ronnie Gilbert's selection and singing of political songs?"

Teach the class "Let Us Break Bread Together," a spiritual found in *Music In Our Life* (Silver-Burdett), and then play Ben Branch's recording of the same song. Discover how his use of the saxophone is very akin to the voice, and how the rhythmic background is distinctively black– pulsating and driving.

Listen for imaginative use of instruments by black instrumentalists: Coltrane's use of the saxophone in his album *Ascensions*; Gillespie and Parker's wizardry in bebop, and Eric Dolphy in *Out to Lunch*.

Use rhythm instruments frequently to locate the pulse in musical examples from spirituals to swing to today's pop music. Challenge the class: "Can a pulse be found in bebop? In cool jazz? In avant-garde jazz?"

Urge talented students to create their own compositions and their own songs in any style they choose. This will continually involve them in analyzing, performing and composing–actually working with the elements of music.

Throughout the study, approach black music as an outgrowth of a culture with its own aesthetics. Correlate, as much as possible, with the students' knowledge of American history; do not evade discussions about the experiences of blacks in America. After all, from these experiences came the music. Without slavery, there might have been no need for spirituals; without the resulting segregation of the races with its poverty, frustration, and despair, there might have been no blues. As beauty is in the eye of the beholder, so beauty in sound is in the ear of the listener.

SELECTED BIBLIOGRAPHY
Books

Blesh, Rudy, and Harriet Janis. *They All Played Ragtime.* NY: Oak Publications, 1966. Standard reference; musical examples.

Chase, Gilbert. *America's Music.* NY: McGraw-Hill, rev. 2nd ed.,1966. Definitive book on the history of music and musicians in America. Gives good coverage to the contributions of black jazz musicians.

Cone, James H. *The Spirituals and the Blues: An Interpretation.* NY: Seabury Press, 1972. Author discusses the theological implications reflected in spirituals and blues.

Courlander, Harold. *Negro Folk Music, U.S.A.* NY: Columbia Univ. Press, 1963. A fine exploration into the development of black folk music in the U.S. with consistent and logical references to connections with the West African tradition. Forty-three very valuable musical examples.

de Lerma, Dominique-Rene, et. al. *Black Music in Our Culture.* Kent, Ohio: Kent State University Press, 1970. Good insight into how black contributors regard their own music. Good curriculum ideas.

Feather, Leonard. *The Encyclopedia of Jazz.* NY: De Capo Press, 1984. Indispensable; contains over 2,000 bios, 200 photos.

Garland, Phyl. *The Sound of Soul.* Chicago: Henry Regnery Co., 1969. Traces soul music from early beginnings to present dominant force in the music industry.

Harding, Vincent. *There Is A River: The Black Struggle for Freedom in America.* NY: Random House, Inc., 1981. Fine, readable history.

Heilbut, Tony. *The Gospel Sound.* NY: Simon and Schuster, 1971. Solid contribution; good discography.

Hasse, John Edward, ed. *Ragtime: Its History, Composers, and Music.* NY: Schirmer Books, 1985. Comprehensive; essays about ragtime.

Hodeir, Andre. *Jazz: Its Evolution and Essence.* NY: Grove Press, Inc., 1956. Careful analysis of the development of jazz.

Hughes, Langston, et.al. *A Pictorial History of Black Americans.* NY: Crown Pub., Inc., 1973. Fine history, engrossing pictures.

The Illustrated Encyclopedia of Black Music. Mike Clifford, Consultant. NY: Harmony Books, 1982. Useful for classroom.

Jones, Bessie and Bess Lomax Hawes. *Step It Down (Games, Plays, Songs and Stories from the Afro-American Heritage).* Athens, GA:Univ. of Georgia Press, 1987. Background, interviews,songs.

Jones-Jackson, Patricia. *When Roots Die: Endangered Traditions on the Sea Islands.* Athens, GA: Univ. of Georgia Press, 1987. Explores the traces of Africa in the traditions of the black Sea Islanders.

Keepnews, Orrin and Bill Grauer, Jr. *Pictorial History of Jazz*. NY: Crown Pub., Inc., 1966. Fine collection of pictures and essays.

Lovell, John Jr. *Black Song: The Forge and the Flame.* NY: Paragon House, 1986. A paperback reprint, this huge tome (704 pp.) thoroughly examines the origins and impact of spirituals.

Murray, Albert. *Stomping the Blues*. NY: McGraw-Hill, 1976. Sensitive and informative treatment of the blues in all its variety.

Oliver, Paul. *The Story of the Blues*. Chilton Book Co., 1969. Contains many pictures of bluesmen and their surroundings. Accompanying essays, by an acknowledged expert, are good.

Rose, Al. *Eubie Blake*. NY: Schirmer Books, 1979. Entertaining life story of a fascinating performer and composer.

Schuller, Gunther. *Early Jazz: Its Roots and Musical Development*. NY: Oxford Univ. Press, 1968. Excellent and comprehensive treatment of jazz from its origins to early Duke Ellington.

Shaw, Arnold. *Black Popular Music in America: from the Spirituals, Minstrels, and Ragtime to Soul, Disco and Hip-Hop.* NY: Schirmer Books, 1986. Excellent; well told and researched.

Southern, Eileen. *The Music of Black Americans: A History*. 2nd ed. NY: W.W. Norton, 1983. The standard reference.

Standifer, James A. and Barbara Reeder. *Source Book of African and Afro-American Materials for Music Educators*. Washington, D.C.: *Contemporary Music Project*, MENC, 1972. A useful book for teachers. Classroom activities are good.

Taylor, Billy. *Jazz Piano: A Jazz History*. Dubuque, IA: W.C. Brown Co., 1982. A very readable history by a fine jazz pianist.

Williams, Martin. *The Jazz Tradition*. NY: Oxford Univ. Press, 1970. An excellent and objective coverage of the outstanding jazzmen, past and present. The introduction, titled "A Question of Meaning," is brilliant.

_____. *The Smithsonian Collection of Classic Jazz.* Washington, D.C.: The Smithsonian Institution, 1973. Comprehensive notes that accompany the collection of the same title.

Articles

Barron, Mary Jo Sanna. "In Retrospect: Bessie Jones," The Black Perspective in Music, Vol. 13, No. 1(Spring '85).

Burnim, Mellonee. "Gospel Music: Review of the Literature," *Music Educators Journal* 69 (May 1983).

deLerma, Dominique-Rene, "Black Music Now!" *Music Educators Journal* 57 (November 1970): 25. Eye-opening article that stresses the place and value of black music in the curriculum.

Ethnomusicology. U. S. Black Music Issue. Ann Arbor, MI: The Society for Ethnomusicology, Inc. Vol. XIX, No. 3, Sept. 1975.

George, Luvenia A. "Lucie E. Campbell and the Enduring Tradition of Gospel Hymnody," Washington, DC: Smithsonian Institution, Program in Black American Culture, 1983.

_____."'The Best of her Service':Lucie E. Campbell in the Development and Diffusion of Afro-American Gospel Songs," *Black Perspective in Music*, Vol 15, Spring 1987.

Reeder, Barbara, "Getting Involved in Shaping the Sounds of Black Music," *Music Educators Journal* 59 (October 1972): 80. Rhythm in black music; clear activities.

Shehan, Patricia K. "The Riches of Ragtime," *Music Educators Journal* 73 (November 1986): 22. Presents basic principles of ragtime form and technique, and makes a case for integrating it into music and appreciation classes.

Maultsby, Portia K. "Afro-American Religious Music: A Study in Musical Diversity," The Papers of the Hymn Society of America, XXXV, 1981.

Williams-Jones, Pearl. "Roberta Martin: Spirit of an Era," Washington, D C: Smithsonian Institution, Program in Black American Cultures, 1981.

Song Collections

The American Heritage Songbook, compiled and arranged by Ruth and Normal Lloyd. NY: American Heritage Publishing Co., Inc., 1969. Part Seven, "Songs of the American Negro," contains thirteen spirituals and folk songs with informative notes about each one.

Carawan, Guy and Candie Carawan, *Ain't You Got a Right to the Tree of Life?* NY: Simon and Schuster, 1966. "The people of Johns Island, South Carolina" in photographs, interviews, songs; background info. on Sea Islands.

Chambers, H.A., ed., *The Treasury of Negro Spirituals*. NY:Emerson Books, Inc., 1963. The book is divided into : "Traditional Spirituals" and "Modern Compositions." The spirituals are tastefully arranged.

Fulton, Eleanore and Pat Smith, *Let's Slice the Ice*. St. Louis: MMB, 1980. Black American children's games/songs.

Johnson, James Weldon, and J. Rosamond Johnson,*The Books of American Negro Spirituals*. NY Viking Press, Inc., 1954. Originally published in 1925, now issued as two volumes in one. The Preface is rich in information – the Johnson brothers were early experts in black music. Useful.

Landeck, Beatrice, *Echoes of Africa in Folk Songs of the Americas,* 2nd. rev. ed. NY: David McKay Co., Inc., 1969. Part Four, titled "Song Roots of Jazz in the United States," has street cries, spirituals and shouts, work and minstrel songs, and blues. Good selections, with notes and suggestions for performance.

Lomax, John, and Alan Lomax, *Best Loved American Folk Songs* NY: Grosset and Dunlap, 1947. Chapter XI has black songs with informative notes.

AUDIO-VISUAL MATERIALS

Films

Afro-American Music—Its Heritage. Color, 16 min.,Communications Group West. Begins with the drums of West Africa and leads into the rhythmic beat of a contemporary jazz ensemble. Explores the evolution of spirituals, blues, ragtime, and Dixieland.

American Music: from Folk to Jazz and Pop. B/W, 46 min, Contemporary, McGraw-Hill. Shows the folk music beginnings of jazz and pop music featuring many performers alive now.

Aretha Franklin, Soul Singer. Color, 25 min., McGraw-Hill. She is shown at recording sessions and performances. Good.

Black Music in America: from Then Until Now. Color, 29 min., LCA. A history of the black contribution to American music. Includes performances by B.B. King, Mahalia Jackson, Billie Holiday, Louis Armstrong, Count Basie, Bessie Smith, various groups. Holds students' interest.

The Blues. Color, 21 min., Brandon Dist. Seven blues singers with interestingly individual styles are featured.

Body and Soul. Color, 30 min. BFA. In Part II, soul music is discussed in detail with poignant insight by Ray Charles. Historical background of black music; stress on sociological aspects.

Buckdancers. B/W, 6 min., produced by Alan Lomax and Bess Lomax Hawes. People shown are from St. Simon's Island.

Discovering Jazz. Color, 22 min., BFA. Traces the history of jazz from nineteenth century to present. Musicians play examples of different jazz styles and techniques.

Ephesus. B/W, 25 min. Audio-Brandon. An actual black church service in all its religious fervor is depicted.

Georgia Sea Island Singers. B/W, 12 min., Film Images (Div. of Radim).

Got to Tell It...A Tribute to Mahalia Jackson. Color, 33 min., Phoenix Films.

Helen Tamiris in Her Negro Spirituals. B/W, 16 min., Nagtan Productions. Miss Tamiris's modern dance interpretations of three spirituals.

Jammin' the Blues. B/W, 10 min., AB. Black musicians sing the blues, instrumentalists engage in a jam session. Good.

Roberta Flack. Color, 30 min., University of Indiana. The popular singer talks informally about her career and sings some of her most popular songs.

Sam 'Lightnin' Hopkins. Color, 16 min. KUHT Film Productions.

Yonder Come Day. Color, 26 min., McGraw-Hill Films. Shows Bessie Jones at home and as Yale Duke Ellington Fellow.

Filmstrips

An Audio-Visual History of Jazz. Educational Audio Visual, Inc., 2 LPs, 4 strips. Survey of jazz from its historic beginnings in New Orleans to the present. Brief musical examples.

Black Folk Music in America. Society for Visual Education, Inc., 2 LPs, 4 strips, color. General correlation of black music with American history.

Listening to Jazz. Educational Audio Visual, Inc., 4 LPs, 4 strips. Billy Taylor, jazz pianist and composer, discusses the basic elements and techniques of jazz.

Recordings
Spirituals

Fisk Jubilee Singers (Folkways FA-2372).
Tuskegee Institute Choir (Westminster 9633).

Ragtime

The Eighty-Six Years of Eubie Blake (Columbia 2S 847).
Max Morath Plays the Best of Scott Joplin (Vanguard VSD 39/40).
Original Rags by Scott Joplin (Jazz Vol. II, Folkways FP 75).
Piano Rags by Scott Joplin, played by Joshua Rifkin (Nonesuch H-71248 and H-71264).

Blues

Rainey, Ma, *Jazz II* (Folkways FP 75).
Smith, Bessie, *Any Woman's Blues* (Columbia G-30126).
Turner, Joe, *Singing the Blues* (Bluesway S-6006).
Williams, Joe, *Something Old, New and Blue* (Solid State 18015).

Jazz

Armstrong, Louis, *Hot Five and Seven* (Odeon Jazz, Jazz Star
    Series OPX 21).
Jazz (Folkways). A definitive eleven-volume collection that traces
    the history of jazz; compiled from out-of-print remastered
    records.
Jelly Roll Morton's Stomp Kings (Folkways 2805).
King Oliver and His Dixie Syncopators (Folkways 2805)
The Smithsonian Collection of Classic Jazz (distributed by W.W.
    Norton & Co.). A fine, comprehensive collection from
    ragtime to modern jazz with annotations by Martin Wil-
    liams. Highly recommended.

Swing

Basie, Count, *Kid from Red Bank* (Roulett 42015).
Ellington, Duke, *Music of Ellington* (Columbia CCL-558).
Tatum, Art, *Solo Piano* (Capitol M-11028).

Bebop

Diz n' Bird in Concert (Roost 2234).
The World of Charlie Parker (Roost LP 2257).

Cool Jazz

Davis, Miles, *Birth of the Cool* (Capitol DT-1974).
Young, Lester, *Giant of Jazz* (Sun 5181).

Boogie-Woogie

Meade Lux Lewis (Folkways FP 73).

Hardbop or Soul Jazz

The Cannonball Adderley Quintet, *Mercy, Mercy, Mercy!* (Capitol T 2663).
Ramsey Lewis, *The In Crowd* (Argo LP-757).

Modern Jazz and Beyond

Coleman, Ornette, *The Shape of Jazz to Come* (Atlantic 1317).
Coltrane, John, *Kulu Se' Mama* (Impulse A-9106).
_____, *A Love Supreme* (Impulse A-77).
_____, *My Favorite Things* (Atlantic 1361).
Hancock, Herbie, *Headhunters* (Columbia KC 32731).
Marsalis, Wynton, *J Mood* (Columbia FC 40308).
Modern Jazz Quartet,*The Modern Jazz Quartet at Music Inn* (Atlantic 1247).
Sanders, Pharoah, *The Best of Pharoah Sanders* (Impulse AS 9229-2).
Scott-Heron, Gil, *The Revolution Will Not Be Televised* (Flying Dutchman BDLI-0613). A striking combination of black poetry and music.
Shepp, Archie, *Black Gypsy* (America 30 AM 6099).
Weather Report, *Sweetnighter* (Columbia KC 32210).

Rhythm and Blues

History of Rhythm and Blues (Atlantic SD 8161).

Black Popular Music

Brown, James, *Greatest Hits* (King 8032-8452N).
Baker, Anita, *Rapture* (Elektra 60444).
Club Nouveau, "Lean on Me," (Warner Bros. 7-28430).
Houston, Whitney, *Whitney* (Arista).
Jones, Grace, "Slave to the Rhythm," (Manhattan Island Records V56012).
Jackson, Janet, *Control* (A & M SP-5106).
Jackson, Michael, *Thriller* (Epic QE 38112).
Klymaxx, "I'd Still Say Yes" (Constellation 53028/MCA).
Mantronix, "Who Is It" (Sleeping Bag Records SLX-25).
Najee, "Najee's Theme," (EMI-America ST 17241).

Prince, "Sign O' The Times," (Paisley Park 7-28399).
Run-D.M.C., "It's Tricky," (Profile 5131).
Shannon, "Do You Want to Get Away," (Mirage 0-96892).
Vandross, Luther (Duet with Gregory Hines), "There's Nothing
    Better than Love," (Alive Records FET 40415).
Wonder, Stevie, *In Square Circle* (Tamla 6134TL).

Gospel

Ben Branch and the Operation Breadbasket Orchestra and Choir,
    The Last Request (Chess LPS-1524).
Cleveland, James, *James Cleveland and the Southern Community
    Choir* (Savoy MG-14284).
Franklin, Aretha, and James Cleveland, *Amazing Grace* (Atlantic
    SD2-906).
The Gospel Sound (Columbia G31086). This collection "documents
    the changes in Afro-American religious music over a
    forty-year period."
Hawkins, Edwin, *Oh Happy Day* (Buddah 5086).
Jackson, Mahalia, *Newport 1958* (Columbia CS 8071).
Richard Smallwood Singers (Onyx International Records
    RO 3833)
Walter Hawkins and the Love Center Choir, *Love Alive II* (Light
    Records/LS 5735).

Georgia Sea Islands

Georgia Sea Island Songs (New World NW 278).The Sea Island
    Singers in a great variety of styles.
So Glad I'm Here: Songs and Games from the Georgia Sea Islands
    (Rounder 2015). Bessie Jones, adults and children.
Step It Down: Games for Children by Bessie Jones (Rounder
    8004). Companion to the book; add'l 26-page booklet by
    Mary Jo Sanna included.

Reggae (albums not previously noted)

Judy Mowatt, *Black Woman* (Shanachie 43011)
Black Uhuru, *Sounds of Freedom* (Greensleeves 23)
BOOK: Davis, Stephen and Peter Simon. *Reggae Bloodlines*. NY:
Random House. Good introduction, wonderful photos.

CHAPTER FOUR

Understanding
American Indian Music

American Indians or, more precisely, native Americans, are members of our society with whom students easily empathize. American Indian music deserves to be studied in its own terms and in its own cultural context for it has survived as a direct result of the Indians' refusal to totally assimilate into American life. Even those Indian songs with English words never have European melodies. Music was an important part of early American Indian life. It was used in healing the sick, before and after battles, in hunting, and in all tasks that needed maximum effort.

We use the word "Indians," but the people tend to think of themselves as, for example, "Dakotas" (*not* Sioux), or "Diné" (the People, *not* Navaho), and so on. In short, they were wrongly called Indians by Columbus and the name persisted. They are really people who belong to the Hopi, Cherokee, Iroquois, Dakotas, and other great nations of the New World.

Each tribe is different from another with its own traditions and cultures. There is a wide variety of music found among the Indian people, which is rather surprising when one considers their relative scarcity in numbers. It has been estimated that the peak North American Indian population never exceeded much over one and a half million persons.

CHARACTERISTICS OF INDIAN MUSIC

In spite of regional variances, there are certain areas of homogeneity in North American Indian music that cut across tribal differences. In *The American Indian Sings,* Ballard (1970) lists the following general characteristics of American Indian music:

1. Oral transmission.
2. Simple, repetitive melodies, linear form. (This writer has heard, in addition, many complex melodies.)
3. Use of many non-Occidental scales and scale combinations in the vocal line.
4. Absence of chordal harmony and fixed counterpoint.
5. Accompaniment is mainly percussive.
6. Instrumental development is in the primary stages.
7. Mainly functional.
8. Chants contain many vocables (no-meaning sounds) as well as words that relate a story or suggest topics.
9. Metric values are primarily in common meter, seldom compound, and rarely irregular.
10. Predominant intervals are fourths and fifths, with the octave as a "backbone" to the structure.

Ballard (1970) maintains that the vocables, or nontranslatable syllables, are "organic" in that they derive from the various tribal linguistic backgrounds and grow out of phrase endings in the chants. The use of vocables is one of the outstanding differences between American Indian and Western music. Barnes' (1925) view is significant. She notes that: "The function of the vocable in the metrical design is nonessential from the intellectual viewpoint; but there is a clear value, from an aesthetic viewpoint, in the full rounded vowels of many syllables. They give tone color to the whole song, and enrich the metrical design." In most Indian songs the main ideas, or the meanings of the songs, are directly presented; vocables sort of surround the meanings.

It is not unusual for a tribe to have between four and five hundred songs in the communal repertoire. There are around two hundred tribes in the United States. When we take into account differences in languages, dialects, and regions, it is obvious that an enormous quantity and variety of indigenous music exists.

In Indian music the rhythm of the drums frequently differs from the rhythm of the songs. Dancers, however, follow the rhythm of the drum. Singers may sing in one tempo and beat the drum in another. This gives an interesting type of syncopation.

Unfortunately, many Western composers have written monotonous rhythmic accompaniments to rather simple pentatonic melodies and called this "Indian music." The vocal characteristics of native American music have been ignored, while these very qualities are the ones that give the music vitality and make it unique.

PRINCIPAL CLASSROOM STRATEGIES

The basic strategies in the study of North American Indian music will be: (1) listening experiences to familiarize students with the vocal characteristics of Indian music; (2) rhythmic activities that will aid in recognition of the true character of Indian percussion as used in connection with the vocal music; and (3) singing for enjoyment and aesthetic enrichment. The listening experiences should focus on the following:

1. What the Indians are singing and why.
2. The vocal characteristics that give the music the sound it has. (Concentrate on two: the tumbling strain wherein the voice begins on a high pitch and tumbles downward, and the one-step melody in which there is only one step either up or down.)
3. The types of instruments used and how they are used.

There are four main types of Indian musical instruments: drums, whistles, flutes, and rattles. Wide varieties are found within each type and they are generally made from natural materials available. Stringed instruments are rare among the native Americans with the Apache fiddle being the only known variety. The drum is the most important Indian musical instrument. Indian drums are always played with sticks and are considered a sacred element. Ballard has observed over a hundred styles of drumming generally within common and compound meters.

The main purpose of the listening is to know what the song means to the singer after which it may have meaning for the listener. In some tribes accuracy in singing is prized. If an error is made in certain ceremonials, the entire affair must begin again. Indian philosophy has a type of spirituality that is found in the meanings of some types of songs. This spirituality is not so much from a theological standpoint but from a deep reverence for nature, order, and harmony in the cosmos.

Ballard (1970) defines the American Indian chant as: "An expression of the soul of the American Indian and each song pulses with the heartbeat of indigenous America, spanning a 30,000 year history on this continent. These songs are as unique and meaningful as a Moslem call-to-prayer from a minaret or the Hebraic Song of Psalms or the many other countless secular and religious tunes of tribal people the world over."

The reverence for nature is evident in Indian legend and poetry in which animals speak and display wisdom. There were tribes that had societies named after various animals with membership in the society dependent upon whether or not the animal had any significance in the member's life such as appearance in a dream or if one were named after it. Some of the most famous ceremonials and dances were named after animals such as Bear Dance, Buffalo Dance, Deer Dance, and others. Certain animals were venerated because of the strength and cunning that enabled them to survive successfully in their environment and they were thus thought to have supernatural powers. As a lead-in to Indian music we can begin with the sounds of the music itself, exposing the students immediately to a world of strange beauty so near us yet sounding so far away.

Lesson One: Orienting the Listener to Varieties of Indian Music

In the first lesson, it is a good idea to let students hear as wide a variety of musical sounds as possible. They will realize right away that the musical stereotypes they have heard so often in motion pictures and on television do not really depict American Indian music at all. (This is also painfully true of the so-called Indian songs still found in some song series.)

Clues for Listening

Procedure:

1. Show film: *American Indian Influence.*

2. Play a prepared tape, or use recordings of music such as the following. Each example could be approximately two minutes long.

a. "Ute Bear Dance Song" (Album: *Great Basin*). A soloist is accompanied by a rasplike instrument; his voice utilizes the tumbling strain.

b. "Shoshone Sun Dance Song" (Album: *Great Basin*). The drum begins slowly and gradually increases to faster tempo. Drum tones are loud, strong and insistent, while group sings repeated phrases in tumbling strains.

c. "Apache Fiddle Melody" (Album: *Music of the Pueblos, Apache, and* Navaho). The sound of the rare Apache fiddle is accompanied by an occasional drum beat.

d. "Night Chant Dance" (Album: *American Indian Dances*). Navaho men are heard singing in pronounced falsetto fashion; their singing is heavily accented.

e. "Forty-Nine Song" (Album: *Pueblo.*) Singing, which includes English words, is accompanied by accented drumming.

f. "The Warrior's Stomp Dance, or Trotting Dance" (Album: *Songs from the Iroquois Longhouse).* Example of responsorial singing, punctuated with vigorous yells.

g. *"Flute* Melody" (Album: *Music of the Pueblos, Apache, and* Navaho*).* Some squeaking can be heard from the cane flute.

h. "Women's Shuffle Dance" (Album: *Songs from the Iroquois Longhouse*). Singers use a complex melody accompanied by a steady beat on the water drum.

i. "Hopi Version of Dixie" (Album: *Pueblo*). Drums accompany male singers in an interesting adaptation of a familiar song.

j. "Legend Songs" (Album: *Kiowa*). Simple, repeated phrases using one-step melodies are sung accompanied by a stick playing in duple meter.

• Define and play examples of tumbling strain, one-step and falsetto singing. Do the same for accented, simple, and complex melodies.

• On a sheet of paper, have the class number one to ten. As each example is heard, they are to write down the vocal characteristics they hear, which you have defined.

• On second hearing, have them indicate the instrument heard on each example such as string, flute, drum, stick, and also place an asterisk beside any selection that includes a yell or yelplike sound. (These activities encourage careful, active listening.)

3. Teach the class a song such as "Navajo Happiness Song" found on page 44 of *Music Educators Journal* 56 (March 1970).

Lesson Two: Music of the Eastern Area Indians

The eastern seaboard Indians were the first native North Americans to come into contact with Europeans. At the time of Columbus, tribal locales ranged from Maine to Florida. These Atlantic seaboard Indians were considered Woodland People; their means of livelihood were farming, hunting, and fishing.

The Iroquois had a form of government that influenced men such as Benjamin Franklin and the framers of our Constitution as the latter were seeking a representative type of government for the American colonies. The eastern Indians comprised many tribes: Cherokee, Choctaw, Chickasaw, Natchez, Creek, and Seminole in the southeast. In the northeastern section were the Delaware, Iroquois, Mohican, Pequot, Powhatan, Fox, Illinois, Menominee, Miami, Winnebago, Ojibway, and a few others.

Some of these were powerful nations, such as the Iroquois and Delaware, consisting of thousands of people. Others numbered in the hundreds and many are now extinct. The Iroquois Confederacy consisted of five nations: Mohawk, Oneida, Onondaga, Cayuga, and Seneca. Fierce fighters and able statesmen, they numbered approximately 10,000 and lived in villages across central New York State. When the Europeans arrived, they called their league of nations "the completed longhouse," which was symbolic of the member tribes living as relatives beneath a single, long roof.

The Iroquois were a matrilineal society; the wealth of the tribes belonged to the women. Political power also came through the female line, and their homes formed the household. On Iroquois reservations there is a council house, or longhouse. Fenton (*Songs from the Iroquois Longhouse*, Album AFS L6) observes that at great councils and twice a year at festivals marking midwinter and the gathering of crops, tribal officers clear the longhouse and set a bench lengthwise in the room. This is the place where many ceremonies and dances are held. Here the Iroquois thank the Creator for life, children, and growing crops, and hold healing ceremonies and religious festivities as was done long ago.

What to Listen For in the Music

Things to listen for in the music:
1. Brevity of songs; yells at the beginning and end of songs.
2. Use of tumbling strains.
3. Strong singing style with a certain amount of tension in the voice along with a feeling of accent or strong pulse.
4. Rather wide range of about an octave.
5. Responsorial or antiphonal pattern in some songs.
6. Repetition of musical phrases or patterns.
7. Water drums are used exclusively; also rattles.

Classroom Strategies and Experiences:
Listening and Performing to Identify Musical Characteristics

Purpose of Activities: Listening and performing to develop aural acuity in distinguishing musical characteristics of certain eastern Indian tribes.

Procedure:

1. Point out on a map the states where the eastern area Indians live.

2. Show film: *The Longhouse People.*

3. Recording: "The Drum Dance" (Album: *Seneca Songs from Coldspring Longhouse,* Side A, Bands 1 and 2). The Drum Dance is named after the type of water drum used in the ceremony. It is a religious dance that the Iroquois believed was given them by their Maker to dance on earth and is also danced in heaven. It forms a thanksgiving celebration because prayers are interspersed between thirty or more short, responsorial songs. The thanks are to the Creator, giver of life and sustenance.
   • A steady drum beat is heard throughout; have the class duplicate this rhythm using handclaps, drums and maracas.
   • Count the number of prayers heard between the songs.
   • Raise hands when a responsorial pattern is heard.
   • Identify the singing as utilizing tumbling strains.

Songs
and Photos

(These songs may be copied for classroom use.)

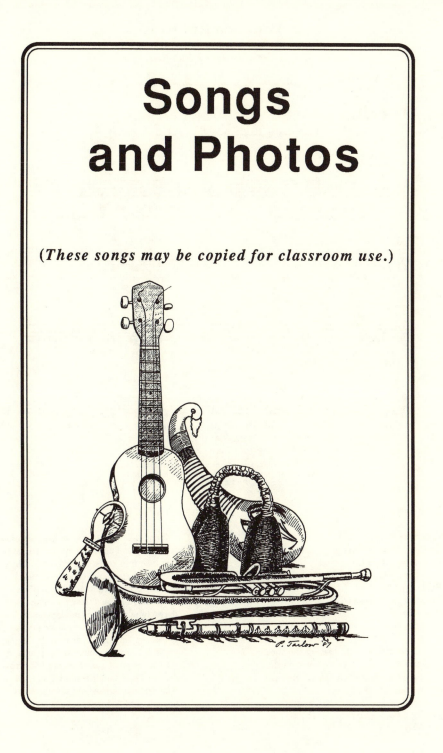

Bantama Kra Kro

An Akan Call-and-Response Stick-Game Song

Bell
(optional)

or

(Sticks) G   G   P   —   G   G   P   —
(Stones) X   →   X   →   X   →   X   →
(L) Leader   (R) Response

Ban - ta - ma kra kro,   mɛ yɛ dɛn na m'an - ya bi ma - dzi
(Bahn - tah-mah krah keer - oh   may - yeh ɑen nah my - ah bee - mahd - zee

(L) G G P G G P
    X → X (R) → X → X →

Kra kro dɛ dɛ iyi, mɛ yɛ dɛn na m'an - ya bi ma - dzi
Krah croh deh day - ee)

(L) G G P G G P
    X → X (R) → X → X →

Kra kro kra kro,   mɛ yɛ dɛn na m'an - ya bi ma - dzi
(Krah croh krah keer - oh)

(L) G G P G G P
    X → X (R) → X → X →

me nyi si - ka,   mɛ yɛ dɛn na m'an - ya bi ma - dzi
(me nee see - kah)

(For stone passing: X = Tap, → = Pass)

To use as a stick game: partners sit facing each other (with short sticks) or stand facing each other (with long sticks).
G = hit the ground, *P* = hit partner's stick. Sticks are held in right hand.

Translation:

Bantama pastries
How can I get some to try?
How delicious are the pastries!
How can I get some to try?
Pastries, pastries!
How can I get some to try?
If you don't have any money,
How can I get some to try?

NOTE: Pastries from the town of Bantama in Ghana are so well known that a traveler in the region will make a special side trip to buy one of them.
This may be used with sticks or as a rock passing game with a simple grab-pass pattern on the beat.

Songs like "Bantama Kra Kro" are used for a variety of activities by children, even into their teen years. Many boys in Ghana take part in an organization very much like the Boy Scouts. They dress in uniform for their activities and learn various skills drawn from ancient and modern times. One activity requires each boy to take a tall staff to bang on the floor in time while singing, or, with a partner, alternately pound the staff on the ground and then raise and cross the sticks with a sharp smacking sound, as if with ancient shields and swords used in protective battle maneuvers.

From: *Let Your Voice Be Heard! Songs from Ghana and Zimbabwe*
©1986 Adzinyah, Maraire, Tucker   Published by World Music Press

(Tucker collection and photo, 1987)

Assorted African instruments:l-r, rear semi-circle: Yemenite *simsimiya;* Drums from Uganda, Senegal, Ghana (*donno*);Kenyan *adeudeu;* Grasslands shakers. Inside, l-r:Gonkogui (Ghana); *kseng kseng* Senegal);*axatse* (Ghana); three types of *mbiras* or *kalimbas* (round:*nyunga nyunga* from Zimbabwe); *axatse* (Ghana). On top of hourglass drum is a firikyiwa, metal castanet and striker from Ghana.

Photo Courtesy Bill Webb

W. Komla Amoaku, Ghanaian master drummer and students playing (l-r) Apentemma drum;
Gankogui double bell; atumpan drums; donno drum

Sheep, Sheep, Don't You Know the Road

Traditional Georgia Sea Islands Spiritual

(A version may be heard on New World 278:
Georgia Sea Island Songs)

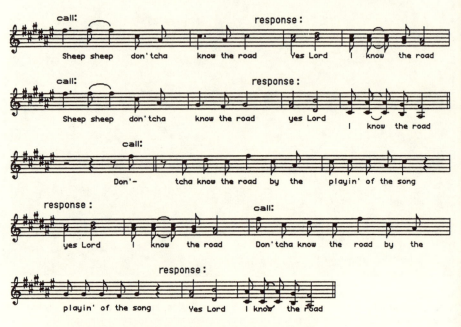

call: response:

Sheep sheep don'tcha know the road Yes Lord I know the road

call: response:

Sheep sheep don'tcha know the road yes Lord I know the road

call:

Don'- tcha know the road by the playin' of the song

response: call:

yes Lord I know the road Don'tcha know the road by the

response:

playin' of the song Yes Lord I know the road

Bessie Jones and the Georgia Sea Island Singers include verses such as the following:

Dont'cha know the road by the playin' of the song?
Dont'cha know the road by the singin' of the songs?
Dont'cha know the road by the prayin' of the prayers?
Dont'cha know the road by the marchin' on home?
Dont'cha know the road by the clappin' of his hands?

Syncopated clapping and stamping add excitement to the sound.

Bessie Jones on her porch – St. Simons Island. The sign was painted
by an admirer. May, 1975 (Photo courtesy Mary Jo Sanna)

Lucie E. Campbell, circa 1955 (Photo courtesy Dr. Amos Jones)

Photo: Luvenia A. George family collection
The Invincible Four Gospel Quartet, Conroe College, Texas 1918-1929
Chicago, 1928; (Top: Floyd Johnson, J.H. James; Bottom: King Spencer, Alvin Thomas)

v

SENECA STOMP DANCES

Recorded by Mary Frances Riemer on
Seneca Social Dance Music (Folkways FE 4072)

by Avery Jimerson
Transcribed by Alan Thrasher
Used by Permission

(/ = vocal shake)

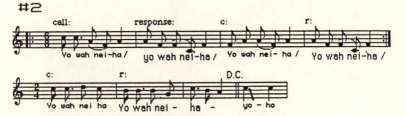

These stomp dance songs as sung by Avery and Fidelia Jimerson, Senecas from the Allegany reservation in Cattaraugus County, NY are traditional trotting or stomp dance songs frequently heard in a group of similar call-and-response songs to kick off an evening of social dancing. The text is composed of vocables, words with no current specific meaning, and the accompaniment is generally only the shuffling and stomping of the feet. Men and women dance single file, counter-clockwise in a circle around the bench where the main singers sit. Stomp dance songs are sometimes used to accompany snake dances as well.

Stomp dance songs may be traditional or recent compositions, and they reflect the vitality of the modern Seneca nation.

ive handsomely clad drummers produce a powerful beat for San Ildefonso singers
nd dancers. (Photo by Roger Sweet, 1973)

Wood and skin drums from Taos Drum
Company (NM); beater is padded with
deerskin ; gourd rattle – l., steer horn
Iroquois rattle – rt.(Tucker)

l-r)Vertical flute, Southern Ute (Miller
Jo. 913); Vertical flute, Sioux (Miller 577);
Vertical flute, Sioux (Miller 526) all 19th Cent.
Library of Congress, Dayton C Miller Collection.

Iroquois water drum
(Rochester Museum & Science Ctr.collection)

EREV SHEL SHOSHANIM

Piano arrangement by Anna Blumstein

EREV SHEL SHOSHANIM ("Evening of Roses")
An old Israeli song of the desert

(a=ah (bar); ai=i (kite); e=eh (set); ey=ay (day); i=ee, ih; o=oh (poke);u=oo(sue); ch=as in "Bach")

[Translation by Sara Kramer]

1.

Erev shel shoshanim	Evening of roses
Neytsena el habustan	Let us go out to the grove
Mor besamim ulevona	Myrrh, fragrant spices and incense
Le raglech miftan	Are a threshold for your feet.

2.

Shachar homa yona	Dawn, a dove is cooing
Roshech maley t'lalim	Your head is filled with dew
Pich el haboker shoshana	Your mouth is a rose unto the morning
Ektefey nu li	I will pick it for myself

Chorus:

Laila yored le'at
Veruach shoshan noshva
Hava elchash lach shir balat
Zemer shel ahava

Night falls slowly, and
The wind of roses is blowing
Let me whisper you a song,
    secretly
A song of love.

viii

(Above) Dancing is an important part of the Israeli culture. Countless folk dance festivals are held, and no social or religious celebration is complete without energetic dancing by all.

(Below)An Israeli clay *tambor* and finger cymbals, often used to accompany dancing. (Tucker '87)

The "shofar" (ram's horn) was used in King Solomon's Holy Temple.It s still blown at the Jewish New Year, at the end of Yom Kippur (Day f Atonement) and on other holy days. It is difficult to blow, and gives ff a raw, powerful sound.   (Independent Picture Service)   *ix*

Aloha Oe
(FAREWELL TO THEE)

QUEEN LILIUOKALANI

Ha- a- heo Ka u- a i- na pa – li Ke hihi a- e- la ka- na-
he- le E ha- ha- i a na i- ka li- ko Pu- a a- hi-hi le- hu-a o
u- ka A- lo- ha oe a- lo- ha oe E-ku o- na- o- na no- ho i- ka
li- po A fond em-brace a ho- i a- e au Un- til we meet a
gain

Translation:
Proudly swept the rain cloud by the cliff
As on it glided through the trees
Still following with grief the liko
The a hi-hi le hua of the vale

Farewell to thee, farewell to thee
Thou charming one who dwells among the bowers
One fond embrace before I now depart
Until we meet again.

x

Young dancers performing at the Polynesian Culture Centre in Oahu.(above)

(l.) Puili Sticks;
(top) kalaau sticks;
(center) ili ili lava rocks;
(bot.) coconut shells

Ipu– traditional gourd drum

ULÍ-ULÍ

Ulí-ulí–traditional gourd rattle commonly
seen decorated with feathers

xi

SI ME DAN PASTELES

Trad. Puerto Rico

SATB, Piano, Guitar, Percussion, Recorders (opt.)

Arrangement by
Alejandro Jimenez
© 1986 Alejandro Jimenez

Verses:(*a* = father;*e*=pen or ay as in day;*y,i* =ee as in meet;*o*=only;u=oo;
   g in *gente*=h; *g* in *guarde*=(g)ood;*j* =h;*que*=kay; roll "r's")

1.

Si me dan pasteles,	If you give me pasteles
Dénmelos calientes.	Give them to me hot.
Que pasteles fríos	Cold pasteles
Empachan la gente.	Make people sick.

2.

Si me dan arroz	If you give me rice
No me den cuchara	Do not give me a spoon
Que mamá me dijo	My mother told me
Que se lo llevara.	To bring it home.

3.

Esta casa tiene	This house has
Las puertas de acero	Iron doors
Y el que vive en ella	And the person who lives within
Es un caballero.	Is a gentleman.

4.

Dios guarde esta casa	God bless this house
Y guarde la familia	And bless the family,
Y que los Santos Reyes	And the three wise men (kings)
También la bendigan.	Also bless the family.

Si Me Dan Pasteles is sung during the Christmas season including the time around January 6th–Three Kings Day. It is a strolling song, sung by groups of people who stroll from house to house while they sing very, very early in the morning. Those within the house exchange food (*pasteles* are a kind of meat pie) and drink for the songs and visit. (The complete choral folio is available from World Music Press. Used by permission)

Illustration by Eli Samuel Rodriguez, 12, Hartford CT

xiii

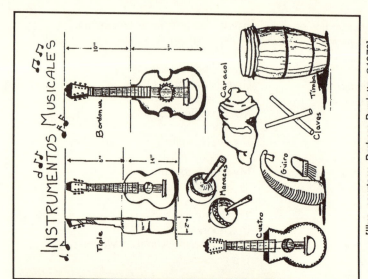

Instruments commonly used in Puerto Rico and Mexico

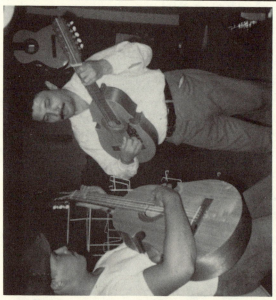

Cristobal Santiago and son in their cuatro and guitar factory in Carolina, Puerto Rico. He has been largely responsible for a resurgence of interest in the cuatro in Puerto Rico. He and his assistants hand build several sizes of fine instruments in their shop.

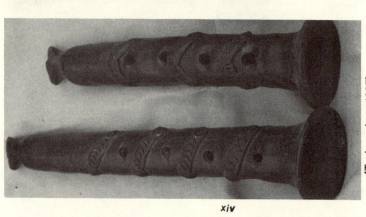

Black clay flutes from Oaxaca, Mexico. They are made in a variety of sizes from small whistles of just a couple of inches long, to dark-sounding flutes over one foot long.

4. Recording: "Bear Society Dance" (Album: *Seneca Songs from Coldspring Longhouse,* Side B, Band 3). This dance is in honor of the bear, which the Iroquois venerated, and is part of a healing ritual. Members of the Bear Society meet certain criteria such as having been cured of an illness during ceremonials of the society, having seen the bear in a dream or vision, etc.

- Have the class listen and try to duplicate the drum rhythms, observing how the drum changes tempo and dynamics in contrast to the meter of the melody.
- Have the class analyze the song using ABA method.

5. Recording: "The Great Feather Dance" (Album: *Songs from the Iroquois Longhouse,* Side A, Band 1). This dance is one of two elaborate religious rituals celebrated by the Iroquois, the Drum Dance being the other.

- Have the class duplicate the sound of the accompaniment, which is the handle of a rattle striking a bench in the longhouse.
- Observe the quaver of the voice; graph the tumbling strains.
- Teach the class "Stomp Dance Song," a Creek-Seminole song found in *The American Indian Sings,* Book 1.

Lesson Three: Music of the Plains Indians

Say the words "American Indian," and it brings to mind brilliantly decorated warriors on fast horses in hot pursuit of either white invaders or the buffalo. This description most aptly suited the Plains Indians whose vanished culture once dominated an enormous area of the North American continent between the Mississippi River and the Rocky Mountains. War, disease, alcohol, and flight has chronicled the demise of many Plains Indians tribes.

Long before the white men came, these people disguised in animal skins hunted the buffalo on foot, cleverly creeping up on herds while serving as decoys to stampede them over cliffs. In the mid 1700s horses brought by the Spaniards to the New World came onto the plains from the southwest. The Indians tamed these animals and replenished their herds through raids upon other tribes as well as upon whites.

The Plains Indians' culture was shaped to a great extent by the horse and the buffalo. The horse enabled them to travel and become a nomadic people, making the buffalo hunt considerably easier while giving them time to develop art and music forms that are popular to this day. Chippewa, Arapaho, Kiowa, Cree, Sioux (or Dakota), Cheyenne, Comanche and Crow became full-time buffalo hunters. They lived in buffalo skin tepees, which were easily assembled and dismantled, and developed military societies with a highly structured system of warfare and raiding.

What the Music Meant to the People

The buffalo and the sun were revered because they provided the food, clothing and shelter that was the source of the people's existence. The buffalo and the sun also inspired much of the art and ceremonials. The Buffalo Dance was used in a religious, or spiritual, manner as part of a ceremony invoking prayer for success in the hunt. The Sun Dance was part of a ceremonial in which vows made to the Creator were publicly acknowledged. This dance included (on occasion) a ceremony of skin piercing, which white people termed to be physical mutilation and was subsequently outlawed by the United States government. (Whites tended to think all Indian dances were war dances and outlawed some that were entirely spiritual in intent.)

Two factors hastened the demise of the Plains Indians: the white man's invasion and the coming of the railroad. This latter factor hastened the extinction of the buffalo, which caused the life of the Indians to change cruelly and rapidly. One of the outcomes of their despair was the Ghost Dance, a religious dance that was part of a movement that began around 1888 when a Paiute Indian from Nevada claimed to be a messenger from God.

His message was that if the Indians would participate in a "holy dance," love all men and lay down their arms, the old days would return. The buffalo would come back, the dead Indians would rejoin them from the spirit world, and, above all, the white man would leave. This was the last hope of the Plains Indians. When they continued their Ghost Dance in spite of government objection, the result was the massacre at Wounded Knee. From then on, until the 1960's, there was little resistance. However, a strong statement of continuing cultural vitality and renewed dedication to Native American rights was made during the occupation of Alcatraz off of San Francisco. Since then many cultural and political movements have blossomed led by knowledgeable elders and young people proud of their heritage. Pan-Tribal Pow Wows draw huge numbers of participants and audiences (both Indian and non-Indian) throughout the United States, and numerous groups similar to the Seneca Allegany Singing Society, the Mohawk Drum, and Tewa ceremonial dancers reveal a resurgence of pride and participation in all aspects of Native American culture.

Things to listen for in the music:
1. Strong vocal tension in the melodies.
2. Pronounced pulsation in the music.
3. Melodies that utilize tumbling strains.
4. Drum accompaniments with even beats throughout a song.
5. Tremolo in drums and rattles.
6. Wide vocal range; repetition in musical form.

Classroom Strategies and Experiences
Activities Designed to Develop Understanding

Purpose of Activities: Listening and performing to develop aural acuity in distinguishing musical characteristics of certain Plains Indians tribes.

Procedure:

1. Point out on a map the states where the Plains Indians lived, and where tribes are presently located.

2. Show films: *Tahtonka* and *Indian Family of Long Ago*.

3. Recording: "Sun Dance Songs" (Album: *Kiowa*, Side A, Band 1). The Sun Dance was the ultimate test of a man's physical and mental endurance. He had to abstain from food and water, dance with his face to the sun during the day, and continue dancing during the night and on succeeding days until he collapsed from sheer exhaustion. The entire ceremony was an intense spiritual experience for both participants and observers.
   ● Have the class duplicate the drumbeat including tremolo, or roll, heard at the end of the song.
   ● Listen for the heavy pulsations in the singing, in whic h only vocables are used.

3.a. Recording: "Crow Sun Dance" (Album: *Sounds of Indian America - Plains and Southwest*, Side 2, Band 4). A short segment performed by one man and one woman at the 1969 Gallup Inter-Tribal Ceremonial. The Crow place emphasis on annual renewal, prayer, thanks and healing with their Sun Dance ritual.
   ● Listen for the eagle bone whistle of the dancer in the background.

4. Recording: "Ghost Dance Songs"(Album: *Kiowa*, Side A, Band 3). The Ghost Dance was considered holy, a spiritual experience.

• Listen for heavily pulsated vocables in the singing.

5. Recording: "Shoshone Sun Dance Songs" (Album: *Great Basin,* Side B, Band 8). Sun Dances were also held to cure the sick. Fasting and continuous dancing was an integral part of the ritual.
• Have the class analyze the recording using ABA method.
• Duplicate drum patterns that change in this recording.
• Listen for repeated phrases; graph tumbling strains as they occur.

6. Teach the class "Sioux Ghost-Dance Song" found in *The American Indian Sings,* Book 1.

7. Show film: *Circle of the Sun.*

Lesson Four: Music of the Southwestern Indians

The Indians of the Southwest still practice their ancient ceremonials to a greater degree than do the Indians of other areas. (The Southwest is also the best-documented area anthropologically and musically.) The Pueblos of New Mexico have one of the oldest continuing civilizations in the Americas. Many of their towns, or "pueblos," were settled before the Spanish occupation. The huge, fortresslike apartments have had the same design for centuries.

Learning About Important Ceremonials

With the Pueblo Indians, spiritual observance is perhaps more ceremonial than that of many other tribes. Each village has large *kivas,* or underground areas where secret religious cermonies are held before the public ones. Their religion centers around the need for rain and many ceremonials are invocations for rain.

The Hopi, whose name means "the peaceful ones," live in the heart of the Navaho reservation, an area in which they have lived for over 1,000 years. The Hopi Snake Dance is world-famous, as are their *kachina* dolls who represent deities. Both the Snake Dance and kachina ceremonials are spiritual in nature. The Taos, Zuni, San Ildefonso and Acoma are other Pueblo tribes that have maintained their culture and ancient beliefs throughout the centuries although nominally Christianized.

The Navaho is the largest tribe in the United States numbering well over 100,000. It is one of the few tribes to have increased significantly in population since contact with whites. The Navaho are an intensely spiritual people with long and elaborately ritualistic ceremonials. They possess a complex mythology interwoven with music, art, and drama. They hold nine-day ceremonies called chants, or sings, for healing purposes and preservation of the integrity of the cosmos. The two most common Navaho ceremonials are Enemyway and Blessingway.

Enemyway is a war ceremonial to protect Navahos from the ghosts of alien peoples such as whites. According to McAllester (1954:12), Enemyway's private ritual contains ghost-killing magic. The public aspect includes the Navahos' only social dancing and a tremendous body of popular songs. Blessingway is the best-loved of the two ceremonies with "songs of good hope" and invocations for good for pregnant women, persons leaving on a journey, and other such instances.

The Apaches are closely related to the Navahos, since both are Athabascan-speaking. The word "Apache" might connote the historical stereotype of fierce warriors roaming the southwestern spaces on horseback, yet today many are accomplished cattle ranchers. They possess the only stringed instrument of the North American Indians, the Apache fiddle. Important ceremonials include puberty celebrations for girls, and healing rituals.

Things to listen for in the music:

1. The sound of the Apache fiddle.
2. Complex rhythms, particularly among the Pueblos.
3. Use of falsetto technique among Navahos and Apaches.
4. Very wide vocal range among Navahos and Apaches.
5. Heavy vocal pulsations and vocal tension.
6. Yelps or shouts in some Pueblo songs.
7. Tumbling strains in some melodies.

Classroom Strategies and Experiences:
Things to Listen For and Do

Purpose of Activities: Listening and performing to develop aural acuity in distinguishing musical characteristics of certain Southwestern Indian tribes.

Procedure:

1. Point out on a map the states in which the Southwestern Indians live.

2. Show films: *Indian Ceremonial Dances of the Southwest* and *Hands of Maria.*

3. Recording: "Zuni Rain Dance" (Album: *Music of the American Indians of the Southwest,* Side 1, Band 4).
   • Have the class analyze the recording using ABA method.
   • Listen for heavy pulsation, wide range of voices.
   • Count how many times yelps are heard.
   • Listen for rich timbre in male unison singers.
   • Listen closely for a quiet cry at the end of the song.

4. Recording: "Hopi Butterfly Dance" (Album: *Music of the American Indians of the Southwest,* Side 1, Band 5).
   • Have the class analyze the song; the structural pattern is easily recognized.
   • Indicate in the analysis in some manner the yells heard in the song.
   • Notate and duplicate the drum rhythm, which is basically steady but starts and stops while accompanying the singers.

5. Recording: "Navaho Enemyway Song" (Album: *Music of the American Indians of the Southwest*). This is music for a Squaw Dance, a rare opportunity for young Navaho men and women to dance together. It is also possibly the most popular part of the Enemyway ceremonial and has been compared to a coming-out party for girls in Western society.
   • Duplicate the strong drumbeat accompaniment.
   • Listen for heavily accented singing.

6. Recording: "Navaho Night Chant" (Album: *Music of the American Indians of the Southwest,* Side 2, Band 1). This music is part of a nine-day ceremonial in which boys and girls are initiated into the ritualistic life of the people. The main figures in the ceremony are two masked adults on stilts.
   • Listen for a rattle at the beginning; use maracas to play along.

- Graph the melodic line of the singers who begin in an unbelievably high falsetto.

7. Recording: "Western Apache Devil Dance" (Album: *Music of the American Indians of the Southwest*, Side 2, Band 3). This dance is part of girls' puberty rites in which the girl dances for hours and is instructed on the observation of certain rituals and tabus that are now in effect for her. These rites are an integral part of Apache life and involve exchanges of gifts and general celebration.

- Have the class analyze the selection using ABA pattern; indicate where "whoo-oo-oo" sounds occur.
- Listen for vocables, which are clearly heard on this recording and are easily distinguished from the words.
- Count the number of yells heard in the song.
- Duplicate the heavy drumbeat and rattle accompaniments.

8. Recording: "Apache Fiddle Melody" (Album: *Music of the Pueblos, Apache and Navaho*, Side 2, Band 2). This recording demonstrates the versatility of the Apache fiddle, which plays with the fluidity of a singing voice.

9. Recording: "Apache Flute Melody" (Album: *Music of the Pueblos, Apache and Navaho*, Side 2, Band 5). The flute is associated with love in Indian lore and life. A young man would play his flute at night and if the girl was receptive she would go out to meet him. (The flute could also be played at other times.) The record notes indicate that the flute heard on this recording is made of river cane and has three stops.

- Listen for the vibrato quality of the flute tone.
- Tell the class about the use of the flute in Western orchestral music to symbolize birds.

10. Teach the class the following songs; "Pueblo Rain Song," an Acoma chant, and the Navaho "Squaw Dance Song," both found in *The American Indian Sings*, Book 1.

11. Show films: *Hopi: Guardians of the Land, Peaceful Ones*, and *The Apache Indian*.

Lesson Five: Indian Music of the Northwest Coast

The Northwest coast area extends, roughly, from northern California to southeast Alaska. Tribes include the Nootka, Bella Coola, Makah, Tlingit, Kwakiutl, Haida and Tsimshian. The cultures were very distinctive, characterized by highly structured social systems and ceremonials related to complex mythology.

The Northwest Indians are great fishermen with a reverence that bordered on the spiritual for the salmon. Salmon was the foremost food, and many tribal beliefs and ceremonies centered around this. Wood was the second most important source of wealth, especially the red cedar.

Curtis (1907:298) notes that the Indians lived in wooden houses painted with beautiful and emblematic animal forms. The totem pole, which is carved from a great tree, looms large in the front of the house with a doorway cut through the pole serving as an entrance. In the Puget Sound area Indians attached great importance to the potlatch feast, which was a favorite ceremonial. The word "potlatch" means "giving" or "gift." A man would invite neighboring villages as well as his immediate tribe to a potlatch, the occasion of which could be the coming of age of a daughter. He would prepare a great feast and distribute gifts to all, sometimes giving away everything he owned to show that material things were insignificant. There would be much singing, music, and dancing throughout.

Things to listen for in the music:

1. Singing of one-step or single-tone melodies, giving a somewhat monotonous effect.
2. Repetition of musical phrases.
3. Some vocal accents; no feelings of tension in the voice.

Classroom Strategies and Experiences:
Identifying Characteristics in the Music

Purpose of Activities: Listening and performing to develop aural acuity in distinguishing musical characteristics of certain potlatch songs.

Procedure:

1. Point out on a map the areas where the Northwest Indians live.

2. Show films: *Dances of the Kwakiutl* and *Hupa Indian White Deerskin Dance.*

3. Recording: "Song in the Canoes" (Album: *Songs of the Nootka and Quileute,* Side A, Band 1). Songs were sung in the canoes by the emissaries who were sent to invite guests to the host's potlatch.
• Duplicate the persistent drumbeat.
• Listen closely for vocal "ooh-ooh" at the end of the song.

4. Recording: "Young Doctor's Canoe Song" (Album: *Songs of the Nootka and Quileute,* Side A, Band 3). This is a dream song given to an Indian when he goes on a solitary quest seeking more power. A song would come to a man in his dream, which then belonged to him exclusively and which he sang in times of danger or other necessity. The singer invariably has a vivid remembrance of the occasion surrounding the dream or vision.
• Listen for the vocal pulsation at the end of the song.

5. Recording: "Song Before Distribution of Gifts" (Album: *Songs of the Nootka and Quileute,* Side A, Band 5). As the gifts were laid out in front of the host, this song was sung before they were distributed to his guests.
• Analyze the song using ABA method.
• Duplicate the steady drum accompaniment.

6. Teach the class "Welcome Song" of the Haida Indians found in *The American Indian Sings,* Book 1.

7. Show films: *Quillayute Story* and *Indian Heritage: The Treasure.*

ADDITIONAL THINGS TO DO AND DISCUSS

Nettl (1965) notes the Indian music tradition to be relatively free of acculturation since they have remained, for the most part, separate from both blacks and whites. This has enabled them to preserve their musical styles through the centuries. The long resistance of certain Indians such as the Plains Indians and other groups to accept Western culture has contributed to the idea that the American Indians refused "civilization." This view is clearly untenable; the Indians had a perfectly functioning culture as far as they were concerned and saw no reason to change. They possessed highly organized social and political organizations and had many values that we now deem to be desirable for modern civilization today.

The songs of a tribe are very important to our understanding because they present a reasonably accurate assessment of its culture. The Plains Indians, for example, had many hunting songs because game was plentiful. There were many healing songs among tribes with access to medicinal herbs, while ceremonial songs of much variety were found in tribes rich in ceremonial traditions. Close communication with nature, not theology, is the basis of Indian spirituality and is a part of Indian music that is basic to any true understanding of the culture. The sounds of nature are frequently heard in Indian songs.

Dream songs, those procured in lonely visions and solitary quests, were the most valued and powerful. They had a distinction of their own and were believed to be given by the spirits of birds or animals that lived successfully in the environment of the dreamer. Thus, a Plains Indian might dream of a spirit buffalo or wolf that gave him success in war and other undertakings.

Songs were property, either of the tribe, or of the individual. They might be bought, exchanged, or received as gifts, but even in such cases credit is always given to the original owner. It is not unusual to find persons who can sing literally hundreds of songs. They are greatly respected and lead the singing. Indian songs, however, are not extemporized; they are always composed and passed on orally.

Constantly emphasize to students that Indians never "sing with expression" as we think of it in terms of Western music. Whatever style is used in the beginning is maintained throughout a song. Another vital point in understanding is to keep in mind that Indian music is, above all, introspective. The only way to really become involved in a culture is to experience it. The following suggestions are idea-stimulators to this end and can be used at any time during a lesson to keep interest high and as a change of pace. They also encourage involvement and discovery on the part of students.

TEN SPECIFIC ACTIVITIES FOR FURTHER ENRICHMENT

1. Use Indian sign language as a five-or ten-minute part of every lesson to involve the students in a different aspect of Indian culture; they absolutely love this! There is a beauty, dignity, and rhythm in sign language that borders on the aesthetic. If done regularly, by the end of the study many will be able to do simple sentences fluently. (Sign language is also a marvelous means of getting a class quiet!) There may be Boy Scouts in class who have knowledge of Indian sign language; have them help teach the class. Sign language was a widely used method of communication between tribes who spoke different languages and between Indians and whites.

2. Enact Indian legends in sign language. This can become a fascinating correlation of music and drama. Indeed, music, art, medicine, drama, and a sense of spirituality are deeply integrated in American Indian life and culture to the extent that many tribes had no separate names for them. Tomkin's book *Indian Sign Language* is recommended for use; it is clearly illustrated and considered authoritative.

3. Perform dances in class. Learn the basic steps and try to practice them frequently, as part of every lesson if possible. Five or ten minutes of dancing in each class period will quickly add up to an impressive variety of steps. Ballard's *American Indian Music for the Classroom* (Canyon)and *Seneca Social Dance Music* (Folkways) have clear dance instructions with accompanying recordings.

4. Learn authentic songs as accurately as possible; again, a few minutes of each class meeting will pay dividends in the end. Ballard's sets, the Bala Sinem Choir recordings, *Seneca Social Dance Music* and Burnett's *Dance Down the Rain Sing Up the Corn* are all excellent sources for songs. Avoid texts with overly romantic sentiment and piano accompaniments studded with musical cliches such as open fifths in the bass register and use of the pentatonic scale in cliche melodies, and rhythms with no basis in actual repertoire.

5. Encourage the artists in class to draw pictures of Indian art; make kachina dolls or dried gourd, papier mache or small tin can rattles painted with symbolic designs; dream shields,masks and tunics. Seek cooperation from appropriate art or home economics thers. This will further involve students in research and discovery.

6. Stimulate those interested to investigate and make reports about Native American art, culture and music in the geographic area closest to your school. The *Eagle Wing Press* and *Akwesasne Notes* publish calendars of ceremonial events throughout the country that both teacher and students would enjoy and benefit from.

7. Make lists of Indian words that have become part of our language. Many of the fifty states have names of Indian origin such as: Alabama, Alaska, Arkansas, Connecticut, Hawaii, Idaho, Illinois, Iowa, Kansas, Kentucky, Massachusetts, Michigan, Minnesota, Mississippi, Missouri, Nebraska, New Mexico, North and South Dakota, Ohio, Oklahoma, Tennessee, Texas, Utah, Wisconsin, and Wyoming.

8. Investigate other areas of Indian influence such as foods. Many classic American dishes such as barbecue, mincemeat pie, succotash, cranberry sauce, and steamed lobster are inherited from the native Americans. With the discovery of America, the rest of the world learned about potatoes, tomatoes, squash, maple sugar, peppers, and many other foods. Many Indians considered corn to be a gift from the gods and there were ceremonies surrounding this versatile food. The use of corn contributed greatly to the successful survival of the American colonists.

9. Keep books, magazines, pictures and artifacts relating to the subject matter on hand throughout the study. Comb the newspapers and listen to the media for current news about Indians; discuss the status of the American Indian and his treatment throughout America's history.

10. Take museum trips; invite Indian residents of your community to visit your class. In short, become immersed in the subject.

Evaluation of learning can be based on aural recognition of differences in vocal characteristics of tribes and identification of certain types of drumming and musical instruments.

It is apparent that unless Indian music is correlated with the lives of the people and the importance it holds in their lives, it will have little value or meaning for students. The music of the American Indian is genuine folk or "people" music and is the strongest thing remaining in their cultures. If the marks of a civilized people are rich legend, noble philosophy, and original art and music, then the North American Indians, even at the time of Columbus, were civilized indeed.

SELECTED BIBLIOGRAPHY
Books

Barnes, Nellie. *American Indian Love Lyrics and Other Verse*. New York: The Macmillian Co., 1925. Sensitive translations of Indian poetry from many tribes.

Bernstein, Bonnie and Leigh Blair. *Native American Crafts Work shop*. Belmont (CA): Pitman Learning, Inc., 1982. Excellent collection of everyday and ceremonial crafts, musical instruments, games and recipes. Clear directions.

Brown, Dee. *Bury My Heart at Wounded Knee: An Indian History of the American West*. New York: Holt, Rinehart and Winston, Inc., 1970. Poignant view of Indian history effectively told by a fine writer.

Cahn, Edgar S., ed. *Our Brother's Keeper: The Indian in White America*. New York: World Publishing Co., 1970. Scathing indictment of America's treatment of the Indian. Timely.

Curtis, Natalie. *The Indians' Book*. New York: Dover Reprints, 1968. One of the best books on the American Indian. Rich in Indian lore, legend, and musical examples.

Fletcher, Alice C. *Indian Games and Dances with Native Songs*. Evanston, IL; Summy-Birchard, 1915, reprinted by AMS Press Inc., 1970. Sections 1 and 2 good for class use.

Hofmann, Charles. *American Indians Sing*. New York: The John Day Co., 1967. Good descriptions of dances with diagrams and directions for performance. Contains songs.

McAllester, David P., "North America/Native America," in *Worlds of Music*, (1984): pp. 12-63. Includes contemporary songs.
_____."North American Native Music," in *Musics of Many Cultures*, (1980); pp.307-331. Both are comprehensive, with bibliography, discography and other references.

Powers, William K . *Here Is Your Hobby: Indian Dancing and Costuming*. New York: G.P. Putnam's Songs, 1966. Costumes that can be easily executed by an average class.

Spicer, Edward H. *A Short History of the Indians of the United States*. New York: D. Van Nostrand Co.,1969. Excellent, traditionally told history that is clearly written. Pbk. Keep several in class.

Sweet, Jill D. Dances of the Tewa Pueblo Indians. Santa Fe: School of American Research Press, 1985. Fascinating introduction (with 15 color photos) to Tewa dances, costumes, songs, meanings and symbolism. (No music transcriptions.)

Tomkins, William. *Indian Sign Language*. New York: Dover Publications, Inc., 1969, reprint of 1931 fifth edition. A clearly illustrated, cross-indexed book of sign language.

Booklets

Bureau of Indian Affairs, U.S. Department of Interior, Washington, D.C. This agency offers a variety of publications about Indians; most materials are free so send for a complete listing. Ask for: *Native American Arts*, an illustrated booklet of Indian art and poetry; *The American Indian Calendar*, which lists dates and places of festivals and ceremonials all over the country, and for booklets about any tribes in which you are interested. Also available and useful is *Three Maps of Indian Country*, which shows locations of tribes around 1500; current culture areas and locations of tribes today; and identifies Indian lands and communities.

McAllester, David P. *Indian Music in the Southwest*. Colorado Springs: The Taylor Museum, 1967. This slender little booklet contains information on North American Indian music in general as well as specifics on Southwestern Indian music.

Nettl, Bruno. *North American Indian Musical Styles*. Philadelphia: American Folklore Society, 1954. A scholarly monograph that divides American Indian music into six musical areas. Contains musical examples.

My Music Reaches to the Sky: Native American Musical Instruments, Washington, D.C.: Center for the Arts of Indian America, 1700 Pennsylvania Avenue N.W. This booklet is part of a kit for teachers of Indian culture and music teachers. Useful.

Article

Ballard, Louis. "Put American Indian Music in the Classroom!" *Music Educators Journal* 56 (March 1970). An impressive rationale for American Indian music in music education. Contains valuable information about Indian music with musical examples from a primary source.

Song Collections
Ballard, Louis W. *The American Indian Sings, Book 1*. Santa Fe, NM:New Southwest Music Publications, 1976. Six songs from various tribes, tastefully arranged. Informative notes for each with suggestions for correct vocal technique. Highly recommended.

Burnett, Millie. *Dance Down the Rain, Sing Up the Corn*. Pittsburgh: Musik Innovations, 1975. Nice variety of songs including game and dance songs with directions, legends for dramatic retelling, ceremonial songs, recipes.

Dawley, Muriel, and Roberta McLaughlin. *American Indian Songs*. Hollywood: Highland Music Co., 1961. Twenty-three songs from wide variety of tribes, some with only English words; notes, bibliography.

Glass, Paul. *Songs and Stories of the North American Indians*. New York: Grosset and Dunlap, 1968. From 5 tribes; all songs with English words; indications for drumming; photos.

Songs of the Wigwam. Delaware, Ohio: Cooperative Recreation Services, Inc., 1955. Ten songs from a cross-section of tribes. Accompanied by notes.

AUDIO-VISUAL MATERIALS
Films

American Indian Influence. Color, 20 min. Depicts how life in the United States has been influenced by the American Indian economically, sociologically, philosophically, and culturally.

The Apache Indians. Color, 10 min., Coronet International Films. Puberty Dance combined with Devil Dance is shown.

Dances of the Kwakiutl. B&W, 10 min., Orbit Films. Depicts British Columbia Indians.

Circle of the Sun. Color, 30 min. Shows present-day existence of the Blood Indians, a Canadian Plains tribe.

Discovering American Indian Music. Color, 20 min., BFA. The music and dance of several tribes is excellently presented.

Dream Dances of the Kashia. Color, 35 min., National Science Foundation. The *Bole-Maru* or Dream religion, of a central California tribe is shown. High school level and above.

Hands of Maria. Color, 15 min. Maria Martinez, the famous potter of San Ildefonso Pueblo, explains the age-old techniques of potting and some of her secrets. Colorful shots of San Ildefonso Pueblo, New Mexico. Good for all ages.

Hopis: Guardians of the Land. Color, 10 min. Filmfair, Inc. Depicts the depth of Hopi feeling for the land, shows kachina dolls, farming, weaving.

Hupa Indian White Deerskin Dance. Color, 12 min., Arthur Barr Productions. Film shows a Northwest California tribe.

Indian Ceremonial Dances of the Southwest. Color, 13 min., Univ. of Oklahoma. Dances and music of the Hopi, Navaho, and Pueblo people.

Indian Dances. Color, 10 min., American Museum of Natural History and Encyclopedia Brittanica. Iroquois "Feather Dance," Pueblo "Deer Dance," Plains "Buffalo Dance" and others are shown.

Indian Family of Long Ago. Color, 14 min., Recreates the life of the Plains Indians in the Dakotas and adjoining territories two hundred years ago. Fascinating.

Indian Heritage: the Treasure. Color, 10 min., King Broadcasting Co. A Northwest Indian father is attempting to preserve his culture and fishing rights. Film is shown through the eyes of his two young sons. Thought-provoking; no music.

The Longhouse People. Color, 23 min., National Film Board of Canada. Depicts life and religious ceremonies of the Iroquois.

More than Bows and Arrows. May be obtained from Bureau of Indian Affairs, Washington, DC.

Peaceful Ones. Color, 10 min., Avalon Daggett Productions. Shows Hopi at daily occupations; Snake Dance is enacted, a kiva is shown. Beautiful film.

Quillayute Story. Color, 25 min., Titania Productions. Present-day life of a Pacific Northwest Indian tribe, including a dance and Shaker religious service.

Tahtonka. Color, 30 min., Charles Nauman. "Tahtonka" is Sioux for "buffalo." A saga of the Plains Indians, the demise of the buffalo and its effect. Students will be spellbound.

Filmstrip

The American Indian: A Study in Depth. Warren Schloat Productions. Six filmstrips with recordings; color. Titles include "Arts and Culture," "The Navajo." Good for school library.

Recordings

American Indian Dances (Folkways FD 6510). Dance notes and descriptions included; good cross section and variety.

American Indian Music for the Classroom, by Louis W. Ballard (Canyon Records). Excellent, useful collection of 4 LPs, maps, bibliography, teacher's guide, spirit masters, photos.

Archive of Folk Culture, American Folklife Center, Library of Congress, Washington, DC. Extensive listing of American Indian recordings; exc. notes. Those used in this chapter are:

Great Basin: Paiute, Washo, Ute, Bannock Shoshone (AAFS L38)
Kiowa (AAFS L35).
Pueblos: Taos, San Ildefonso, Zuni, Hopi (AAFS L43).
Seneca Songs from Coldspring Longhouse (AAFS L17).
Songs from the Iroquois Longhouse (AFS L6).
Songs of the Nootka and Quileute (AAFS L32).

Branch to Branch by Leon Redbone (Atco EC-38136). Rock sounds by a contemporary Indian music ian.

A Cry from the Earth: Music of the North American Indians (Folkways 7777). Book and record set by John Bierhorst.

Flute Songs of the Kiowa & Comanche by Tom Mauchahty-Ware (Indian House 2512) Cassette with booklet. Traditional flute technique; good notes.

Love Songs of the Lakota (Indian House 4315) by Kevin Locke.

Music of the American Indians of the Southwest (Folkways FE4420). Good notes; varied selection.

Music of the Pueblos, Apache, and Navaho (The Taylor Museum of the Colorado Springs Fine Arts Center). Varied; notes; bib.

Pueblo Songs of the Southwest (IH 9502)Inc. Hopi, Zuni, Laguna.

Seneca Social Dance Music (Folkways 4072). Notes by Mary Reimer. Contemporary singers, traditional styles. Useful.

Music of the American Indian (New World series):
Songs and Dances of the Eastern Indians from Medicine Spring and Allegany (NW 337). Good instrumental sounds.
Songs of Earth Water Fire and Sky (NW246) Notes by Heth.

Songs of the Chippewa - Vol. 1(Folkways 4392).

Sounds of Indian America-Plains & Southwest (IH 9501). Exc. variety, notes.

SOURCES

Canyon Records, 4143 N. 16th. St., Phoenix, AZ 85016

Children's Book and Music Center, 2500 Santa Monica Blvd. Santa Monica, CA 90404.

Indian House (Recordings), Box 472, Taos, NM 87571

Iroqrafts Ltd. RR#2, Ohsweken, Ontario NOA 1MO Canada

Museum of the American Indian, Heye Foundation, 155th St. NYC, NY

Taos Drum Co., Box 1916, Taos, NM 87571

US Dept. of the Interior, Bureau of Indian Affairs, Washington, DC 20240. Source of numerous free pamphlets, booklets etc.

CHAPTER FIVE

Effective Strategies for Teaching Jewish Song

In order to understand and enjoy any aspect of the music of a people, some knowledge of their sociocultural history is necessary. This is particularly true of the Hebrew people who, due to the many countries in which they have lived, have many cultures. These various communities differ widely from one another, yet all share the common heritage of the Pentateuch, the five books of Mosaic law. Even a cursory examination of Jewish song will unearth a tremendous variety of music, for here we find the songs of a people who are living all over the world.

BIBLICAL REFERENCES TO MUSIC

The Old Testament portion of the Bible is not only our richest source of reference for ancient music and musical instruments, it is also a priceless storehouse for information about the ancient Israelites and their musical life. The First Temple in Jerusalem boasted an orchestra of enormous size with a corps of professional musicians. Idelsohn (1929:17) states that the First Temple choir of male singers equalled the number of instruments. (In biblical times, it was customary for Hebrew song in the temple to be accompanied by instruments.)

The Bible also refers to the musical instruments played: cymbals, small drums, small bells, rattles, stringed instruments, flutes or pipes, and the trumpets and shofar. The shofar, which is usually a ram's horn, alone has survived to this day and is still used on the High Holy Days. The shofar today is becoming more symbolic of a variety of traditional lore and function. Dancing was also important in ancient temple worship. In the Bible there is mention that King David "danced before the Lord with all his might" (II Samuel 6:14).

The psalms are not only indicative modes of musical expression, viz. singing and dancing, but they remain beautiful examples of religious poetry. Gradenwitz (1949:2) notes that David's psalms are "sublime examples of shepherd poetry and song." There is an impressive variety of psalms, many of which have been used and loved in Christian churches through the centuries. There was, in fact, such an established relationship between pre-Diaspora temple music and worship that the psalms associate coming into the temple with that of making "a joyful noise unto the Lord; sing praises unto Him with the timbrel and harp" (Psalm 81:1,2).

The ancient pre-Diaspora Israelites also used music outside religious worship: at the coronation of kings, to celebrate victories of their many wars, as love songs, work songs, dance songs, and for other purposes. Idelsohn (1929:21) notes that rhythm played an important part in secular music and handclapping was used to emphasize it. He further observes that the secular music was similar to the Arabic music still heard in Israel and the Near East.

MUSIC DURING THE DIASPORA

The dispersion of the Hebrew people that began after the destruction of the First Temple resulted in settlements in places such as Babylonia and Persia. When the Second Temple was destroyed in 70 A.D., the Diaspora (dispersion) was continued. The Jewish people were scattered and began their wanderings throughout the world. Some went to parts of the Roman Empire; some were taken captive or sold into slavery, but they managed to hold fast to their religious heritage. This heritage was firmly rooted in their belief in one God (which made them unique in the ancient world) and their adherence to Mosaic law.

Displaced and uprooted from many countries, the Hebrew people traveled on with their songs, however varied through acculturation, through the ages against varied backgrounds of historically shattering events. These events ranged from the Spanish Inquisition, the ghettos of Europe, the trauma of the Nazi holocaust, to the wars of the present State of Israel. Today their descendants are found all over the world.

Eisenstein (1972:55) states: "Wherever Jews have lived, they sang their folk songs in the language of the vernacular." Acculturation occurs when there is continued contact between different cultures. Since Jews have lived all over the world, there has been a great deal of acculturation in their music. The inevitability of acculturation is always a force to be reckoned with in the study of the music of any culture, and in Jewish music this makes for a uniquely complex musical picture. In the large body of folk songs, the only thing distinctively Jewish about the music seems, in many instances, to be the language—Yiddish (Judeo-German) used by eastern Europeans and their descendants; Ladino (Judeo-Spanish) used by eastern Mediterraneans; Hebrew—and, inevitably, the sentiments expressed in the words of the songs.

The one facet of Jewish music that has remained nearly universal and identical everywhere is the liturgical song, or chant and cantillation, but musically even this has been affected. The Hebrew language was used in cantillation in Jewish worship (prayer and Holy Scripture) and now, in Israel, as a vernacular tongue.

PRINCIPAL CLASSROOM STRATEGIES

The main purpose of this sampling of Jewish song is to help students discover the diversity to be found. This will involve classroom strategies that strengthen and develop aural acuity and rhythmic response. The obvious differences between Jewish and non-Jewish song seem to be found in the liturgical chants, or cantillation, and some predilection toward use of the minor mode in folk song among selected Jewish cultures. All Jewish songs, in keeping with Hebrew origins, have a close affinity to music of the Oriental world, particularly the Near East. The chapter organizations will be in two sections, Liturgical Chant and Folk Song.

Lesson One: Orienting the Listener to Variety in Jewish Song

Purpose of Activities: Listening to distinguish between cantillation (chants) and folk song.

Clues for Listening

Procedure:

1. Play a prepared tape (or use recordings) of a variety of Jewish chants and folk songs, each example approximately two minutes long. A sample tape could include examples such as the following:

   a. "A Song of Work." A melodic folk song accompanied by guitar that moves easily between major and minor, ending in minor. (Album: *A Harvest of Israeli Folksongs* by Theodore Bikel)

   b. "Cantillation of the Prophets" (Samuel 1-15). An Ashkenazic chant. (Album: *Jewish Music: Unesco Collection*)

   c. "I Have a Pair of Oxen." A humorous Yiddish folk song. (Album: *Jewish Folk Songs* sung in Yiddish by Mark Olf)

   d. "En Este Mundo." A melodic Sephardic folk song with flute obbligato. (Album: *Ladino! Folk Songs of the Sephardic Jews)*

   e. "Kol Nidre." A chant full of meaning for Yom Kippur, the Day of Atonement, an important Jewish High Holy Day. (Album: *Kol Nidre Service* by Richard Tucker)

   f. "Love Song." A lively folk song by two Yemenite girls accompanied by percussive rhythms played on a kerosene tin. (Album: *In Israel Today*, Vol. 3)

   g. "Squares" or "Little Boxes." A delightful Yiddish folk song that includes imitations of animal sounds. (Album: *Jewish Children's Songs and Games* by Ruth Rubin)

   h. "Psalm 16." A very florid, melismatic cantillation from the Near East. (Album: *Jewish Music: Unesco Collection)*

   i. "My Father Lit the Candles." A Hanukkah song with traditional folk melody. (Album: *Holiday Songs of Israel* by Geula Gill)

   j. "Thou Didst Form." In this chant, the cantor is accompanied by vigorous male chorus. (Album: *The Art of the Cantor*)

2. On the chalkboard write the words "chant" and "folk song" and give a brief definition of each word. Have the class number from one to ten on a sheet of paper and as each example is heard they are to write "chant" or "folk song" as it sounds to them.

3. When this is done, listen to each example again and this time tell what each one was. This can serve as an aural introduction to the varieties of music found in Jewish song.

Lesson Two: Learning About Liturgical Chants

The tradition of chanting or cantillating the Jewish scriptures instead of just reading them is a very old one (Rothmuller 1967:101). Established in the fifth century B.C., the chant is (with the exception of the musically notated equivalent) "the oldest type of Jewish ritual music used for reading the prose books of the Bible" (Harvard Dictionary:445). These chants are a veritable treasure of Jewish song in the oral tradition, with many melodies and variations still in use in synagogues and temples around the world.

According to Gradenwitz (1949:41): "The present-day cantillation of the Scriptures and prayers substantially follows the modal theory of the Orient in the eastern as well as the western Jewish communities." The liturgical chants are sung in successions of melodic formulas which can be recognized upon careful listening. Called *nusachim* (noose-ah-*cheem;* "ch" as in Bach), these melodic patterns are represented by written marks in the texts, either above or below the words. Example (a) is a portion of a chant while example (b) isolates the melodic patterns used in the chant.

(Translation: "Blessed art Thou, O Lord our G-d, King of the Universe" (Ruth Srago Newhouse).

Cantillation is characterized by free rhythm and a semi-cadence (half pause) and a full cadence (complete stop) after each verse with few exceptions (Eisenstein 1972:35). As a rule, the liturgical songs are sung in Hebrew all over the world. The cantors who sing these chants in American synagogues and temples today are usually trained musicians and, according to Central European Jewish tradition, usually have been tenors.* They are adept at improvisation and embellishment, which they use to give spiritual expression to the scriptures and prayers. Cantorial singing also employs frequent use of coloratura and falsetto, phrases that pass easily from major to minor (and vice versa) and from key to key.

Classroom Strategies and Experiences:
Ways of Discerning Differences in Chants

Purpose of Activities: Listening for melodic patterns and use of voice in Jewish liturgical chant; discovering differences in the sounds of chants from various parts of the world.

Procedure:

1. Show film: *Israel: The Story of the Jewish People.*

2. Recording: "Cantillation of the Prophets" (Album: *Jewish Music: Unesco Collection,* Side 1, Band 10). This chant is Ashkenazic. (The Ashkenazim are descended from the Jewish communities of western, central, and eastern Europe.) Approximately eighty-five percent of American Jews are of Ashkenazic descent.
   - On the piano, play examples of Ashkenazic tunes for prose texts (Idelsohn 1929:148-156). (Play example of *nusachim* on page 148.)
   - Since the recording is short, tell the class you will play it twice and that they are to listen for vocal runs and melodic patterns. On the first hearing they are to write the letter "R" each time they recognize a vocal run. On the second hearing they are to write "MP" each time they recognize a melodic pattern.
   - Explain that a chant of this type could possibly be heard in an American synagogue.

_____
*(Today, particularly among Reform congregations, many women are being ordained as Cantors.)

3. Recording: "Prayer of Penitence" (Album: *Jewish Music: Unesco Collection*, Side 1, Band 2). This chant is from Yemen, sung by a cantor and a group of singers in antiphonal fashion, which is frequently used by Yemenites. Yemenite chants are the oldest surviving types of chant and are possibly closest to those sung in Biblical times.

- On first hearing, have the class raise hands when the shofar is heard.
- On second hearing, have the class raise one finger when the cantor sings and two fingers when worshippers "answer" or respond.
- Explain that the shofar is used in synagogues all over the world (not always in the same format, however), but that the types of singing done by the Yemenites on the recording are not likely to be heard in the United States.
- Ask: "Can you describe the sound of the singers' voices?" (The sound is high and shrill, which is not unusual in the Near East.)

4. Recording: "Kol Nidre" (Album: *Kol Nidre Service* by Richard Tucker, Side 1, Band 1).

- Ask the class to listen to this famous Jewish chant and try to absorb the pathos and fervor in the singer's voice. The Kol Nidre recalls the tragic periods in history when Jews were forced to accept other faiths or suffer great persecution or death. The chanting of the Kol Nidre ushers in the Day of Atonement (Yom Kippur), the most sacred day in the Jewish year.

5. Challenge talented members of the class to create a simple chant. They can devise several melodic patterns (nusachim) of three or four notes, connect them in various orders and sing them on a word such as "alleluia." (Eisenstein (1972:9-16) has an excellent illustration of this procedure.)

Lesson Three: Introducing Oriental Jewish Folk Song

During the many hundreds of years of the Diaspora many Jews moved to such places as Yemen and Turkey. As minorities in

Muslim societies, their lives were filled with the misery of poverty, neglect, and second-class citizenship, but their songs reflected a spiritually beautiful character.

Idelsohn (1929:24) reminds us that Jewish music is a part of the Oriental world, coming to life in the Near East. As such it has the following characteristics of the musics that surround it: Oriental modality, emphasis upon ornamentation, rhythms that are free-flowing rather than metered, use of instruments such as the *'ud* (Arabic lute), use of quarter tones, and absence of harmony.

Rothmuller (1967:168) observes that many folk songs of Oriental Jews are religious or ceremonial songs. For example, the Yemenite Jews (and others) have many songs in connection with their elaborate wedding ceremonies that last for days.

Classroom Strategies and Experiences: Finding Out About Near Eastern Jewish Music

Purpose of Activities: Listening for characteristics of Near Eastern music in the songs of Oriental Jews.

Procedure:

1. Show film: *Gestures of Sand.*

2. Recording: "Elohim Eshala" (Album: *Shoshana,* Side 2, Band 4). A Yemenite song sung by Shoshana Damari, an Israeli singer originally from Yemen. The music has many Near Eastern characteristics.
  • Have the class listen for ornamentation in the voice, quarter tones, and a shrill vocal timbre. Listen also for rhythms in the accompanying drum.

3. Recording: "Song of the Henna" (Album: *Jewish Music: Unesco Collection,* Side 1, Band 4). A very interesting recording. Traditionally, the Yemenites have used no musical instruments since the destruction of the temple. The practice of mourning over the destruction of the temple was once observed by all Jews long ago. The Yemenites, as a "mode of compromise," developed the art of playing common household utensils to accompany certain

songs. On this recording, the singer is accompanied by copper vessels or trays which are beaten very loudly and rapidly. The effect is the sound of a drum.

- Encourage use of pencils or hands on desks to duplicate the sounds of the household utensils.
- Tell the class that this "Song of the Henna" is one of the many rituals that accompany a Yemenite wedding. (Henna is a substance that turns bright green which is placed on the hands of the bride and groom to bring them good luck.)

4. Recording: "Love Song" (Album: *In Israel Today, Vol 3*). This song is sung in Arabic by two young Yemenite girls. They are accompanied by the percussive sound of a kerosene tin, which is absolutely fascinating.

- Use drums and tops of desks to duplicate the rhythm of the kerosene tin.
- Clap the basic meter of the song.
- Ask: "What is the total effect of the singing and accompaniment on your ears?" Teach the Yemenite song "Kol Dodi" on page 107 of *Sound, Beat, and Feeling*.

Lesson Four: Discovering Sephardic Folk Song

Prior to their final expulsion from Spain in 1492, the Sephardic Jews experienced what could be considered a golden age of Jewry in that country. Centuries of brilliant scholars, centers of learning and magnificent accomplishments were part of their heritage on Spanish soil, a heritage that had to be scattered and abandoned under the dreaded Inquisition.

As a result, these Jews were further dispersed around the shores of the Eastern Mediterranean, but they took with them their customs, folklore, and their songs, which are still sung today in Ladino (Judeo-Spanish) by their descendants. As traditional Ladino songs, they evoke memories in the Sephardim of the land in which they once lived so proudly. These songs have certain characteristics: some of them show a blend of sophisticated Spanish culture and popular folk song, while others appear to combine these elements with cantorial style singing.

Classroom Strategies and Experiences:
Identifying Distinguishing Characteristics in Sephardic Music

Purpose of Activities: Becoming aware of Sephardic folk songs in Ladino as one variety of Jewish music; listening for the blend of Spanish-Jewish characteristics in the songs.

Procedure:

1. Recording: "La Soledad" (Album: *Ladino! Folk Songs of the Sephardic Jews*, Side A Band 2).
   - Ask the class to listen for anything in the music that sounds Spanish to them. (The flamenco guitar is one sound that will be easily identified; ask for others. The melody has a strong Spanish flavor.)

2. Recording: "Noches Noches" (Album: *Ladino! F olk Songs* , Side B, Band 3). This interesting song describes night in Spain.
   - Ask: "Does the soloist's voice remind you of any Jewish singing we have heard before?"
   - Compare the sound of the flamenco guitar with the chantlike singing. Ask: "What is the total effect upon your ear?"

3. Recording: "At One" (Album: *Ladino Folk Songs,* Side 1, Band 6). This is the song of a young man on his way to war bidding farewell to his love.
   - Listen for vocal ornamentation and rubato that seem to resemble some facets of cantorial singing. The song maintains a strongly Spanish flavor due to the process of acculturation.

4. Teach class a song such as "Little Sister," a Sephardic melody, found on page 124 in *Heritage of Music* by Judith K. Eisenstein.

5. Use selections from album *Sephardic Jews* for more examples.

Lesson Five: Becoming Acquainted with Yiddish Folk Song

The Yiddish language is based on old German with a generous mixture of Hebrew and Slavonic elements. It has an extensive literature and many songs. Yiddish is a product of East European Jewry, and Rothmuller (1967:172) states: "The songs still sung today may have come into existence at any time since the middle of the nineteenth century."

Idelsohn (1929:391) identifies Yiddish songs as the folk songs of the Ashkenazim in Eastern Europe. Since such a large percentage of American Jewry is of Eastern European descent, the Yiddish songs are the musical heritage of a significant number of people. These songs are songs of the ghetto dwellers and reflect the varied facets of life found therein. Many songs are those of Jewish women who as young girls, wives, and mothers poured out their hopes, dreams, loves and sadness in their songs.

A characteristic of the Yiddish song is the use of the minor key, particularly in the cadences. Traditionally we tend to associate minor keys with sadness, but this is by no means always the case in Jewish folk song; many lively and infectiously humorous songs are in minor. Yiddish is very much alive today; it has a strong linguistic impact upon a large number of people.

Classroom Strategies and Experiences:
Discovering Diversity in Yiddish Song

Purpose of Activities: Becoming aware of Yiddish folk song as part of the diversity of Jewish music.

Procedure:

1. Show film: *Bar Mitzvah.*

2. Record album: *Fiddler on the Roof,* preferably the original cast recording.
   - A good lead-in to Yiddish music would be to let classes listen to the album *Fiddler on the Roof,* which is based on stories by Sholom Aleichem, one of the classic recorders of Yiddish folk stories. The story has a good deal of humor, and Sholom Aleichem, while describing what is going on at that time, shows the great respect for tradition the Jewish people have. The attitudes portrayed in the musical are also very familiar to Jews of Ashkenazic descent, particularly of Eastern Europe.
   - Teach the classes songs from the musical such as "Sunrise, Sunset" and "Fiddler on the Roof."

3. Recording: "Quadrille" (Album: *Jewish Life "The Old Country"* by Ruth Rubin, Side 1, Band 14). This is a very gay and lively song sung by a woman teaching a dance to a group of young people.
  • Have the class clap the heavily accented rhythms as they listen.

4. Recording: "Lullaby" (Album: *Jewish Children's Songs and Games* by Ruth Rubin, Side 1, Band E). This song is both lullaby and love song. In it a young girl sings to a baby she is caring for while the mother works in order that the father may study at the synagogue. Point out to the class that in Europe it was common in Jewish tradition for women to support their husbands while they studied Mosaic law and commentary at the synagogues or schools of higher learning, since such education was valued greatly.
  • Read a translation of the song before playing the recording.
  • As the music is playing, have the class raise hands when the chorus is heard. (Verses have a melody distinct from the chorus.)
  • Ask: "By the *sound* of the singer's voice, how do you think the young girl felt at having to care for a baby all day, every day?"

5. Recording: "Bay Dem Shtetl" (Bye Dem Sh*tay*tel—pronunciation) (Album: *Jewish Folk Songs* by Ruth Rubin, Side 1, Band G). This song is about a family's life in a Russian village in the restricted Pale and their possessions (small house, a few animals).
  • Ask the class to listen for and identify the sounds of animals imitated.
  • Clap the basic meter of the very fast rhythm on second hearing.

6. Teach the class "A Geneyve" in its English translation in Ruth Rubin's *A Treasury of Jewish Folksong,* page 130. The melody of this song is easy to learn, and the words tell about a thief who unfortunately broke into the home of a poor rabbi. The song depicts a sense of humorous irony found in many Yiddish texts.

7. Let the class sing "We Survive" by Glik, which is a stirring song of the Jewish underground during World War II. It is found in Ruth Rubin's *Jewish Folk Songs,* pages 82-83.

Lesson Six: Recognizing the
Blending of Cultures in Israeli Song

In the wake of the Nazi holocaust came a vast migration to Israel. This great "ingathering of the exiles" has added a multiplicity of cultural traits to the young country that are reflected in the music of its inhabitants. There is quite a body of music coming out of Israel including new songs composed for annual song festivals, songs devoted to the Israeli battles, and a growing collection of Israeli pop tunes. Hundreds of songs of all types are especially for children; in fact, there is much creative musical activity for youngsters. The term "Israeli Music" has become a part of the impetus to rebuild a secure homeland for all Jews.

The Israelis sometimes use Yemenite themes and jazz them up; they become danceable in a land where the people greatly enjoy dancing. Rhythms, many syncopated, seem to be a feature of Israeli folk song. Israel is a melting pot of Jewish music that can be compared to a river with many tributaries (Yemenite, Sephardic, Ashkenazic, Western, Moroccan, Tunisian, African, etc.) that came together. It is a culmination reminiscent of a delta. Songs in Western popular music styles are created, along with songs that show Near Eastern and central European characteristics.

Rothmuller (1967:290) describes the tendency of Israeli folktunes "towards a gay and optimistic expression, which is mostly achieved by vivid rhythmic patterns." Many Israelis tend to sing without vibrato (adding vibrato at will, however) and use a straight, somewhat nasal singing tone. While this is not a national characteristic, it is heard in many songs.

Classroom Strategies and Experiences:
Ways of Exploring the Inherent Vitality in Israeli Song

Purpose of Activities: Listening, singing, and using instruments to discover the fusion of cultures in Israeli folk song.

Procedure:

1. Show films: *Israel: The Land and the People* and *Karmon-Israeli Dancers and Theodore Bikel.*

2. Recording: "Give Us Wine" (Album: *A Harvest of Israeli Folksongs* by Theodore Bikel, Side 1, Band 3). This is the music of a *hora* (dance) and is very gay and rhythmic.
   - Have the class analyze the song using ABA pattern on a sheet of paper.
   - On second hearing, let everyone clap the basic meter and shout "Hey!" with the singer on the recording. (Bikel shouts emphatically at the ends of phrases.)

3. Recording: "Hills and Slopes" (Album: *A Harvest of Israeli Folksongs* by Theodore Bikel, Side 2, Band 7). A love song.
   - Have the students use a few small drums to duplicate the drum pattern heard at the beginning of the recording.
   - Ask: "Does the song sound more Near Eastern or Western?" (Answer: Near Eastern because of acculturation.)
   - On second hearing, let everyone clap the lively rhythm as the drums play.

4. Recording: "Harvest's End" (Album: *Holiday Songs of Israel* by Geula Gill, Side 1, Band 3). A song of feasting to celebrate a good harvest.
   - Have the class clap the rhythm; add soft tambourine.
   - Analyze the song using ABA pattern.
   - Identify the accompanying instruments (accordion and recorder).

5. Recording: "Pancakes" (Album: *Holiday Songs of Israel* by Geula Gill, Side 1, Band 4). A charming, lively Hanukkah song. The pancakes, called *latkes*, are potato pancakes usually served with sour cream or applesauce. Delicious!
   - Place the translated words of the song on the chalkboard. Encourage the class to clap rhythms and sing along with the recording.

6. Recording: "Milk and Honey" (Album: *Martha Schlamme Sings Israeli Folk Songs,* Side 1, Band 2). This song is so sprightly it probably accompanies a hora dance.
   - Have the class clap the basic meter softly, then clap quite loudly when the music requires it. (They will be able to tell when.)

7. Teach the popular Israeli song "Havah Nagilah."

8. Play a recording of Smetana's *The Moldau.* The melody is similar to the Israeli National Anthem. (Note in Idelsohn (1929:222) that the Israeli National Anthem is "Hatikvah," No. 4; Smetana uses No. 9.)

9. If possible, collaborate with the physical education department in your school to incorporate Israeli dance during the study (See Berk, 1972).

10. Let the class hear the narrated recording *Israel, Its Music and Its People.*

11. Show films: *Shalom* and *Sallah.*

ADDITIONAL THINGS TO DO AND DISCUSS

The roots of Jewish music are very deep; they can be compared to a tree whose boughs spread throughout the world. The liturgical music utilizes melodic patterns called nusachim to give expression to worship or prayer service in the synagogue. There are different systems of nusachim depending on the holidays, Sabbath, or week-day services and also which portion of Scripture is being chanted. There are differences between morning and evening services, between the musical sounds of High Holy Days and those of the rest of the year.

The melodic patterns also differ depending on whether the synagogue or temple is Ashkenazic, Sephardic, orthodox, con-servative or reform tradition. Gradenwitz (1949:12-13) affirms the fact that the Torah, together with the prayer chant, have kept Jews united throughout the world. The Torah, in an inclusive sense, includes the five books of Moses, the writings of the prophets, and all the commentaries connected with same. (Basi-cally the Torah is the *Chumach,* the five books of Mosaic Law [Pentateuch]. Commentaries include post-Torah discussion, Haftorah, Talmud, etc.) There can be little doubt that the melodies used for the cantillation of the Torah have had a great influence upon the development of Jewish song.

The sounds of the folk music are as diverse as the countries in which Jews live, or have lived, for they incorporate the various local musical characteristics into their folk song. In short, the music assumes the coloration of the country of its origin. Throughout the long period of the Diaspora, the Jewish people and their melodies have moved, often perforce, throughout the world.

The Yemenite community is greatly loved and highly regarded in Israel. Their folk life and music tradition reveal remnants of an ancient Jewish civilization that has survived nearly intact from ancient to modern Israel. Their songs are not written down, but are passed on by oral tradition. The Sephardic communities have a long, deep tradition; their Ladino songs are gems of ancient fifteenth-century Spanish balladry. Young girls were treasured and protected by their families, and many of the love songs reflect the longings of anxious lovers. The music has a very strong Spanish flavor, but elements of cantorial style singing, which can be found in many of the songs, give them a refreshingly unique character, along with the texts.

The Yiddish folk songs absorb all the joys, sadnesses, hopes, dreams, and absurdities of a people confined in ghettos. One thread seems to be woven throughout many of these songs: a great reverence and respect for learning. Jewish mothers sing to their sons in their cribs of their hopes that they will be scholars; girls aspire to marry the rabbi's son; mothers sing of working to support husbands who are studying the Torah. When Jews came to the United States in such large numbers during the 1880s and '90s, America suddenly became a major center of Jewish population. These immigrants brought Yiddish song with them. It took root in the New World and adapted new tunes with new meanings.

Inspired by the musically active Sabras (native-born Israeli), the new Israeli folk songs remind one of youth. They seem to resemble the roots of both ancient trees and the promising boughs of recently planted olive trees. The songs are newly born in the Hebrew language and reflect the challenges of a new land with spirit and a sense of hope. Community singing and dancing are important to today's Israelis when there is time for music-making, a situation not uncommon to other cultures. There is an active amount of musical activity in Israel now with some Israeli musicians believing that future Jewish music will be inspired by Oriental sources rather than Eastern European ones.

SEVEN MORE SPECIFIC ACTIVITIES FOR
STUDENT INVOLVEMENT

Since young people like to *make* music above all, it seems important to involve them in as many activities as possible that enable them to do this.

1. Utilize the many good collections of Jewish songs available to augment what is found in classroom series books. Include instruments such as a drum, tambourine, recorder, small cymbals, guitar, and an accordion, if available, to accompany the singing. Let youngsters decide which combinations of instruments will be used, and don't forget handclapping.

2. Because carefully guided listening is the strategy that will probably be of most long-term value, use listening as a basis for evaluation. Challenge youngsters to let their ears and understanding of concepts of Judaism be the judge of what makes the music sound Jewish (or not) to them. Ask questions like: "Is it the melodic motifs, instrumentations, use of the voice, or words of the texts that make the music sound like Jewish music or not?" Encourage discussion and listening at home; loan recordings used in the lessons for interested students to take home.

3. Organize at least one lesson that will involve listening to music of certain Near Eastern countries and compare with Israeli music. The classes will hear many similarities; let them point them out. Encourage further research in Jewish music.

4. If possible, arrange for those interested to visit different synagogue services and report to the class on the music they heard.

5. Encourage reading about Jewish holidays and teach some of the songs sung on these occasions. For example, many Jewish families sing together in their homes on certain holidays, Passover being one of the most outstanding musically. The Passover Seder (meal, service and ceremony) commemorates the flight of the Israelites from Egyptian bondage. (Many youngsters have seen the movie *The Ten Commandments* where this is shown.) Frequently songs are sung during the meal that have been handed down orally through the years. It has been suggested that the Last Supper of Jesus and His disciples was probably a Passover Seder (Zeitlin: 444-449). Encourage students to find out as much as they can about this major home holiday generally observed by orthodox

Jews in America and all over the world. The recording *Passover Seder Festival* sung by Richard Tucker with narration could be played.

6. There are other holidays (some historical, some liturgical) that could be studied such as Hanukkah and Purim. There is a Hanukkah ceremony in the home in which cnadles are blessed and presents are frequently exchanged each night for eight nights. Purim is a jolly holiday involving masquerades and the exchange of gifts. There are delightful songs for both these holidays wherein art and drama could be incorporated to make an enlightening and enjoyable student presentation.

7. Those interested could find out what is taught in the Jewish Day Schools, and also the Hebrew schools many Jewish youngsters attend after three o'clock. These schools develop a deep knowledge of and appreciation for Jewish cultural and religious traditions.

8. Jewish summer camps and day schools frequently have Israeli staff members teaching singing, folk dance and conversational Hebrew. Contemporary Israeli folk and popular music is an interesting and exciting blend of traditional Middle Eastern influences and Western instrumentation. A workshop in your class led by such a teacher familiar with traditional and modern Israeli folk music would be an enjoyable eye-opener for all participants.

This type of active exploration will unearth a good deal of information about Jewish history and life as well as more about the music. Besides glimpsing the great variety and diversity in Jewish music, students will learn that Jews have given to the world the Old Testament, an exemplary code of laws and ethics, and outstanding poetry. They will come to realize that the Jewish community shares a proud history, deep respect for tradition, and great love for music.

SELECTED BIBLIOGRAPHY

Books

Berk, Fred. *Harikud: the Jewish Dance.* New York: The Union of American Hebrew Congregations, 1972. An excellent guide for dance explorations; contains illustrations, discography.

Birmingham, Stephen. *Our Crowd.* New York: Harper and Row, 1963. About the immigration and establishment of German Jews in the United States.

Brod, Max. *Israel's Music.* Tel Aviv: Sefer Press, 1951. Good general reference.

Eisenstein, Judith Kaplan. *Heritage of Music.* New York: Union of American Hebrew Congregations, 1972. An outstanding presentation of the history and development of Jewish music.

Ellis, Harry B. *Israel: One Land, Two Peoples.* New York: Thomas Y. Crowell, 1971. Informative and interesting.

Encyclopedia Judaica: Vol.12, "Music." Jerusalem: Keter Publishing House, Jerusalem, Ltd., 1972, pp. 554-678.

Fitch, Florence Mary. *One God: The Ways We worship Him.* NY: Lothrop, Lee and Shepard, 1954. Describes Jewish, Roman Catholic and Protestant ways of worship.

Gradenwitz, Peter. *The Music of Israel.* NY: W.W. Norton and Co., Inc., 1949. A survey of Jewish music from ancient to modern times; a dependable source.

Idelsohn, A.Z. *Jewish Music in Its Historical Development.* NY: Schocken Books, 1929. Standard work; scholarly. Rich in musical illustrations.

John, Robert. *Israel.* NY: Time, Inc., 1965. Beautiful photographs of Israel accompany a well-written text.

Kamm, Josephine. *The Hebrew People, A History of the Jews.* NY: McGraw Hill, 1968. A well-written history for young people.

Levin, Meyer. *The Story of Israel.* NY: G.P. Putnam's Sons, 1966. Good for student reading.

Manovers, Ande. *Poor Cousins.* NY: Coward, McCann, 1963. Concerns the influx of Russian and Polish Jews to the United States and their struggle.

Margolis, Isidor, and Sidney L. Markowitz. *Jewish Holidays and Festivals*. New York: Citadel Press,1962. Good for understanding the significance of Jewish commemorative days.

Rothmuller, Aaron Marko. *The Music of the Jews*. New York: A.S. Barnes and Co., Inc., 1967. Excellent overview of Jewish music; good resource for teachers.

Schwadron, Abraham, "On Jewish Music," in *Musics of Many Cultures*, Elizabeth May, ed., Berkeley: Univ. of California Press, 1981. Pp.284-306.

Sendrey, A. Bibliography of Jewish Music. New York: Columbia Univ. Press, 1951. Standard work; classified bibliography of 5,854 items. Somewhat dated, but still valuable.

Steinberg, Milton. *Basic Judaism*. New York: Harcourt, Brace and World, 1947. Concise introduction to the beliefs and practices of the Jewish people.

Tor, Regina. *Discovering Israel*. New York: Random House, 1960. Contains references to religious festivals and music.

Weisser, Albert.*Bibliography of Publications and Other Resources on Jewish Music*. Revised and enlarged edition.

Wigoder, Geoffrey, ed. *Jewish Art and Civilization*. 2 vols. New York: Walker and Co., 1972. Essays by distinguished scholars magnificently illustrated.

NOTE: Both *The New Harvard Dictionary of Music* and *The New Grove Dictionary of Music and Musicians* have excellent articles on Jewish Music.

Article

Zeitlin, Solomon. "The Liturgy of the First Night of Passover," Jewish Quarterly Review 38 (April, 1948)

Song Collections

Carp, Bernard, editor.*The Jewish Center Songster*. New York: National Jewish Welfare Board, 1949. A good, inexpensive collection. Songs are unaccompanied.

Challis, Evelyn. *Fun Songs, Rounds and Harmony*. New York: Oak Publications, 1974. Contains several folksongs in Hebrew.

Coopersmith, Harry. *The New Jewish Song Book*. New York: Behrman House, 1965.

_____.*The Songs We Sing*. New York: United Synagogue Commission in Jewish Education, 1950.

_____. *Companion Volume to The Songs We Sing*. New York: United Synagogue Commission in Jewish Education, 1950.Three useful collections for young people.

Deutsch, Leonhard, collector and arranger. *A Treasury of the World's Finest Folk Song.* New York: Crown, 1967. Includes section of Yiddish folk songs.

Eisenstein, Judith, and Freda Prensky. *Songs of Childhood.* New York: The United Synagogue Commission on Jewish Education, 1955. Although primarily for children aged four to eight years, some of the songs are suitable for older children. Useful.

Rubin, Ruth, editor. *Jewish Folksongs in Yiddish and English.* New York: Oak Publications, 1965. Very useful; brief informative material given about most songs. Illustrated with poignant photographs. Accompanied by chords only.

───────. *A Treasury of Jewish Folksong.* New York: Schocken Books, 1967. Fine collection of a variety of Yiddish songs.

Slobin, Mark, ed. & trans. *Old Jewish Folk Music: the Collections and Writings of Moshe Beregovski.* Philadelphia: Univ. of Pennsylvania Press, 1982. Songs in Yiddish with translations and background; a scholarly work.

Schwartz, Teddy, ed. *Tumbalaika and 16 other Jewish Songs for Singing in English.* NY: Hargail, 1956. Charming; useful.

AUDIO-VISUAL MATERIALS

Films

Bar Mitzvah. B & W, 14 min., NFBC. Depicts the preparation and training for a boy's bar mitzvah. The ceremony is shown, including cantillation.

Gestures of Sand. B & W, 18 min., UCLA. Dancer Margalit Oved interprets Jewish life in Aden.

Israel: The Land and the People. B & W, 15 min., Coronet International. Possibly designed for geography classes, this film would serve as a background for information about the Jewish people. Music is negligible.

Israel: The Story of the Jewish People. Color, 50 min., Julian Bryan and the International Film Foundation. An excellent film for a condensed history of the Jewish people from ancient to modern times.

Karmon-Israeli Dancers and Theodore Bikel. Color, 30 min., Warner Bros. Hollywood, but with some redeeming features, especially Bikel.

Sallah. B & W, 105 min., Audio/Brandon. A poor family secures housing in Israel; both humorous and moving.

Shalom. Color, 74 min., Audio/Brandon. Featuring film footage and photographs, the people and events that formed Israel are brought vividly to life.

Recordings

The Art of the Cantor (RCA Victor; VCM 6173). Liturgical music sung by outstanding cantors; good notes included.

Bikel, Theodore, *A Harvest of Israeli Folksongs* (The Elektra Corp. EKL 210-A). Good variety of songs done in Bikel's inimitable manner.

Fiddler on the Roof (RCA Victor LSO-1093). The original Broadway cast recording.

Gill, Geula, *Holiday Songs of Israel* (Folkways FC 7738). Notes accompany recording.

In Israel Today (Westminister Recording Co., 1963-64, 4 vol.). Interesting notes accompany this valuable collection of field recordings.

Israel: Its Music and Its People (Desto D-503). A narrated recording that utilizes a storytelling format.

Jewish Children's Songs and Games, by Ruth Rubin (Folkways FC 7224). Fourteen Yiddish folksongs popular in Eastern Europe. Notes, texts included.

Jewish Folk Songs, by Ruth Rubin (Oriole XTV 20577). Seventeen Yiddish and Israeli songs; texts and notes included.

Jewish Life: "The Old Country," by Ruth Rubin (Folkways FG 3801). Many songs sung by men and women who remember them from Eastern Europe.

Jewish Music (Unesco Collection Musical Sources, Religious Psalmody IV-I, Phillips 6586 001). Primarily Near Eastern Jewish music; some notes.

Jo-Amar-Oriental Favorites (Hed-Arzi Ltd. AN 47-91). Many interesting songs and sounds; unfortunately, no notes are given.

Ladino! Folk Songs (Collectors Guild CGL 605). Judaeo-Spanish ballads and songs of love sung by Raphael Yair Elnader, a cantor. This collectio has grace and elegance.

Martha Schlamme Sings Israeli Folk Songs (Vanguard VRS 9072). A fine variety of songs, sung with great verve.

Pizmon: Syrian-Jewish Religious and Social Song. (Meadowlark 105). Songs from the Syrian-Jewish community of Brooklyn, NY; features Hebrew lyrics set to melodies in the Arabic tradition; interesting.

Sephardic Jews - Ballad, Wedding Songs (Folkways FE 4208).

Shoshana (Vanguard VSD 2144). Shoshana Damari is one of Israel's best known singing stars; her choice of selections is very enjoyable.

Tucker, Richard, *Kol Nidre Service* (Columbia MS 6085). Composed and conducted by Sholom Secunda, this is a very moving album.

Tucker, Richard, *Passover Seder Festival* (Columbia MS 6336). Narration that accompanies music explains meaning and significance of the Passover seder.

Recordings from Canada

Gerineldo, *Chansons traditionnelles judeo-espagnoles* -   Vols. I and II (Traditional Judeo-Spanish Songs)   (Education Resource Center, Montreal, 1983 and 1985).

What It Means to be Jewish (Kids Records, 68 Broadview Ave., Suite 303, Toronto, Ontario Canada M4M 2E6) Explores the many aspects to Jewish life in North America including history, values, holidays. Wonderful resource for teachers and students.

Sources for Music

A Harvest of Jewish Music
    Tara Publications Catalog of Books. Records and Tapes
    29 Derby Ave., Cedarhurst, NY 11516
B'Nai B'Rith Adult Jewish Education
    1640 Rhode Island Ave. N.W., Washington, DC 20036
Transcontinental Music Publications
    838 Fifth Ave, New York, NY (Send for Master Catalog).

CHAPTER SIX

Studying Varieties of Hawaiian Music

Our fiftieth state is probably the only state in the Union whose very name is nearly synonymous with the word "music." Mention Hawaii and visions of lovely girls dancing the hula, the sound of steel guitars and ukuleles providing languorous, memorable melodies, and the rhythm of surf against sand come almost immediately to mind.

The Hawaiian islands were discovered in 1778 by Captain James Cook, an Englishman, who named them the Sandwich Islands. Cook was thought by the natives to be the god Lono, and he and his crew were warmly welcomed. He brought with him articles the people had never seen before such as iron and firearms, and his large ships were looked upon as magical structures. Cook was killed by the natives during a skirmish when they discovered he was not a god but a mortal who could be wounded.

Hawaii consists of 122 islands that extend 1,610 miles from west to east. Only seven islands are actually inhabited: Oahu, Hawaii, Maui, Kauai, Molokai, Lanai, and Niihau. Kahoolawe makes the eighth main island. Of these, Oahu is by far the best-known island; it has the largest population, the capital city of Honolulu, and Pearl Harbor.

The population of the islands is approximately 800,000 with only about 10,000 persons of pure Hawaiian blood. The state is a genuine melting pot with persons of Japanese, Chinese, Okinawan, Philippine, Korean, Polynesian, Portuguese, and Puerto Rican ancestry, as well as Caucasians and blacks from mainland United States, and northern Europeans. The native Hawaiians are of

Polynesian descent and are now a minority in their own country, a situation similar to that of the American Indian.

Many of the races maintain their own musical cultures in Hawaii today, with festivals throughout the year, such as Philippine and Tahitian dances, Japanese *Bon* dances, Chinese and Korean opera. Smith (1959:50) states that contributing factors to the stability of these varied musical traditions are the nature of and use of the music in society, the number of people sharing the culture and the extent of their education in it, plus the length of residence in the islands.

TYPES OF EARLY SONG AND DANCE

Hawaiian music can generally be classified into two broad categories, ancient and modern. Ancient Hawaiian music is that music indigenous to the islands prior to their discovery by Cook in 1778, and modern Hawaiian music is that which has been developed and acculturated since contact with Western civilization. In ancient Hawaii music, dance, drama, and gesture, as well as speech, were the means of communication among the people since they had no written language. Their history, geneologies, values, religion, and an extensive body of history and myth were all passed down in the oral tradition.

Much of this was done in the form of a song, or chant, called the *mele*, a word that also includes all forms of poetry. There were two types of mele: the *mele hula* and the *mele oli*. The mele hula is a dance, and the mele oli is a chant. To the Hawaiians, the principal charm of the mele is in the words, many of which have more than one meaning. The hula gives bodily expression to what the words are saying. What is seen today are adaptations of the early hulas, since Emerson (1909) notes that the ancient hula was a religious service combining poetry, music, pantomime, and the dance. According to Hawaiian mythology, the goddess Laka was the patron of the hula, and her sister Hiiaka danced the first hula.

To become an accomplished performer, long and diligent training in both song and dance and observance of many tabus to guard against profanities were required. In ancient Hawaii, the hula was not engaged in for personal amusement, but was under strict priestly supervision, supported by royalty. The dancers entered a dance school and took vows of chastity for the length of their stay there. The meles and hulas they learned were often sacred, as well as the chants and prayers, for they were dedicated to Laka and Pele, goddess of the volcano.

Special halls were built in which to perform the hula, with the performers being divided into two classes, the *olapa* (agile ones) and the *ho'o-paa* (steadfast ones). The olapa, the dancers, were the young men and women considered the most graceful and beautiful, while the ho'o-paa were older men and women who played the heavier instruments while sitting or kneeling. The ho'o-paa also sang along with the dancers. Today, the mele hula is sung and danced by one or more persons with instrumental accompaniment and a regular rhythmic beat.

The mele oli is sung unaccompanied by a soloist and has irregular rhythms, depending upon the words. The oli has very little melodic variation, but requires at least two things: great breath control (breathing is allowed only at certain logical points in the chant) and a pronounced vibrato, or trill sound, in the singer's voice. Ancient prayers were probably all done in this style. Emerson (1909) believed that the oli was in a strict sense the lyric utterance of the Hawaiians. They used the oli to express every emotion imaginable: joy, love, humor, sarcasm, etc. The mood of the singer determined the type of oli.

The Hawaiians are adept in use of the gesture; the hands of the hula dancer are always in motion, the body swaying, the face full of expression. The ancient method of learning the gesture has been described as follows: the teacher had fixed the mele or oli in the minds of his pupils; someone would recite the words while the class watched the gestures of the *kumu* (teacher) and listened closely at the same time to the words. They had to pantomime the kumu's gestures until he was satisfied. The next step was to combine recitation with gesture. Grace and elegance were desired in the performance of the hula. Hulas performed in a sitting position were called "gesture" hulas; the hands, always gracefully moving, told the story. In standing hulas, the hips and feet kept rhythm while the hands and facial expressions told the story.

Following Cook's discovery of the islands, many ships began to use Hawaiian ports. It was during this period that the natives became familiar with Western music, including whaling songs and sea chanties, and musical instruments. This, too, they assimilated into what became Hawaiian folk music.

THE IMPACT OF WESTERN INFLUENCE ON HAWAIIAN MUSIC

After the first missionaries arrived from New England in 1820, they suppressed the ancient music (including dancing), which they considered "heathen," taught the natives to sing in harmony, and called their songs *himeni* to distinguish them from the pagan meles. The hymns added many more notes to Hawaiian music, and their style of singing was adapted enthusiastically by the music-loving Hawaiians. Today, any song not danced to is generally called himeni and is not necessarily religious, while songs and chants are known as hulas.

In the 1800s the Portuguese brought the guitar and ukulele to the islands, and these instruments became associated with Hawaiian music in the latter part of the century. The steel guitar was invented by a Hawaiian schoolboy in the 1890s, and ushered in what could probably be called the modern era of Hawaiian music. The steel guitar is considered the most significant contribution to Hawaiian music since it introduced to the Western world a unique style of stringed instrument playing. This style of playing is accomplished by sliding a steel bar along the guitar strings.

The "slack-key" style is also used in Hawaiian guitar playing. This is done by lowering the lowest strings to D and G and plucking them. Many other tunings are possible in the slack-key style, and some performers are instantly recognized by the tunings they use.

The steel guitar style is also found in the voices of Hawaiian singers—the sliding from note to note. Some women singers have low-pitched, throaty voices, while falsetto is characteristic of some male singing. Contemporary Hawaiian music is an intriguing combination of American pop, jazz, and South American rhythms, with the vocal characteristics and guitar playing that give the music a distinct sound.

PRINCIPAL CLASSROOM STRATEGIES

Basic classroom strategies in the study of Hawaiian music will be: (a) aural recognition of differences between two styles of ancient Hawaiian vocal music, mele oli and mele hula; (b) aural recognition of the two styles of Hawaiian guitar playing, steel and slack key; (c) aural recognition of ancient Hawaiian musical instruments such as the *ohe hano ihu* (nose flute), *uli-uli* (gourd rattle), *ili ili* (two smooth lava pebbles), *ipu* (gourd drum), the *pahu* drum and others; (d) recognition of songs as being *hapahaole* (lyrics part English and part Hawaiian), and (e) aural recognition of percussion characteristics that sound Hawaiian. (Drumming was a prominent feature of Hawaiian music prior to the introduction of the guitar.)

The outstanding differences between ancient Hawaiian and Western music seem to be the use of the voice in meles and olis; the limited range of notes in the melodies; the form of mele hulas, which include use of *kaheas*, spoken phrases within the chant, and repetition. As a lead-in to the study of Hawaiian music, let the students hear, in the very first lesson, as wide a variety of musical styles as possible. This will be the first step in going from the general to the specific and will open the way for involvement and discovery.

Lesson One: Orienting the Listener to Variety in Hawaiian Music

Purpose of Activities: Listening to distinguish between ancient and modern Hawaiian music.

Clues for Listening

Procedure:

1. Play a prepared tape (or use recordings) of a variety of Hawaiian musical styles, each example approximately two minutes long. A sample tape could include the following:
   a. "Blue Hawaii" (Album: *Hawaii in Hi Fi*). Well-known Hawaiian song in typical contemporary style; two ukuleles, one rhythm guitar, two steel guitars.
   b. "Hawaii-Kawika" (Hula Olapa) (Album: *Music of the World's Peoples*, Vol. V). A mele hula sung by several voices; only two tones are used. High and low drums accompany.
   c. "Ula Noweo" (Album: *Music of Hawaii from the Missionaries through Statehood*). Originally a mele hula.

d. "Hawaiian Wedding Song" (Album: *Romantic Instrumentals of the Islands*). Sound of steel guitar and surf against sand. Contemporary, languid style.

e. "E Pele, Pele, Pele" (Hawaiian Drama-Hula) (Album: *Hawaiian Chants, Hula and Love-Dance Songs*). Soloist accompanied by drum; limited range of notes.

f. "Ohe Hano Ihu" (Album: *Hawaiian Chant, Hula, and Music*). The very interesting sound of the bamboo nose flute.

g. "Hawaiian Wedding Song" (Album: *Hawaii Calls: Greatest Hits*). Full chorus arrangement of an all-time favorite; includes male-female duet.

h. "My Little Grass Shack" (Album: *Hawaii Calls: Favorite Instrumentals of the Islands*). Lyrics are part English, part Hawaiian (hapa-haole), a common feature of modern Hawaiian music.

i. "Hele Mai A Kalani Hele Mai" (Album: *Hawaiian Chant, Hula, and Music*). A mele oli with singer showing great breath control and use of trills. Unaccompanied.

j. "Hula Ili Ili" (Album: *Hawaiian Chant, Hula and Music*). Singer accompanied by two smooth lava pebbles called *ili ili*.

2. Have the class number from one to ten on a sheet of paper. As each example is played, have them write either "ancient" or "modern" according to how the music *sounds* to them.

3. On a second hearing, the class could indicate "melodic" or "percussion" according to the predominance of the background instrumentation. (There will be one selection unaccompanied.)

4. Show film: *Hawaii Calls*. Contains beautiful visuals of the eight main islands, with music interwoven throughout.

Lesson Two: Learning About Ancient Hawaiian Music

The ancient Hawaiians had a pantheon of gods and goddesses that have been compared to those of the Greeks. Kane was the chief god of the pantheon, while Pele, the goddess of the volcano, was the most feared. (Throughout Hawaiian mythology, Pele seems to emerge as the goddess with the most immediate relationship to the Hawaiians.) Laka, the goddess of the hula, was like a spirit of the trees, and there were also myriads of wilderness gods who had to be placated. Some of the most beautiful meles (poems upon which the chants are based) are about the various gods and goddesses.

Roberts (1967) classifies the meles into four divisions: (1) religious chants and prayers; (2) funeral dirges; (3) name songs in honor of the birth of a chief and citing the greatness of his ancestors, and (4) love songs. There are many subgroupings to be found under the four divisions.

Typical of the mele hula is a brief spoken introduction to the chant, called *kahea*. This is usually immediately followed by the sound of instruments to be used in the mele, and then the singer begins with the accompaniment continuing throughout. Many of the meles have kaheas interspersed throughout the chant. The kaheas usually end with a rising inflection of the voice, typical of Hawaiian speech. (There is frequently a subtle change in the rhythmic patterns of the accompanying instrument following a kahea.)

Classroom strategies will evolve around recognition of the form of the mele hula, and identifying, notating and duplicating the basic rhythmic patterns. Show pictures of the instruments used in each recording; excellent pictures are found in "Musical Instruments" (Arts and Crafts of Hawaii) by Te Rang Hiroa and in *Hawaii: Music in Its History* by Hausman.

Classroom Strategies and Experiences: Learning About the Mele Hula

Purpose of Activities: Listening and performing to develop aural acuity in distinguishing the form, vocal and rhythmic characteristics of the mele hula.

Procedure:

1. Show pictures of Hawaiian hula dancers and of the pahu.

2. Recording: "Kahiki Lau Lani" (a hula pahu) (Album: *Hawaiian Chant, Hula, and Music,* Side 1, Band 2). Many mele hulas are named after the musical instruments used in the accompaniment, as in the case of this hula pahu. The pahu is a type of standing

drum in various sizes with a sharkskin head and is played with the hands. This chant describes the movements of gods and goddesses "from Kukulu o Kahiki," which were pillars that helped support the sky. Two pahus are heard on this recording.

- Have the class analyze the chant using ABA pattern.
- Notate and duplicate drum patterns.
- Divide the class into two groups; one group playing the high drum pattern on desks, the other the low pattern while recording is heard.
- Use two drums, one high-pitched and the other low to play along with the recording.

3. Recording: "E Pele, Pele, Pele" (a hula Pele) (Album: *Hawaiian Chants, Hula and Love-Dance Songs,* Side 1, Band 1). This mele hula is in honor of Madame Pele, the goddess of the volcano, and tells how she chose Hawaii as her home after a long search.

- The chant utilizes only a few notes. Have the students find the tones used on the piano or resonator bells.
- The drum accompaniment follows the rhythm of the voice in this mele; challenge the class to clap the drum pattern. (They will have to be alert: the rhythms change from slow to fast.)

4. Recording: "Anoai" (a hula ulí ulí) (Album: *Hawaiian Chants, Hula and Love-Dance Songs,* Side 1, Band 4). This mele hula is named after its accompanying instrument, a gourd rattle usually decorated with feathers, the ulí ulí. The chant tells two stories: one of the beauty of two ancient hula teachers, and one of the lehua blossom in the rain. Show a picture of an ulí ulí.

- Challenge students to find and clap the basic pulse of the gourd rattle; some could play along using maracas.
- An occasional stomping sound is heard; how often?
- Find the notes used in the melody on the piano.

5. Recording: "Maika´i Kaua´i" (a hula *ili ili*) (Album: *Hawaiian Chant, Hula and Music* Side 2, Band 10). Two smooth lava pebbles, called ili ili, provide the accompaniment for this chant. The song is about the beauty of Kauai island. Show a picture of an ili ili.

- Have several students use pebbles to duplicate the rhythm.
- Count the number of kaheas heard during the chant.

6. Recording: "Kona Kai Opua I Ka La'I" (a hula *papa hehi*, or treadle board dance) (Album: *Hawaiian Chant, Hula, and Music*, Side 2, Band 11). Three layers of sound (voice included) comprise this interesting mele hula. The performer strikes two lengths of wood while operating the treadle board with one foot; two distinct rhythms are produced. The chant tells about the beauty of the Kona district on the island of Hawaii.
   • Challenge the class to notate and clap the rhythm of the *kala'au*, the two lengths of wood.

7. Recording: "Pihanakalani" (a hula *ka'eke'eke*) (Album: *Hawaiian Chant, Hula, and Music*, Side 1, Band 4). The ka'eke'eke are bamboo stomping tubes, also called a bamboo organ. They produce fascinating resonant sounds in this mele hula, whose text is romantic. Show a picture of a ka'eke'eke.
   • Challenge the class to notate the rhythmic pattern, which is produced by two sounds, one high and one low.

Example:

Low	High	Low	High	Low	High	Low	High

   • Divide the class into two sections, one clapping the high rhythms, the other the low. Use backs of hands to clap low, palms together for high. (Experiment with other sound sources, as well as drums.) Close listening is required since the rhythms change subtly after each kahea.

8. "Ohe hano ihu" (Album: *Hawaiian Chant, Hula, and Music*, Side 2, Band 14). The haunting sound of the nose flute, the only true wind instrument of ancient Hawaii, is heard here.
   • Challenge a student to graph the contours of the melodic line.

9. Teach the class songs of the following types:
   a. "Aia O Pele I Hawaii" ("Pele Is at Hawaii"), an ancient Hawaiian hula found in the book *Hawaii: Music in Its History* by Hausman, page 14. Use the Hawaiian words (key to pronunciation is on page 103). Let the class decide what instruments and rhythm patterns to use.

b. "He Mele O Ke Kahuli" ("Song of the Land Shell"), *Hawaii: Music in Its History,* page 15.

c. "I Went to Hilo." Found in *Folk Songs Hawaii Sings* by Kelly, page 32. This is a hapa-haole (half-white) hula song that combines characteristics of the ancient mele hula with those of Western music.

d. "Who Is Knocking?" An ancient Hawaiian chant on page 19 of *Hawaii: Music in Its History.*

e. Challenge the class to sing the excerpt from the following mele hula using two notes a minor third apart, D and F for example.

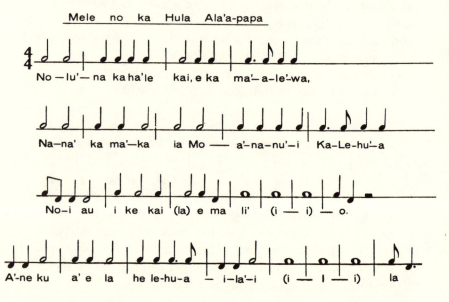

(The complete mele hula may be found on page 156 in *Unwritten Literature of Hawaii* by Emerson.) The hula *ala-a-papa* is one of the dignified hulas, comparable to an old-fashioned courtly minuet in its stateliness and dignity. Below is the translation of the song.

> From mountain retreat and route-woven ladder
> Mine eye looks down on Goddess Moana-Lehua
> Then I pray to the sea, be thou calm; would
> there might stand on thy shore lehua.

10. Show film: *Ho'Olaulea,* which illustrates performances of ancient Hawaiian dances and chants.

11. Listen to album: *Legends of Hawaii.* Absolutely fascinating stories.

Lesson Three: Learning to Play the Ipu Drum

The following illustration shows how to play the *ipu.* (A large empty plastic Clorox bottle can be substituted for the ipu if a gourd is not available.)

Drum Rhythms for the Ipu (by Yona Nahenahe Chock)

Pa'i   = single slap with fingers.
Pa   = finger, thumb, ground, pause, slap.
Kahela = finger, thumb, ground, slap, slap.
Kuku   = finger, thumb, ground; finger, thumb, ground; finger, thumb, ground; slap, slap.

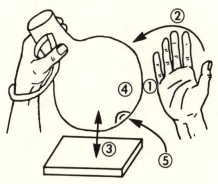

Hold ipu in left hand.

① *Finger: Lift the gourd up with a sharp tap of the little finger.* ② *Thumb: Put it down with a hard thump of the thumb. This sound should be distinct from the "Pa" sound when the ipu strikes the mat.* ③ ④ *Pa'i or slap with the fingers on the lower half of the ipu.* ⑤ *Be careful never to strike the piko, or soft center, of the gourd. It will crack.*

Challenge students who become adept at playing to keep up with the ipu on the recording "He Wahine Holo Lio."

Recording: "He Wahine Holo Lio" (a hula *pa ipu)* (Album: *Hawaiian Chant, Hula and Music*, Side 1, Band 3). In this mele hula the chant is accompanied by rhythmic patterns played by the gourd drum, ipu, after which the hula is named. The mele praises the horsemanship of a member of the royal family.

Have the class listen closely and count how many kaheas are heard; listen for the chant to continue after each kahea with the words previously spoken.

Ask: "The chant sounds repetitive; how many notes are used?" Listen for glottal stops and vocal subtleties that add interest.

Let those who became adept at playing the ipu play along with the recording.

Use drums, desk tops, or rhythm sticks to duplicate the very rhythmic ipu accompaniment.

Lesson Four: Recognizing Characteristic Features in Modern Hawaiian Music

The arrival of missionaries from New England in 1820 marked the beginning of many changes in Hawaiian life. Important from the musical standpoint, the missionaries initiated the choral tradition by establishing singing schools, a tradition that was enthusiastically accepted by the Hawaiian natives and which flourishes today.

There were members of the Hawaiian royal family, as well as many lesser-known musicians, who composed songs in the himeni style. Smith (1959) states that these old Hawaiian songs are generally learned by oral tradition.

The Hawaiians seemed to have always been a music-loving people and quickly included new sounds in their music. In fact, one of the outstanding characteristics of Hawaiian music is that the influences are borrowed. They enjoyed the sounds of band music; a Prussian bandmaster, Henry Berger, led the Royal Hawaiian Band for approximately forty years and enjoyed great popularity in the islands. Berger also wrote the state song, "Hawaii Ponoi." After the introduction of the himeni style of singing, certain members of the monarchy composed songs that are still sung today.

The many foreigners who came to Hawaii enriched the musical culture of the islands. Using the study of Hawaiian music as a starting point, it is interesting (as well as logical) to delve into the music of a wide variety of cultures touched by the Pacific Ocean.

Classroom Strategies and Experiences: Discovering Unique Sounds in Hawaiian Music

Purpose of Activities: Listening and performing to become familiar with the himeni and other popular styles of Hawaiian music, including the sound of the ukulele and steel and slack-key guitar playing.

Procedure:

1. Recording: "Aloha Oe" (Album: *Hawaii in Hi-Fi,* Side 2, Band 5). Written by Queen Liliuokalani, the last of the Hawaiian monarchs, this is perhaps the most famous of the old Hawaiian songs in the himeni style. This recording uses hapa-haole (both English and Hawaiian words).
   - Alert the class to listen in the recording for the sound of the steel guitar with its characteristic glissandi and arpeggios.
   - Note the use of familiar Western instruments. What are they?
   - Teach the class the song "Aloha Oe" (included here).
   - Teach "Sweet Lei Le Hua" as an example of a song in   hapa-haole (page 42 in *Hawaii: Music in Its History*).

2. Recording: "Tomi Tomi" (Album: *Trade Wind Islands,* Side 2 Band 4). A lively song, in rapid tempo, sung in Hawaiian.
   - Have the class count the number of phrases played solo by the steel guitar.
   - Ask: "What other instrument is prominent?" (Flute.)
   - Name other instruments used.
   - Note the deep, throaty voice of Haunani, the female singer.

3. Recording: "Hoonani I Ka Makua Mau" ("Praise God from Whom All Blessings Flow") (Album: *Music of Hawaii from the Missionaries through Statehood*, Side 1, Band 1). Sung in Hawaiian, this song is an excellent example of the synthesis of Hawaiian and Western influences by a contemporary arranger.

- Ask: "What effects do the trumpets and chorus give to the song?"
- Ask: "Does anything beside the words *sound* Hawaiian? What?"
- Let the class sing the opening phrase in Hawaiian.
- Sing "A Charge to Keep I Have" in Hawaiian (page 30 in *Hawaii: Music in Its History*).

4. Recording: "Blue Hawaii" (Album: *Hawaii Calls: Greatest Hits,* Side 1, Band 1). Good song for typical languorous, sensual, Hawaiian sounds.
- Listen for the remarkable tenor-to-soprano range of the female singer, and the sliding vocal line.
- Listen for the steel guitar solo with its characteristic glissandi throughout and at the end of the song.
- Analyze the song in ABA pattern.

5. Recording: "Hiilawe" (Album: *Hawaii Calls: Greatest Hits,* Side 1, Band 2). Sounds of the slack-key guitar with ipu, *pu-ili* (split bamboo) and pahu (drum) providing authentic Hawaiian rhythms.
- The percussion instrument sounds can be duplicated by the class: divide students into three groups to play ipus, pu-ilis, and pahus.
- As these instruments alternate in accompanying the singers on the recording, let each group play as their instrument is heard. Turn the volume of the recording down, and let the groups play together.
- Ask: "How does the sound of the slack-key guitar differ from that of the steel guitar?"

6. Recording: "King's Serenade" (Imu Au Ia Oe) (Album: *Hawaii Calls: Greatest Hits,* Side 2, Band 3). This is the theme from the movie *Bird of Paradise.* A delightful listening experience, the chorus and steel guitar are heard against background sounds of the waves of Waikiki.
- Have the class analyze the song in ABA pattern.
- Ask: "How would the sounds of waves be indicated?"
- Teach "The Thirsty Winds of Kohala" (page 30 of *Folk Songs Hawaii Sings*).

7. Recording: "Hawaiian War Chant" (Ta-hu-wa-hu-wai) (Album: *Hawaii Calls: Greatest Hits,* Side 2, Band 2). Drums and chanters begin in solid rhythm in this familiar song. Singers occasionally use syncopation in a manner reminiscent of the ancient Hawaiian drum style.
   • Have the class raise hands when they hear the syncopated rhythms.
   • After several listenings, duplicate the drum rhythms.

8. Recording: "Hawaiian Wedding Song" (Album: *Hawaii Calls: Greatest Hits,* Side 1, Band 3). This is probably the second most famous Hawaiian song, heard here in full-chorus arrangement with male-female duet.
   • Listen for sliding voices, similar to instrumental playing style.
   • Ask: "Why do you think this song is such a favorite?"

9. Recording: "The Hukilau Song" (Album: *Hawaii Calls: Greatest Hits,* Side 1, Band 5). The *hukilau* is a fishing party. Large nets, strung with leaves, are used to drive fish to the shore.
   • Teach the class "The Hukilau Song"; the words can be learned easily from the recording (also on page 130 in *Growing with Music 8,* Prentice-Hall, Inc., 1966).

10. Recording: "Some Enchanted Evening" (Album: *Hawaii Calls: Exotic Instrumentals,* Side 1, Band 1). The familiar song from the musical *South Pacific* is played in Hawaiian style. Steel guitars play melody, vibes play solo phrases, accompanied by the steady rhythm of the pahu drum.
   • After playing this recording, play the same song from the original cast album or any other instrumental arrangement available. Have the class list differences in sound and style between the two.
   • Ask: "What makes one *sound* instantly Hawaiian, and the other not?"

11. Sing other popular Hawaiian songs found in collections or in sheet music; include the state song, "Hawaii Ponoi."

12. Show film: *Hawaii: Crossroads of the Pacific.*

ADDITIONAL THINGS TO DO AND DISCUSS

Assign students projects that require research into the history of Hawaii, our only state that was once a monarchy. For islands of such serene beauty, their past was very turbulent, indeed. The story of Kamehameha I, the first king of the islands, is a fascinating one. Each of the main islands has a distinct personality; assign a different one to volunteers for investigation. How and when Hawaii became a territory and then a state also makes interesting research. The story of the development of the major agricultural industries such as sugar and pineapple will lead into the discovery of how and why some of the many different nationalities came to the islands. Perhaps cooperation with the social studies department in your school could be arranged. There is always, of course, further research into Hawaiian music for those interested.

There is a great deal of interest in Hawaii today in reviving the ancient premissionary chants and dances. The singing of meles, the ancient chants, required vocal mannerisms that some authorities believe are found on occasion in the styles of some modern Hawaiian singers. The ancient Hawaiians used percussion instruments effectively, with drumming being particularly outstanding. The great wealth of ancient legend and lore provided an almost infinite amount of subject matter on which mele hulas and mele olis were based.

In the classroom, youngsters are adept at picking up the drum rhythms and while playing along with the recordings they become familiar with the style of mele hula chant singing at the same time. In fact, an average class can sing an authentic-sounding chant with percussion accompaniment by the end of the study.

While the hula is generally associated with women, male hula dancers were common in ancient Hawaii. After the discovery by Westerners of the islands when the ports became open to seamen from around the world, it became immediately obvious that the foreigners preferred women dancers. Thus the tradition began and has persisted.

In performances of the ancient hula the dancers usually wear *kikepa,* sarong-type dresses with one end passed over the right shoulder, flowing freely in the back. (The grass skirts commonly seen are Tahitian.) The Hawaiian dancers would also generally wear a feather lei in their hair and have leis of either fragrant fruit or leaves around their necks. Sitting hula gestures could be learned by a class. An excellently illustrated example of one is on pages 76-77 in the October 1972 issue of the *Music Educators Journal*. Others can be found in *Polynesian Dance* by Adrienne Kaeppler. The drawings of stick-people dancing facilitate learning. The more complex hip-wriggling hulas use combined hand and torso gestures, but are fun.

When teaching children Hawaiian songs, always include the Hawaiian words--youngsters enjoy them. Since there are many repetitions and duplications in the Hawaiian language, the words are rather easily pronounced with practice; the language contains only twelve letters: 5 vowels (*a,e,i,o,u*) and seven consonants (*h,k,l,m,n,p,w*). Classes could begin by singing the major diatonic scale in Hawaiian: *pa, ko, li, ha, no, la, mi, pa*. If possible, obtain a Hawaiian hymnbook; a large number of hymns from the Judeo/ Christian tradition are included, and many students will recognize and enjoy singing them in Hawaiian.

Encourage the classes to keep accurate notes. Correct spellings, definitions, and other information you want them to remember could be kept in the music section of their notebooks and reviewed for a few minutes each day. Evaluation, however, should be based on the recognition of the musical *sounds* of the various ancient and modern instruments and the singing styles in mele hulas and mele olis. This type of evaluation gives all students an equal chance, since *sound* in any music is the important thing.

- Construct Hawaiian musical instruments.
- Do lots of drumming, following examples on records.
- Perfect a sitting hula, complete with music and costumes, incorporate songs and instruments, and present an assembly combining Hawaiian history and music.
- Learn to play the ukulele, which is plucked. (On occasion, slack-key style is used in ukulele playing.)
- Learn to play the guitar in slack-key style.
- Try sliding a steel bar up and down guitar strings to achieve a Hawaiian sound. Use the two methods to accompany songs.

Beginning with the turn of the century, many ballads extolling the beauty of the islands began to be written. This has continued to the present. Motion pictures helped to popularize the nostalgia music that poured from the islands. It is little wonder that

Hawaiian music is recognized and heard almost all over the world. This music undoubtedly played a significant part in helping tourism develop into an important industry for the islands.

Hawaiian popular music is performed with more interpretive freedom than is customary in Western popular music; many of the songs are never performed twice in exactly the same way. In fact, the music becomes Hawaiian in *performance*, the origin of the melody or the lyrics notwithstanding. One of the reasons why this music is so distinctly Hawaiian is the fact that the sounds seem honestly to reflect the great charm and warmth of a people to whom the word "aloha" (even in ancient times) meant a genuinely friendly nature and sincere hospitality.

SELECTED BIBLIOGRAPHY
Books

Colum, Padraic. *Legends of Hawaii*. New Haven:Yale Univ. Press, 1937. A classic collection.

Elbert, Samuel H., and Noelani Mahoe. *Na Mele o Hawaii's Nei* (101 Hawaiian Songs). Honolulu: Univ. of Hawaii Press, 1970. An excellent guide to pronunciation, meaning, and tradition of Hawaiian speech and song; no music.

Emerson, Nathaniel B. *Unwritten Literature of Hawaii*. Washington: Bureau of American Ethnology, 1909. Standard work; an exhaustive early survey of ancient Hawaiian music.Contains music examples. (Translations not always accurate.)

Feher, et al. *Hawaii: A Pictorial History*. Hawaii: Bishop Museum Press, 1969. Expensive, but very valuable book. History of the islands from the first inhabitants through statehood. Stunning photographs.

Graves, William. *Hawaii*. Washington, D.C.:National Geographic Society, 1970. Detailed coverage of the islands; good photos.

Hargrave, Helena May. *Fragments of Song from Hawaii*. Honolulu: Maurice Kidjel, 1939. A slender volume with much precise, pertinent information about Hawaiian music. Four chants with music and translations are given. Good.

Hausman, Ruth L. *Hawaii: Music in Its History*. Rutland, VT: Charles E. Tuttle Co., 1968. Traces Hawaiian music history in an easy-to-read manner; valuable for classroom use; contains music examples.

Hiroa, Te Rang (Peter H. Buck). "Musical Instruments" Section IX in *Arts and Crafts of Hawaii*. Honolulu: Bishop Museum Special Publication #5, 1945. Beautiful pictures of instruments.

Judd, Gerrit P. *A Hawaiian Anthology*. New York: The Macmillan Co., 1967. Writings about Hawaii from primary sources.

Kaeppler, Adrienne L. *Polynesian Dance: With a Selection for Contemporary Performances.*. Honolulu: Alpha Delta Kappa, 1983.(Avail. from Bishop Museum.) Accessible, interesting, easy to use, varied. Recording included.

_____."Polynesian Music and Dance", in *Musics of Many Cultures,* ed. Elizabeth May. PP. 144-150: "East Polynesia-Hawaii."

Kanahele, George S., ed. *Hawaiian Music and Musicians*. Honolulu:The Univ. Press of Hawaii, 1979. Encyclopedia with app. 200 entries; major articles on all aspects of Hawaiian music; excellent bibliography.

Kuykendall, Ralph S., and A. Grove Day. *Hawaii: A History.* New York: Prentice-Hall, Inc., 1948. Standard work on history of Hawaiian islands; valuable for classroom reference.

Michener, James. *Hawaii.* New York: Random House, 1959. Fascinating saga of the islands.

Roberts, Helen M. *Ancient Hawaiian Music.* Honolulu: Bishop Museum, 1926. Dover reprint, NY, 1967. Standard work; detailed descriptions of Hawaiian music and musical instruments. Contains many music examples; no illustrations.

Stoneburner, Brian C. *Hawaiian Music: An Annotated Bibliography.* Westport, CT:Greenwood Press, 1986. Over 500 annotated entries on the music of Hawaii, including musicians.

Westervelt, William D. *Hawaiian Historical Legends.* New York: Revell, 1923.

_____.*Hawaiian Legends of Ghosts and Ghost-Gods.* Boston: Ellis, 1916. Classic collections.

Articles

Gillett, Dorothy K. "Hawaiian Music for Hawaii's Children," *Music Educators Journal 59* (October 1972). Excellent article with many good suggestions for presenting Hawaiian music to children.

Smith, Barbara B. "Folk Music in Hawaii," *Journal of the International Folk Music Council XI* (1959). Well-written article; good overview of Hawaiian music from past to present.

Song Collections

Criterion's Hawaiian Song Book. NY: Criterion Music Corp., 1965. Contains twenty-six songs with both Hawaiian and English words for voice, piano, uke, guitar. Many of the songs have been recorded. Useful.

Hawaiian Sampler. Delaware, OH: Cooperative Recreation Service, 1963. Booklet containing good songs for classroom.

Kelly, John M., Jr. *Folk Songs Hawaii Sings.* Rutland, VT: Tuttle, 1963. Contains songs not only of Hawaii and other Polynesian areas, but has section on Asian music. Valuable for classroom use; excellent notes.

King, Charles Edward. *King's Book of Hawaiian Melodies.* Honolulu: Charles E. King, 1948.

_____.*King's Songs of Hawaii.* Honolulu: Charles E. King, 1950.

Two useful collections.

Na Himeni Haipule Hawaii. Honolulu: Hawaii Conference, 2103 Nuuanu Ave., 1972. Standard hymnbook containing hymns in the Hawaiian language.

Roes, Carol. *Eight Children's Songs from Hawaii.* Honolulu: 988 Kealaolu Ave., 1958. Good for elementary and young secondary classes; has some fine rhythm songs.

_____. *Introduction to the Hula.* Honolulu: Mele Loke Publishing Co., 1961. Dance movements to accompany book *Eight Children's Songs from Hawaii.* Two forty-five rpm records can be ordered. Useful.

AUDIO-VISUAL MATERIALS

Films

A Child of Hawaii. Color, 15 min., Journal Films. Good for view of life in Hawaii through a youngster's eyes; some music in background. Holds student interest.

Artifacts of Old Hawaii. Color, 15 min., Bishop Museum. Outdoor scenes portraying how the ancient Hawaiians lived before the discovery of the islands by foreigners.

Arts of Polynesia. Color, 15 min., Bishop Museum. Basically a visual arts film showing extensive carvings. Hawaiian art is emphasized.

Hawaii Calls. Color, approx. 10 min., Cate and McGlone. Hawaii Visitors Bureau. A travel film with music skillfully interwoven throughout. Good; holds student interest.

Hawaii: Crossroads of the Pacific. Color, 40 min., Cate and McGlone Films, Hawaii Visitors Bureau. Primarily a travel film, this contains a goodly amount of Hawaiian music and dance. Holds student interest.

Hawaii: Pacific Paradise. Color, 35 min., Hawaiian Airlines, Cate and McGlone Films. Another travel film, with an appreciable amount of Hawaiian music and dance. Mention is made of Pele and other gods. Very good; students enjoy this.

Ho'Olaulea. Color, 22 min., Bishop Museum, P.O. Box 6032, Honolulu. Beautiful film showing ancient Hawaiian dances, chants and musical instruments; holds student interest.

Sports of Old Hawaii. Color, 15 min., Bishop Museum. Some of
   the ancient Hawaiian games and sports are shown.
Ula Noweo. Color, 30 min., Bishop Museum. Authoritative; instructions for hula, with accompanying record.

Recordings
A. Ancient Hawaiian

*Call of the Morning Bird; Chants and Songs of Palau, Yap, and
   Ponape, Collected by Iwakichi Muranushi, 1936.* (Audio
   Recording Collections, Bishop Musium ARCOS-2. Cassette). Historic cylinder recordings of a 1935-36 expedition.
   61 page booklet contains music transcriptions; chants in
   original languages with transcriptions; photos, maps and
   bibliography.
Hawaiian Chant, Hula and Music (Folkways, FW 8750). Excellent
   examples of a variety of instruments accompanying chants.
   If only one recording can be purchased, let this be it. Notes
   are scanty.
Hawaiian Chants, Hula and Love-Dance Songs (Folkways, FE
   4271). Very good musical examples; scanty notes.
Let's Hula (with hula instructions) (Hula 500). Nina Kealiiwaha-
   mana. Fun for classroom dancing!
"Music of Hawaii" (Side IV of *Music in World Cultures,* included
   in Music Educators Journal, October, 1972).Fine example of
   chant accompanied by *ili ili*; magazine includes notation.
Music of the World's Peoples (Ethnic Folkways Library Vol.V,
   No.78). Contains example of hula *olapa,* "Hawaii-Kawika."

B. Modern Hawaiian

Favorite Instrumentals (Capitol DN 16170). Contains popular standards; good for classroom listening.
Hawaii - A Musical Memento (GNP 34E).
Hawaii Calls: Exotic Instruments (Capitol ST 1409). Music includes instruments of different Asian nations; Japan, China, the Philippines, etc. Interesting as "lead" to further
   study of Asian musics.
Hawaii Calls/ Greatest Hits, by Webley Edwards (Capitol SN
   16171). A two-volume set; one with vocals, the other instrumental; good.
Hawai in Hi-Fi, Leo Addeo and his orchestra (RCA Camden CAL
   510). Standard examples of popular Hawaiian music.
Hawaiian Slack Key (Waikiki Records Co., LP 320). Good examples of slack-key guitar style.

Hawaii to Hong Kong - South Sea (Request 10106). Good for introduction to contemporary Asian music.

Legends of Hawaii (Kamokila Record Co., Honolulu; Monaural K-100; two volumes). Narrated by Kamokila. Absolutely spell-binding legends told by a master storyteller; students are enthralled. Highly recommended.

Music of Hawaii from the Missionaries through Statehood by Jack de Mello (Ala Moana, SR 35-7849). Excellent variety; very good notes.

Na Mele Hawaii No Na Keiki: Hawaiian Songs for Children (Hula Records Stereo HS-510). Fourteen songs and booklet with Hawaiian words and English translation; good for classroom use.

Trade Wind Islands (Capitol T1203). Songs sung by Haunani in her fascinatingly deep, throaty voice.

SOURCES

For Hawaiian Records and Sheet Music: House of Music, Ltd., Ala Moana Center, Honolulu, Hawaii.

For Hula Instruments: Hula Supply Center, 2346 S. King St., Honolulu, Hawaii, 96822.

Hawaiiana Resource Units, Mitchell, Kamehameha Schools, 1969. Bishop Museum Education Department, PO Box 6037, Honolulu, Hawaii, 96818. (THE BISHOP MUSEUM IS AN EXCELLENT SOURCE OF A VARIETY OF MATERIALS AND MANY OF THE BOOKS AND RECORDS IN THIS CHAPTER; WRITE FOR LIST OF AVAILABLE ITEMS.)

CHAPTER SEVEN

Learning About Mexican and Puerto Rican Folk Music

I. THE MEXICAN AMERICAN MUSICAL HERITAGE

United States citizens of Mexican or Spanish Indian origin form the second largest racial minority in this country. They number approximately four million persons with more than eighty-five percent of them living in the American Southwest. Mexican Americans generally reside in *barrios*, or communities not unlike the ghettos of black Americans. The largest barrio in America is in East Los Angeles, which is home to over 500,000 men, women, and children.

Who are the Mexican Americans? They are described by many names: Latino, Chicano, Mexicano, etc., but they are not a totally immigrant population. They are descendants of the original *mestizos* (persons of mixed Spanish and Indian parentage) who came to this country after the Spanish conquest of Mexico. Lesson One will help orient students to the sounds of some of the folk music representative of the Mexican American heritage.

Lesson One: Orienting the Listener to Variety in Mexican Folk Music

Purpose of Activities: Listening for distinguishing characteristics in Mexican folk music.

Clues for Listening

Procedure:

1. Show the class a map of Mexico and the United States. Point out the areas of the Southwest that were part of Mexico before

the Mexican War (1846-1848). Those areas were Texas, California, New Mexico, Colorado, Arizona, and parts of Utah, Wyoming, and Nevada.

2. Show film: *Mexican American Culture, Its Heritage.*

3. Play a prepared tape (or use recordings) of a variety of folk music, each example approximately two minutes long. The following musical suggestions will demonstrate characteristics of Mexican music such as the following: the piercing trumpets and slightly off-pitch sound of violins in the *mariachi* (mah-ree-*ah*-chee) band; the lively stomping and vocal explosions of the musicians in the *son* (sohn); the so-called primitiveness of Yacqui Indian music; the singing in thirds and sixths in "La Cucaracha"; the gentle, romantic style characteristic of Mexican balladeers in "Voy a Cantar Un Corrido" and a Tarascan song, "Male Rosa," sung by descendants of the original Indians of the area, which shows both Spanish and Indian characteristics.

    a. "Cuerdas de Mi Guitarra" ("Strings of My Guitar") (Album: *Mexican Mariachi Pasadobles*). Typically lively, noisy music of a mariachi band.

    b. "El Pajaro Cu" ("The Cu Bird") (Album: *Mexican Panorama*). An example of a type of ballad called a *son*. The singer asks a beautiful bird to take a message to his sweetheart. Includes Latin exclamations of exuberance and very rhythmic sounding instruments.

    c. "Baile del Venado: El Tecolate" (Album: *Folk Music of Mexico*). This song is of pre-Hispanic origin. It is sung here by a Yaqui Indian accompanied by a water drum and two notched sticks over gourd resonators.

    d. "La Cucaracha" ("The Cockroach") (Album: *Mexico y Su Folklore*). Accompanied by guitars, a male trio sings this familiar favorite of the Revolution of 1910.

    e. "Voy a Cantar Un Corrido" ("I Shall Sing a Corrido") (Album: *Songs of Old Mexico*). Tenderly sung by a man recalling memories of a friend shot during an escapade of the Revolution.

    f. "Male Rosa" ("Senorita Rosa") (Album: *The Real Mexico in Music and Song*). Three girls harmonize unaccompanied in this charming song.

4. As they listen, have students list as many as possible of the instruments heard during this lesson.

Lesson Two: Exploring the Roots and Sounds
of Mexican Indian Music

The ancestors of today's Mexicans were the Aztec and Mayan Indians who had very advanced civilizations. The Aztec capital, Tenochtitlan, was located where Mexico City now stands. The Aztec high civilization had a musical tradition so well developed it amazed the early Spanish historians. Their dancing was expertly choreographed and done to the sound of reed flutes, gourd rattles, and possibly drums. Music was a vital part of ceremonies and rituals, frequently in connection with sun worship and battles. From the reconstruction of ancient musical instruments, the pentatonic scale seems to have been predominant, although some flutes have been found that can produce diatonic and chromatic intervals.

The Aztecs had a wide variety of instruments, some of them made of human as well as animal bones. Flutes, conch shell trumpets, rasps, drums, rattles, and whistles of varying sizes, all individually designed, were used. Many have come down to us in nearly perfect condition.

Characteristics of Aztec Music

Stevenson (1952:17-19) draws the following conclusions about Aztec music: music was used solely in a functional capacity, dealing with religious and cult rituals; music was a communal, not an individual expression; some instruments such as the *huehuetl* (whay-*whay*-tul) and *teponatzli* (teh-poe-*naht*-zlee) drums were considered sacred. Obviously there was a considerable amount of music among the Aztecs long before the arrival of the Spaniards. The singing of choruses, dramas that used music, and orchestras with a wide variety of instruments have all been documented. Undoubtedly the influence of all of this music reached into the villages and affected the native folk music. Much of the native Indian music heard in Mexico today is still functional.

Certain elements of music such as melody, rhythm and tone color were used by the ancient Mexicans. (An example of tone color can be heard in the singing of the Huichol Indians in the "Fiesta de la Calabaza" described in Lesson Three.) Some idea of how Aztec music might have sounded can be heard in the music of present-day Indian tribes who have remained outside the mainstream of contemporary life such as the Cora and Huichol Indians. Aztec singing was seemingly characterized by monophonic, pentatonic vocalizations that were rhythmic and accompanied by wind instruments and drums. Aztec drumming has been described as a succession of steady beats in rapid tempo.

Before the arrival of the Spaniards there were no stringed instruments. Many types of drums have been discovered along with other percussion instruments such as clay bells, rattles, and rasps. Hundreds of wind instruments have been discovered, more than any other variety. The two favored drums of the Aztecs, the huehuetl and teponaztli, were made out of hollowed sections of tree trunks. The former was played vertically and the latter, horizontally.

Classroom Strategies and Experiences: Recognizing the Music of Selected Mexican-Indian Tribes

Purpose of Activities: To recognize sounds of the music of certain Mexican Indian tribes.

Procedure:

1. Show film: *Mexico's History.*

2. Explain to the class that the music they are about to hear could very possibly be similar to the kind of music the Aztecs sang and played before the Conquest. The tribes singing and playing instruments on the recordings were selected because they are the least influenced by contemporary civilization.

3. Recording: "Son de Semana Santa" (Album: *Folk Music of Mexico,* Side A, Band 5). The Cora Indians of the Mexican State of Nayarit participate in both ancient pagan rites and Christian services. The instruments used for pagan rituals are different from those used in the Christian ceremonies.

• Have the class do the following: (a) identify the two musical instruments heard, (b) describe the tempo of each instrument,

(c) chart the melodic line of the flute and indicate where tremolo occurs.

- Show pictures of the Cora Indians and their instruments: a reed flute and a drum covered by a woolen cloth (the pictures are inside the record jacket). Explain that during Holy Week it is a custom in this area to cover the drum.

4. Recording: "Fiesta de la Calabaza" ("Fiesta of the Squash") (Album: *Folk Music of Mexico,* Side B, Band 4). This is the music of the Huichol Indians who pray to the gods through their shamans (tribal priest and/or medicine man) for overall contentment and a successful harvest.

- Show pictures of the three-legged huehuetl Aztec drum (found in the recording notes).
- Have the class analyze the recording using ABA or other pattern.
- Teach the song "Aztec Hymn to the Sun" (page 5 of *Latin American Folk Songs*). Add dance steps as suggested and include costumes and instruments.

Lesson Three: Introducing Selected Forms of Mexican Folk Music

The Aztec civilization fell to the Spanish invaders in 1521 and with it a great culture. The Spaniards, however, came not only to colonize but to convert the Indian population. In pursuit of this goal they vigorously suppressed the native arts and "pagan" music was expressly forbidden. The Catholic Church sent many missionaries to Mexico, some of whom placed great emphasis on the musical training of the Indians as a part of the total educational structure. (This was necessary since music was an integral part of church ceremony.)

The natives were good pupils not only because music was a motivating factor in their conversion, but also because they had been accustomed to elaborate rituals before the Spaniards arrived. A Franciscan missionary, Pedro de Gante, taught the natives Gregorian chants and in 1524 founded a music school in Mexico. This was the first such school in the New World.

During the 300 years of the Colonial Era and the years following independence in 1810, the acculturation process was a continuing one. This process involved the rhythms and melodies of Indians, Spaniards, and blacks to produce a music that eventually evolved into distinctly Mexican (or mestizo) forms. The Spanish influence has remained dominant as is obvious in the folk music forms that show definite Spanish characteristics and derivations.

Eight of the forms selected to be discussed in this chapter are: the *alabanzas,* a religious form; the music of the mariachi band, which developed during the era of Emperor Maximilian (1864-1867); folk dances such as the son, the *huapango* (wah-*pahng*-oh), which shows some black rhythmic influences, and the *jarabe* (hah-*rah*-bay), the national dance of Mexico; the *corrido* (koh-*ree*-doh), a favorite type of ballad during the Revolutionary period that began in 1910; the *cancion* (cahn-see-*ohn*), and the *valona* (vah-*lohn*-ah).

Since many Mexican folk songs are dances and many dances are songs, a lively tempo is a characteristic of much of the folk music. Another identifying feature is the use of the major keys for the vast majority of the songs. Many religious folk songs have remained almost unaltered due, perhaps, to the pervasiveness of Catholicism in the life of the people. To discover some of the things that make these musical forms sound Mexican in character will form the basis of the classroom strategies and activities in the following lessons.

Identifying the Alabanza, A Type of Religious Folk Song

After Cortes's conquest, the Spaniards brought their own music to Mexico. During this long period, masses, magnificats, and other church-related forms were faithfully copied. Mexico was the first country in the western hemisphere to publish a book with musical notation; it was an Ordinary of the Mass, printed in Mexico City in 1556.

There was a gradual synthesis of native and Spanish elements into the music of this time. The Europeans enlarged the scale from the prevailing pentatonic and introduced harmony. The Spanish conqueror "imposed not only his religious beliefs and social administration, his customs and language, but also his musical practices, liturgical, secular, popular and dances" (Mayer-Serra 1960:26). The folk music of Mexico became, and has remained, overwhelmingly in the musical tradition of Spain. Some of the native religious folk songs show evidences of the influence of the liturgical music of the Catholic church. In the alabanzas (Christian praise songs) native instruments are used.

Classroom Strategies and Experiences

Purpose of Activities: To become aware of the alabanza as a type of Mexican folk music.

Procedure:

1. Show filmstrip: *Man and His Music: Mexico.* Show film: *Marimba Music of Mexico.*

2. Give a definition of *alabanza:* "Originally, a Spanish hymn in praise of the Eucharist, brought to the New World by the Franciscans, probably during the seventeenth century. It became a hymn in praise of Jesus, the Virgin Mary, and other saints. Some forms of (*alabanza*) have survived in numerous Roman Catholic communities of Mexico, New Mexico, etc . . ." (Harvard Dictionary 1969:26). The word "alabanza" means "praise."

3. Recording: "Alabanza a Juan Diego" (Album: *Mexican Panorama*, Side 1, Band 5). Guitars made of the shells of armadillos and gourd rattles accompany the singing and dancing.
   • Have the class clap the steady rhythm of the instruments.
   • Have the class describe the singing. Ask: "Is the singing major or minor? Is there harmony? Does the music sound simple or complex?"

4. Recording: "Alabanza a la Virgen" (Album: *Mexican Panorama*, Side 1, Band 6). The description of this recording states that it was sung at three a.m. Women are heard singing unaccompanied in high nasal tones.
   • Play a recording of a Gregorian chant, then let the class hear "Alabanza a la Virgen." Ask: "Do you hear any similarity in mood and texture between the two songs?"

Recognizing Selected Types of Folk Music

From the period of independence to contemporary times, music has continued to be a vital part of Mexican life. One of the most popular forms of Mexican music today is the music of the mariachi band, an ensemble of itinerant folk musicians. A typical band will include at least a *guitarron* (a large, five-stringed guitar), two violins and a trumpet, trombone, or clarinet. Sometimes guitars of other sizes are added and occasionally a harp will be used instead of a trumpet. The guitar players usually sing also.

The size of the bands varies from three to about twelve players wearing "the distinctive *charro* (horseman) garb of boots, tight-fitting pants, bolero jacket trimmed with silver ornaments and *sombrero* (wide-brimmed hat)" (Gomez 1973:xiii).

Besides the mariachi bands there is the *son*, a folk dance considered "as one of the most genuinely Mexican of all folk genres" (Behague 1973:201). The word "son" can also designate any song or part of a song. *Sones* are always included in mariachi band repertoires.

The corrido is a "Mexican type of narrative folk ballad derived from the Spanish *romanze*" (Harvard Dictionary 1969:207). The texts are about historical figures (Pancho Villa, for example), with essentially the same music for each stanza. The *cancion* is a lyrical Mexican song of Spanish origin that can be sung in a number of ways. Another folk dance is the *huapango*. Modern huapangos are frequently accompanied by song as well as instrumental ensembles that range in size from two in number to a large mariachi band. The word "huapango" is also used to refer to any Mexican dance.

The *valona* (or *balona*) is a type of song that has a "lyrical, declamatory form which appeared early in colonial times . . . and is still a favorite mestizo expression" (Yurchenko: Nonesuch). Valonas have many topics from serious to humorous. The Mexican Hat Dance, as it is known in this country, is a traditional Mexican dance called the *jarabe*. It has a delightful section in which a man pursues a girl as she skillfully dances in the sombrero he has laid on the ground.

Behague (1973:202) states: "The most typical performance characteristics of Mexican folk music comprise a high tension of the voice; . . . a slight continuous nasalizing of the voice and a preference for high pitch, frequently passing into falsetto; instrumental pieces often beginning in a slower tempo than is used in the main body of the piece, with a gradual acceleration to the desired tempo, which is then maintained rigorously until the final cadence." Mexican folk dance songs have other characteristics that include easily recognizable features such as: violins playing together slightly out of tune; the inevitable use of strings (especially the guitar); many selections ending with a brisk V-I cadence, use of cross-rhythms, and a generally happy, noisy sound.

Classroom Strategies and Experiences:
Activities Designed for Involvement and Discovery

Purpose of Activities: Listening for distinguishing characteristics in seven traditional forms.

Procedure:

1. Show film: *Discovering the Music of Latin America.*

2. Recording: "El Relicario" ("The Locket") (Album: *Mexican Mariachi Pasadobles,* Side 1, Band 2). Sounds of a typical mariachi band: guitars, violins, trumpets in a lively rendition.
  • Show a picture of a mariachi band (found on record jackets).
  • Let the class clap the basic rhythm pattern of the composition both with and without the recording:

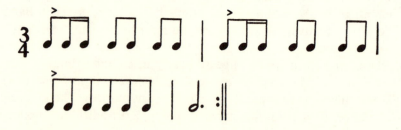

  • Analyze the recording using ABA pattern.
  • While listening, observe how trumpets and violins alternate melody as guitars provide the continuing rhythmic accompaniment.

3. Recording: "El Pajaro Cu" ("The Cu Bird") (Album: *Mexican Panorama*, Side 1, Band 3). Example of a *son;* singers are accompanied by a harp and two small guitars. This brisk, gay song is about a lover who asks a beautiful bird to take a message to his sweetheart.
- Observe spoken exclamations at intervals during song such as "ah-ha!" etc. This type of vocal explosion is frequently heard in Mexican and Latin American folk music.

4. Recording: "Mexico: Sones of Huasteco" (Album: *Music of the World's Peoples*, Side 1, Band 33). This male duet is a classic example of a *son.*
- Listen for the singers' use of falsetto, harmonies in thirds and sixths, and joyous vocal explosions.
- A violinist accompanies with frantic rhythms, embellishes generously and occasionally strums his instrument like a guitar.

5. Recording: "Vay a Cantar Un Corrido" ("I Shall Sing a Corrido") (Album: *Songs of Old Mexico*, Side 1, Band 1). A typical ballad in the corrido form. All verses have the same melody with guitar accompaniment; the text is of a topical nature. This corrido is typical of hundreds of corridos that have been written about incidents that occurred during the Revolution, in this case about an execution.
- Teach the class "Las Chaparreras," a corrido (page 71 in *Folk Songs of the World*).

6. Recording: "En La Mañana Cuando El Sol Se Despierta" ("In the Morning When the Sun Rises") (Album: *Songs of Old Mexico*, Side 1, Band 3). A romantic *cancion;* a lover longs for his beloved. Male singer accompanied by guitar.
- Listen for a slow beginning followed by an abrupt change to much faster tempo, a characteristic of Mexican folk music.
- Teach the class "La Paloma Azul" ("The Sky-Blue Dove") (page 72 in *Folk Songs of the World*). This love song has some cross-rhythms. Add instruments to emphasize this.

7. Recording: "La Bamba" (Album: *Mexico!* Side 1, Band 1). This is a good example of a modern huapango. The music is lively and filled with cross-rhythms. The instruments (guitar, guitarron, and harp) create a good deal of noisy excitement.

• Listen for the different rhythmic patterns used by the instruments and their independence from the soloist. One instrument plays in 3/4 time, another in 2/4, and another in 6/8. Discover which ones are playing what meter.

8. Recording: "Los Tiradores" ("The Wastrels") (Album: *The Real Mexico in Music and Song*, Side 1, Band 1). An excellent example of the popular *valona* form.

• Listen for singing in a recitative-like, somewhat declamatory fashion while instruments play rhythmically between verses.

ADDITIONAL THINGS TO DO AND DISCUSS

The Hispanic people have left a great impact on the Southwest where the vast majority of them live. This is apparent in the architecture, customs, and words that have become a part of our language. Some of the words are: Negro, mosquito, potato, barbecue, chocolate, mustang, parasol, hurricane, paragon. Even the great American hero, the cowboy (who came into being around 1836), is a direct descendant of the Mexican *vaquero* who supervised sheepherders on horseback.

The Mexican American population in the United States grew when the revolt in 1910 led by Pancho Villa and others precipitated a large migration to this country. The lure of jobs in the vegetable fields and fruit orchards in the 1920s (plus further internal disorder) brought thousands across the border. Not all of the immigrants stayed. Many would come to work during the harvest seasons and return home, while others were sent back by the government during the Depression. It is important to discuss with students how the Mexican immigration differed from that of any of the other groups who came to this country. The blacks were brought as slaves from Africa and the Europeans voluntarily crossed an ocean. The Mexicans, on the other hand, only had to cross a comparatively small land barrier and upon arrival found a compatible life in the barrios.

The Hispanic culture, which includes language, dress, food, music, family structure, religion, and outlook on life and life style is closer to that of Mexico than that of the United States. The younger people consider themselves Chicanos or La Raza (the Hispanic race) and are increasingly proud of their Latin heritage.

Mexican music is a collage of sounds that reflects the Spanish heritage in harmonies and melodies, but the rhythms and vocal characteristics are unique to the mestizos. Certain musical instruments show similar cross-cultural exchanges: the strings, for example. The guitars and violins introduced by the Spaniards were sometimes adapted to local tastes or convenience.

Large guitars with added strings and/or with armadillo shells can still be found. These changes give the instrument an entirely different and original sound. Cross-rhythms are frequently found in Mexican folk music which, when combined with vocal characteristics and mariachi instrumentation, give the music a unique and easily distinguishable sound and texture.

Mexican folk dance is among the most colorful and exciting in the world. The swirling bodies of women dressed in colorful, flowing attire and the agile movements of both sexes present a truly extraordinary picture of natural grace. Here again we find the blending of two cultures. The "hauteur" of Spain (somewhat reminiscent of flamenco dancers) can be seen in the erect, elegant carriage of the dancers combined with the exuberant abandon of the mestizos traceable to Indian and black influences.

FOURTEEN ADDITIONAL ACTIVITIES
FOR LEARNING STRATEGIES

1. Teach the class Mexican songs such as "Cielito Lindo," "La Calandria," "Las Mañanitas," all found in *Sound, Shape and Symbol* by the American Book Company ("Las Mañanitas" is a favorite birthday song). "La Cucaracha," the famous fighting song of Pancho Villa, is liked by young people. It would be best to sing the songs in Spanish; if necessary, work with the Spanish teacher in your building. Use guitar accompaniment whenever possible. (There are many other fine songs in the collections listed in the Selected Bibliography in this chapter.

2. Collaborate with the physical education department and arrange for classes to learn Mexican dances. A useful source is the album *Pan American Folk Dances,* which includes descriptions and steps for the dances along with photographs of appropriate costumes.

3. Play Mexican children's games. Descriptions with the accompanying music are in the album *Latin American Children's Game*

Songs. See also "Children's Games" by Luis Garcia in *Mexican Folkways* 7 (1932).

4. Arrange a class trip to a good Mexican restaurant. Or collaborate with the home economics department to prepare a Mexican meal.

5. Arrange a museum trip to see native Mexican craft and artifacts.

6. Include a lesson on Christmas in Mexico. Toor (1947) notes: *"Posadas . . .* is the designation given to the nine days of Christmas celebration in commemoration of the difficult journey of Mary and Joseph from Nazareth to Bethlehem begging for lodging each night along the way. The most important fun-making element of the *posadas* involves the breaking of the *piñata,* a papier-mâché figure covering an earthen jar filled with toys and sweets." Many lovely songs accompany this Christmas tradition. Some can be heard on the album *Cantos de Las Posadas and Other Christmas Songs.* Teach the songs "Humildes Peregrines" and "La Piñata" (pages 6 and 8 of *Latin American Folk Songs*).

7. As a class project, investigate other Mexican folk dance songs.

8. Dress dolls in colorful Mexican clothing.

9. If there is a Spanish-speaking radio station that features music in your area, spend portions of class periods listening to it. You will hear modern Hispanic rock groups as well as some traditional music.

10. Take the class to see a Spanish language motion picture, preferably a musical.

11. If there is a Spanish-speaking section of your city, visit it and find out what cultural events are open to the public.

12. Plan an assembly featuring Mexican song and dance.

13. Show film: *Chicano from the Southwest.* Discuss problems facing Mexican Americans today.

14. Make several piñatas; each class could design and make one. Have a Christmas party anytime!

It is reasonable to assume that Mexican music of the future will bear strong Indian characteristics due to the large and growing Indian population. Interestingly enough, native Mexican Indian music sounds different from much native North American Indian music. (Play a selection of each type and let students list the differences they hear.)

If one acknowledges the existence of a Mexican American subculture, one must inquire as to its roots. The arts of a people are indicative of their character and it is generally accepted that music is one of the strongest manifestations of a living culture. The music of Mexico is exciting and easily captivates the imagination and enthusiasm of young people. The study of this music can bridge a gap that may exist not only between our understanding of our closest Latin American neighbor, but our understanding of a significant number of our fellow countrymen.

SELECTED BIBLIOGRAPHY

Books

Behague, Gerard. "Latin American Folk Music" in *Folk and Traditional Music of the Western Continents*, 2nd Edition, by Bruno Nettl. Englewood Cliffs, NJ: Prentice-Hall, Inc., 1973.

Chase, Gilbert. *A Guide to the Music of Latin America,* 2nd Edition. Washington, D.C.: Pan American Union, 1962. Standard reference; general information and annotated bibliographies for 27 Latin American countries; section on Hispanic elements in the United States.

Gomez, David F. *Somos Chicanos: Strangers in Our Own Land.* Boston: Beacon Press, 1973. Should be read by all who wish to understand the Chicano subculture.

Grove's Dictionary of Music and Musicians, 5th Edition. New York: St. Martin's Press, 1954. A good survey of Mexican musical traditions by Nicolas Slonimsky is found under "Folk Music: Mexican." (See also the *New Grove Dictionary of Music and Musicians* entry under "Mexico.")

Harvard Dictionary, 2nd edition, by Willi Apel. Cambridge: The Belknap Press of Harvard Univ. Press, 1969. Contains entries on most Latin American countries. (See also the *New Harvard Dictionary of Music* entry under "Mexico.")

Lewis, Oscar. *The Children of Sanchez*. NY: Random House, 1963. A modern classic about a Mexican family.

Mayer-Serra, Otto. *The Present State of Music in Mexico*. Washington, D.C.: Pan American Union, 1960. Concise observation that includes historical information.

Paredes, Americo. *A Texas-Mexican Cancionero: Folksongs of the Lower Border*. Urbana: Univ. of Ill. Press, 1976. Excellent discussion of the historical eras associated with specific song forms; songs and translations included.

Rosaldo, Renato, and others. *Chicano: The Evolution of a People*. Minneapolis, MN: Winston Press, 1973. Series of monographs detailing the history of Mexican Americans. Good background for understanding the culture.

Simpson, Lesley Byrd. *Many Mexicans*. Berkeley: Univ. of CA Press, 1966. Informative reading for students and teacher.

Slonimsky, Nicolas. *Music of Latin America*. NY: Thomas Y. Crowell Co., 1945. Standard reference.

Stevenson, Robert M. *Music in Aztec and Inca Territory*. Berkeley: Univ. of CA Press, 1968. Scholarly presentation of the "musics of the two high American cultures."

_____. *Music in Mexico*. NY: Thomas Y. Crowell Co., 1952. A fine survey of the history of Mexican music.

Toor, Frances. *A Treasury of Mexican Folkways*. NY: Crown, 1947. Valuable for resource material.

Wolf, Eric. *Sons of the Shaking Earth: The People of Mexico and Guatemala...Their Land, History, and Culture*. Chicago: Univ. of Chicago Press, 1967. Interesting and informative; good for school library.

Articles

Lieberman, Carol, "Moctezuma's Musicians" in *Inter-American Music Bulletin* 73 (September 1969). Article details research done on pre-Columbian musical instruments in Mexico and Central America.

Music Educators Journal 59 (October, 1972). See "Music of the Americans," p.54.

Booklets

Music of Latin America. Washington, D.C.: Pan American Union, 1960. A valuable survey with information from the pre-Columbian era to the present. Extensive bibliography, discography and song collections.

Pan American Union, General Secretariat, Organization of American States, Washington, D.C. Publishes some free information about Latin America, including music. The following can be purchased at nominal cost:

> *Cancionero Popular Americano.* Seventy-five songs from the American republics; in Spanish, no translations.
> *Some Latin American Festivals and Folk Dances.*
> *Folk Songs and Dances of the Americas,* Nos. 1 and 2.
> *Christmas in Latin America.*
> *Folk Songs and Stories of the Americas.*
> *The Inter-American Music Bulletin.* (The *Bulletin* has discontinued publishing; send for a complete listing of available issues.)

Song Collections

Favorite Spanish Folksongs, compiled and edited by Elena Paz. New York: Oak Publications, 1965. Traditional songs from Spain and Latin America. Contains Mexican corrido on page 7.

Folk Songs of the Americas, edited by A.L. Lloyd. New York: Oak Publications, 1966. A collaboration of UNESCO and the International Folk Music council. Contains seven Mexican folk songs with music, texts, and translations.

Haywood, Charles. *Folk Songs of the World.* New York: John Day, 1966. Has two Mexican folk songs along with information about Mexican music.

Jacovetti, Raymond N. *Escuchar y cantar.* New York: Holt, Rinehart and Winston, 1965. Songs recorded on thirteen seven-inch 33-1/3 rpm long-playing records. Countries of origin not indicated.

Krone, Beatrice and Max. *Cantamos en espanol,* Books 1 and 2. Park Ridge, Illinois: Neil A. Kjos.

_____. *Inter-Americana.* Park Ridge, ILL: Neil A. Kjos.

McLaughlin, Roberta. *Latin American Folk Songs.* Hollywood, CA: Highland Music Co., 1969. Contains four Mexican songs with information about the songs and suggestions for interpretation.

Millan-Krone. *Mexican Folksongs.* Park Ridge, ILL: Neil A. Kjos.

Robb, John Donald. *Hispanic Folk Songs of New Mexico.* Albuquerque: The Univ. of New Mexico Press, 1954. Interesting variety of folk songs arranged for voice and piano with accompanying information.

Spanish and Latin American Songs. (SATB) Park Ridge, ILL: Neil A. Kjos.

Yurchenko, Henrietta. *A Fiesta of Folk Songs from Spain and Latin America.* NY: G.P. Putnam's Sons, 1967. Obviously collected for young children, there are nevertheless some songs that all can enjoy.

AUDIO-VISUAL MATERIALS
Films

Chicano from the Southwest. B&W, 15 min. Encyclopedia Britannica Educational Corp. Shows the effect of transition on a migrant family as they move to the city. Provocative; some Mexican music in background.

Chulas Fronteras (Beautiful Borders). Brazos Films; color;Spanish.

Discovering the Music of Latin America. Color, 20 min., BFA Educational Media. Ancient and modern instruments, traditional and modern dances of selected countries. Music is presented from aspects of pre-Columbian and Spanish influences.

Marimba Music of Mexico. B&W, 8 min. Univ. of WA Press. Four men play three *sones* on different parts of a single marimba.

Mexican-American Border Songs. B&W, 29 min. Indiana Univ. Audio-Visual Center.Songs are shown being recorded.

Mexican-American Culture, Its Heritage. Color, 18 Min., Communications Group West. History showing various influences; lots of music; traditional dancers, singers, instruments.

Mexico's History. B&W, 16 min., Coronet Films. Concise history spanning Mayan civilization to social revolution of 1910.

Musica. Video, color, 58 min. Latin American Music in Alternative Spaces, P.O. Box 2207, NY, NY 10027.Latin music in US.

Filmstrip

Mexico: Indian and Spanish Influence. A Keyboard Publication. Consists of: "A Land of Contrasts," "Its Music," "Its Art," "An Ancient Land," "Its History." Good for overview of Mexican culture.

Recordings

Cantos de las Posadas and Other Christmas Songs. (Folkways FC 7745). Fine collection of traditional Christmas songs.

Festivals of Chiapas and Oaxaca (Nonesuch 72070). Lively and exciting music.

Folk Music of Mexico, edited by Henrietta Yurchenko (Archive of Folk Culture, Library of Congress AFS L19). Music of so-called primitive Mexican tribes. Exc. notes with photos.

Los Peludos. (Ambiente AMB 103). A fine collection of Mexican corridos with excellent notes.

Marimba Music from Tehuantepec (Univ. of Washington Press; HWP-1002). Very good accompanying notes.

Mexican Mariachi Pasadobles (Capitol ST 10331). Mariachi band.

Mexican Panorama, 200 Years of Folk Song (Vanguard VRS 9014). Excellent variety; notes included.

Mexico! (Monitor MFS 431). Popular and folk music by Maria Buchino accompanied by instrumental ensemble. Texts with English paraphrases.

Mexico y su Folklore (Mercury SR 90522). Music performed by a number of Mexican ensembles. Spanish and English notes.

The Real Mexico in Music and Song (Nonesuch H-72009). A varied collection of Mexican Indian folk songs. English texts included; good notes.

Songs of Old Mexico, edited by Lillian Mendelssohn (Folkways FTS 31304). Songs with guitar accompaniment; English translations of first verse of each song are included.

The Texas-Mexican Conjunto by Manuel Pena (Folklyric 9049). Companion to book (published by Univ. of Texas Press) by same name about the musicians, music and social setting of the *conjunto,* a popular contemporary style.

Traditional Songs of Mexico (Folkways 8769). Useful songs for classroom.

II. THE PUERTO RICAN MUSICAL HERITAGE

When Puerto Rico was discovered by Columbus in 1493, the island was inhabited by the Borinquen, or Arawak, Indians. Historians have chronicled the musical instruments, singing and dancing of the native Indians and concluded they made especial use of rattles and log drums. Fewkes (1970:210) describes both the early music of the West Indian islanders and the Puerto Ricans in the following observations. The West Indian islanders accompanied their rhythmic *areitos*, or dances, with instruments, among which were bells, tinklers, rattles, and drums. They had a hollow calabash with notches cut on the exterior, which, when scraped with a stick or stone, emitted a rasping, rhythmic sound for the step of the dance. A similar instrument was used by street musicians in Puerto Rico. The native drum was most likely made of a hollow log of wood.

The Puerto Rican Indians were practically extinct by the mid-1500s and seemingly no influence of their music has remained on the island. Since Puerto Rico remained under Spanish rule for nearly four centuries, the music retains a close affinity with the Spanish heritage, while at the same time there is a strong black tradition in certain distinct musical forms. The first African slaves arrived on the island in 1502 and brought with them rhythms, singing, and dancing styles that were different from those of both the Spaniards and the Indians. Black rhythms are found in *plena* (*play*-nah) and *bomba* (*bohm*-bah), accented by the African-like use of drums and polyrhythms. Call-and-response patterns of singing with a shouting vocal effect are other black traditions. In the Christmas *aguinaldos* (ah-gwin-*ahl*-dohs), the harmonies, melodies, and rhythms of Spain are evident along with the use of the guitar.

Plenas, bombas, and aguinaldos are very representative music of the island and are heard nearly everywhere. Many of the folk songs are reminiscent of the Puerto Rican manner of speech, which tends to be very rapid and spoken in a Spanish dialect that sounds different from Mexican speech. Much of the music shows an acculturation of elements from other Caribbean islands, particularly Cuba, along with strong jazz influences from the United

States. This is particularly true in contemporary versions of the traditional forms. Overall, Puerto Rican music (both traditional and contemporary) has a distinctly Latin American sound.

Lesson One: Orienting the Listener to Three Puerto Rican Folk Music Forms

Purpose of Activities: Listening to discern certain Hispanic and African influences in Puerto Rican music.

Clues for Listening

Procedure:

1. Find Puerto Rico on a map so that the class can see its location in relation to mainland United States.

2. Show film: *Puerto Rico: Its Past, Present and Promise.*

3. Play a prepared tape (or use recordings) of aguinaldos, plenas, and bombas, each example approximately two minutes long. A sample tape could include examples such as the following:

   a. "Aguinaldo Cagueño" (Album: *Songs and Dances of Puerto Rico*). A joyfully sung aguinaldo rhythmically accompanied by guitars and maracas.

   b. "Plena" (Album: *Folk Songs of Puerto Rico*). Sung in call-and-response pattern with distinctive rhythms. Male singers accompanied by guitar.

   c. "Bomba Rhythms" (Album: *Folk Songs of Puerto Rico*). Two drums provide very exciting African-sounding rhythms.

   d. "Bomba Music by the Parilla Family" (Album: *Folk Songs of Puerto Rico*). Enthusiastic singers and African-sounding drumming.

   e. "Christmas Carol" (an aguinaldo). Two women sing accompanied by neighborhood children using ordinary objects as musical instruments.

   f. "La Plena Viene de Cidra" (Album: *Folk Songs of Puerto Rico*). Male singers accompanied by guitar.

4. Have the class number from one to six on a sheet of paper and

write "Spanish" or "African" as each example sounds to them. (The bomba music will be decidedly African in sound while the plenas and aguinaldos sound Spanish.)

5. Briefly explain to the class the basis of the Hispanic and African influences on Puerto Rican music.

6. Teach the class "Fresh Fish Today" (page 80 in *Echoes of Africa in Folk Songs of the Americas*), "San Severino" (page 25 in *Latin American Folk Songs*) and "The Pearl" (page 132 in *Folk Songs of the Caribbean*).

Lesson Two: Learning About Aguinaldo, A Type of Folk Song

The aguinaldo is a Puerto Rican song form of Spanish origin considered very folk (or country) and much loved by the Puerto Rican people. Many aguinaldos follow the conventional refrain-stanza-refrain pattern. Some are in the form of the *decima* (*day*-see-mah), an eight-syllable ten-line stanza of Spanish origin. Aguinaldos have simple melodic structures and are frequently accompanied by drums, guitars, and maracas.

The equivalent of Christmas carols, aguinaldos are sung and played during the holiday season, especially during the time of the Three Kings just before Christmas day. At this time, local musicians go from house to house singing aguinaldos until they are invited in for refreshments. They then sometimes invite members of each house they visit to go with them and by the time they arrive at the last house the entire group is in a decidedly holiday mood and having a grand time.

The music of the aguinaldo is melodically Spanish. The use of the Spanish language further solidifies the Spanish heritage as does the decima structure and certain rhythmic characteristics.

Classroom Strategies and Experiences:
Developing Aural Acuity by Performing and Listening

Purpose of Activities: To become aware of the aguinaldo as one variety of Puerto Rican folk song that reflects the Spanish heritage.

Procedure:

1. Show film: *Puerto Rico and the Virgin Islands.*

2. Recording: "De las Montañas Venimos" ("We Come from the Mountains") (Album: *Songs and Dances of Puerto Rico,* Side 1, Band 1). This lively aguinaldo follows the refrain-stanza-refrain pattern common to this song form. The words are about abundant food and Christmas presents. The singers are accompanied by guitar, drums, and maracas.
   • Have the class do the following: Analyze the song in ABA pattern. (Note that in this song the refrain is in a minor key, the stanzas are major.)
   • Duplicate drum and maraca rhythms.
   • Listen for Spanish-sounding melody; the harmonies in thirds (common in Spain) are heard.

3. Recording: "Aguinaldo Cagueño" (Album: *Songs and Dances of Puerto Rico,* Side 2, Band 2). A male singer with a very high voice sings this joyful aguinaldo accompanied by a guitar and maracas. The song is in the form of a decima.
   • Have the class clap the basic meter while listening to the recording.
   • Listen for singers' use of "lah-lo-lah" as a fill-in while he thinks of another verse. (Raise hands when this is heard.)
   • Listen for spoken comments during instrumental passages.

4. Recording: "Three Aguinaldos" (Album: *Folk Music of Puerto Rico,* Side A, Band 1). These songs are typical of those sung by strolling musicians who occasionally wear costumes during the holiday season.
   • Have the class clap the basic meter of the infectious guitar rhythms as they listen.

5. Recording: "Aguinaldo Tradicional" (Album: *La Tuna (Estudiantina) De Cayey,* Side B, Band 4). This is a modern aguinaldo as heard in the overall sophistication of the arrangement. A vocal ensemble is accompanied by guitars.
   • Compare this selection with the more traditional aguinaldos. List similarities and differences heard.

6. Teach the class aguinaldos such as "Come Shepherds" ("Venid Pastores") (found in *Puerto Rican Folk Songs* by Ruth Allen Fouche) and "We Come from the Mountains" (p. 78 in *Echoes of Africa in Folk Songs of the Americas*). Use maracas and softly played drum for accompaniment; add guitar if available.

Lesson Three: Finding Out About Bomba, A Singing, Drumming, Dancing Expression

The music of the bomba is of strong African influence. It is still played in Loiza Aldea, the only all-black town in Puerto Rico. When the slaves came to the island they brought the first skinhead drums, called "bombas" (sometimes "bombos") with them. They also introduced the call-and-response style of singing along with distinctly different rhythms.

Among the blacks, bomba played an important part; it could be used as a type of social objective. Members of the community could be praised or censured within the structure of bomba. Usually there is the rhythm of two drums: a lead drummer who improvises and an accompanying drummer. Rattles are also used. Singing, enthusiastic and rhythmic, is call-and-response while a solo dancer sometimes performs until exhausted.

Classroom Strategies and Experiences:
Recognizing African Characteristics in Bomba Music

Purpose of Activities: To identify the African influence in the music of bomba.

Procedure:

1. Show film: *Puerto Rico, Showcase of America.*

2. Find Loiza Aldea on a map of Puerto Rico.

3. Recording: "Bomba Rhythms" (Album: *Folk Songs of Puerto Rico,* Side 2, Band 1). On this recording we hear two locally made wooden drums.
   • First, play at least one recording of African drumming and singing. Next, play "Bomba Rhythms" and encourage class to point out the similarities they hear.

4. Recording: "Bomba" (Album: *Bomba! Monitor Presents Music of the Caribbean,* Side 2, Band 1). The words of this bomba are in Spanish, but many bomba words sound like African dialect.
- Have the class analyze the record in ABA pattern indicating where drum rhythms change.
- Challenge the class to improvise a bomba rhythm; select a lead drummer and an accompanying drummer. When performers are satisfied with their sounds, add maracas, claves, and handclapping.

Lesson Four: Investigating Plena, Puerto Rico's Favorite Folk Music

The *plena,* of Puerto Rican origin, is a topical ballad about real-life events. "The vocal part of the *plena* consists of a four-line verse answered by a chorus, usually for two voices singing in parallel thirds, sixths, or unison with occasional octaves . . . the lyrics tend to contain social comment or (often sharp) comment on girls and other subjects of general appeal" (Roberts 1972:102). Plenas are even sung in political elections, at which time the wittiest lyrics and catchiest music give a politician or party a distinct advantage.

As in the Trinidad calypso, the words focus on real people and happenings and challenge the singers to create skillful verses. The uninhibited way in which the leader shouts out the words of a song is characteristic of the plena, which means "full." The rhythms are steady and uncomplicated which allows for improvisations and syncopated accents by the instruments. The plena is a dance for couples and is the most popular folk music on the island.

Classroom Strategies and Experiences: Discovering the Sounds That Make the Plena Unique

Purpose of Activities: To recognize those musical characteristics that make the plena a unique dance song.

Procedure:

1. Show film: *Manuel from Puerto Rico.*

2. Recording: "Santa Maria" (Album: *Bomba! Monitor Presents Music of the Caribbean*, Side 1, Band 1). This plena is a plea to the Virgin Mary for protection from natural disasters such as hurricanes, which occur seasonally in the Caribbean. The rhythm is lively and quite danceable.

- Instruct the class to listen for the following characteristics of the plena: The abandon with which the leader sings his verses and comments (in Calypso-like fashion) during the instrumental interludes.
- Syncopated, off-beat accents of the *pandereta*, a small tambourine-type drum.
- Improvisation of the *sinfonia*, a small accordion-type instrument.
- Call-and-response manner of singing; harmonies in thirds and sixths.
- The upbeat character of the music even though the words have serious intent, which is typical of the plena.
- Use a tambourine and small drum to play along with the recording; let others clap softly the following rhythmic pattern characteristic of plena:

3. Recording: "Plena" (Album: *Folk Songs of Puerto Rico*, Side 1, Band 4). This song is about a fighting cock. (Cock fights are popular in Puerto Rico.)

- Call attention to the high voices of the two singers. (Male singers with high voices are prized in Puerto Rico.)
- Have the class analyze the song in ABA pattern.
- Use tambourine and handclapping to capture the rhythm while listening.

4. Recording: "Candela es" (Album: *Folk Music of Puerto Rico*, Side B, Band 1). This lively plena is sung by a well-known soloist, called a *plenero* (play-*nay*-roh), accompanied by maracas, guitar, and sinfonia.

- Have the class analyze the recording using ABA pattern.
- Discover that the pronounced percussion effect heard during the last half of the recording is produced on the guitar.
- Let the class sing the refrain with the recording (text and translation are included in the album).
- In all plenas listen for a brief chorus sung repeatedly by a group in response to a soloist who sings the verses.
- Teach the class "Baquine" and "The Seven Daughters," two *plena* dances (pages 75 and 76 of *Echoes of Africa in Folk Songs of the Americas*).

  The following recordings in sections 5 through 9 are examples of modern plenas. This style of plena became popular after World War II and has remained a favorite on the island ever since.

5. Recording: "Plena Navidena" (Album: *La Tuna (Estudiantina) De Cayey,* Side A, Band 4). Call-and-response between two groups of singers; vocal explosions. Song is about the good times of Christmas. Guitars, maracas and modern band instruments improvise.

6. Recording: "A La Plena" (Album: *La Plena y El Bolero de Puerto Rico,* Side A, Band 1). Modern band, playing in sophisticated, contemporary style. Frequent instrumental interludes. How many?

7. Recording: "Plena en Ponce" (Album: *La Plena y El Bolero de Puerto Rico,* Side A, Band 3). Modern dance band; chorus answers leader in accented, repeated phrases.

8. Recording: "El Club de las Cuatro Patas" (Album: *La Plena y El Bolero de Puerto Rico,* Side A, Band 5). Sections of instruments engage in call-and-response; reminiscent of swing band style.

9. Recording: "Plena en San Juan" (Album: *La Plena y El Bolero de Puerto Rico,* Side B, Band 5). Bell sound provides heavy accents; vocal call-and-response. Modern Latin band sound.

- Listen for the following similarities and differences in traditional and modern plenas:

Traditional	*Modern*
1. Call-and-response singing; frequent repetition of chorus between verses.	1. Same; plus call-and-response between instruments playing in sections showing influence of American jazz. Longer instrumental interludes.
2. Free and uninhibited singing of soloists and vitality of chorus.	2. Same.
3. Folk instruments such as guitar, maracas, sinfonia.	3. Modern band instruments such as trumpets, saxophones and drum sets added.
4. Accented syncopated rhythms.	4. Same.
5. Overall lively, upbeat character of the music; distinctively Latin American sound.	5. A more contemporary, "sophisticated" Latin sound; still infectiously rhythmic.
6. Instrumental improvisation.	6. Same, with jazz influences.

Encourage the class to cite any other similarities and differences they hear in traditional and modern plenas.

• Suggest dancing of couples to the music of the contemporary plenas.

ADDITIONAL THINGS TO DO AND DISCUSS

Mexico and Puerto Rico were the topics of this chapter because of the large percentage of American citizens of such ancestry, but students could investigate the other Hispanic influences felt in this country. In 1917 Congress granted citizenship to the people of Puerto Rico. This meant they could travel freely to the United States without restrictions. Since then there has been a steady migration to the mainland (primarily to New York City), which peaks during periods of economic prosperity when workers are needed.

Most Puerto Ricans leave their island in the hope of finding better jobs and educational opportunities for themselves and their families. Many return home after saving enough to live better than before, but most of the migrants remain in the US. Today more than 1,500,000 Puerto Ricans live on mainland United States, the majority in New York City barrios where every tenth person in Manhattan is Puerto Rican. "El Barrio," or Spanish Harlem is the center of Puerto Rican culture in New York City. Here Spanish is spoken, there are Spanish language newspapers, grocery stores, shops, movie theaters, churches, cultural centers and dance halls, which are quite popular. In addition, there are increasingly large communities of Puerto Ricans in Florida, (joining with Cubans to form a tremendous Hispanic population in Miami), and in Hartford, Connecticut.

Many New York-based musicians and pop singers such as Tito Puente, Jose Feliciano and Tito Rodriguez, Argentine folk singer Suni Paz, and band leaders and members of musical groups including Hector Rivera, Victor Montañez and Israel Berrios present varied Puerto Rican (and Afro-Cuban) musical traditions. Some work with a blend of Latin sounds, including the exciting and popular *salsa*. A sampler of some of these top New York Latino musicians is the album, *Caliente=Hot (Puerto Rican and Cuban Musical Expression in NY)* (NW 244). The Puerto Rican teen poprock group Menudo is wildly popular. Listen to recordings by these and others and assign students to read about other musicians, artists, athletes, politicians etc., and report their findings to the class.

Play other examples of Puerto Rican music such as "Puerto Rico-Bacquine," a dance tune (found in *Music of the World's People*, Side 1 Band 37). Identify and duplicate the drumming patterns, which alternate between duple, triple, and quadruple meters.

Teach the class the Puerto Rican National Anthem, "La Borinqueña" (pg. 25 of *Favorite Spanish Folksongs*).

Have interested students do research on the relationship of Puerto Rico to the United States; occasionally there are timely newspaper articles.

Since the times require an approach to understanding the minorities in our midst different from the approaches used by other disciplines in areas such as sociology, psychology, or anthropology, we can do no better than turn to the humanities. The Puerto Ricans are a proud, sensitive people whose musical heritage provides a reliable insight to their nature.

SELECTED BIBLIOGRAPHY

Books

Alford, Harold J. *The Proud Peoples*. NY: David McCay Co., Inc., 1972. Documentation of the Hispanic presence in the United States, 1500 to present.

Behague, Gerard. "Latin American Folk Music" in *Folk and Traditional Music of the Western Continents*, 2nd ed. by Bruno Nettl. Englewood Cliffs, N.J.: Prentice-Hall, Inc., 1973. Contains information about Puerto Rican folk music.

Fewkes, Jesse Walter. *The Aborigines of Puerto Rico and Neighboring Islands*. NY: Johnson Reprint Corp., 1970. Originally published in 1907 by the Government Printing Office. Early documentation of the history of the island.

Landeck, Beatrice. *Echoes of Africa in Folk Songs of the Americas*, 2nd revised edition. NY: David McKay Co., Inc., 1969. Section on Puerto Rico has notes about the music of the island, songs, and suggestions for instrumental accompaniments.

Mendez, Eugenio Fernandez, ed. *Portrait of a Society: Readings On Puerto Rican Sociology*. Univ. of Puerto Rico Press, 1972. A collection of readings that give a comprehensive overview of Puerto Rican society, life, and culture.

The Music of Puerto Rico: A Classroom Music Handbook. Developed by Lloyd Schmidt, Leonor Toro, and Alejandro Jimenez. Hartford: CT State Dept. of Education. Obtain copies from: Ethnic/Arts Migrant Project, Hamden-New Haven Co-op. Education Center, 1450 Whitney Ave., Hamden, CT 06517. Very handy. Includes history, good section on musical styles and dances, composers, instruments, a few songs.

Roberts, John Storm. *Black Music of Two Worlds*. NY: Original Music, n.d. and Folkways LP(FE4602-3 records). Chapt. 5 "The Caribbean," has information about Puerto Rican music.

_____.*The Latin Tinge*. NY:Original Music, nd. Excellent history of the profound influence of Latin music in the US.

Wagenheim, Kal. *Puerto Rico: A Profile*. NY: Praeger, 1970. Overview of the people, their culture, and history.

Booklet

Fouché, Ruth Allen. *Canciones Puertorriqueños*. 1967. Unfortunately no other publication data is available, but it is worth seeking in libraries, bookstores, etc. Contains songs, pictures of musical instruments, and informative notes about Puerto Rican music.

Song Collections

Favorite Spanish Folksongs (Traditional songs from Spain and Latin America), compiled and edited by Elena Paz. NY:Oak Publications, 1965. Two Puerto Rican songs, including "La Borinqueña," the National Anthem, are in this collection.

Folk Songs of the Caribbean, collected by Jim Morse. NY: Bantam Books, 1958. Some information about Puerto Rican music; one very melodic song, "The Pearl," on page 132.

The Griot Sings: Songs from the Black World, collected and adapted by Edna Smith Edet. NY: Medgar Evers College Press, 1978. (Available from Folkways.)Wonderful collection of game and story songs including 7 from Puerto Rico.

Para Chiquitines, compiled by Emma Jimenez and Conchita Puncel. Glendale, CA: Bowmar Publishing Corp., 1969. Songs, poems and fingerplays in Spanish; glossary of phrases and directions in English and Spanish. For all ages.

AUDIO-VISUAL MATERIALS
Films

Manuel from Puerto Rico. B&W, 14 min., Encyclopedia Britannica. Shows difficulties of adjustment for a New York-born child of Puerto Rican parents.Increases understanding of problems.

Puerto Rico and the Virgin Islands. B&W, 11 min., Coronet Films. Shows Puerto Rico's strategic location and imp. landmarks.

Puerto Rico: Its Past, Present, and Promise. Color, 20 min.,Encyclopedia Britannica. Places the island in perspective as an important part of the US, explains its government and value Puerto Ricans still place on their Spanish cultural heritage.

Puerto Rico, Showcase of America. Color, 18 min., Leonard Peck Prod. Focuses on development of industry on the island.

Recordings

Caliente=Hot: Puerto Rican and Cuban Musical Expression in New York (New World Records, NW244). Produced by Rene Lopez. Exc. collection, complete notes, five groups.

Canciones Para el Recreo, sung by Suni Paz (Folkways FC 7850). Paz is an Argentinian musician living in NY. Songs in Spanish including several from Puerto Rico. Some English words. Booklet includes translations, notes on instruments.

Folk Music of Puerto Rico, ed. by Richard A. Waterman (Archive of Folk Culture, Library of Congress, AFS L18). Excellent notes; fine selection of traditional music.

Folk Songs of Puerto Rico (Asch Records, No. AHM 4412). Recorded by Henrietta Yurchenko. Interesting variety. Includes notes, texts, translations.

La Plena y El Bolero de Puerto Rico (Carino Records DBMI-5807). The music of Cesar Concepcion's Band, an island favorite for many years. Contemporary sound.

Latin American Children's Game Songs (Asch Records, No. AHS 751). Charming collection of Mexican and Puerto Rican songs, among others. Descriptions of the games, notes, texts, and translations.

La Tuna (Estudiantina) De Cayey (Hit Parade HPKL 065). Contemporary Puerto Rican music.

Music of Latin America (MENC Sounds of the World Vol.2).Set. Three tapes on the music of Mexico, Ecuador, Brazil; teachers guide by Dale Olsen, Daniel Sheehy, Charles Perrone.

Nuestra Musica by El Gran Combo (Combo RCSLP 2045). Includes plena, bomba, jibaro styles and rhythms. Modern.

Puli Toro Sings Favorite Hispanic Songs ("Alma Hispana") (Folkways FW-8730). Fine collection, good variety.

Return on Wings of Pleasure, Pedro Padilla y Su Conjunto (Round5003). Interesting selections; students enjoy these.

Songs and Dances of Puerto Rico (Folkways FW 8802) Interesting variety of "musica tipica" (folk music). Notes, texts, and translations are included.

Appendix

SELECTED LIST OF ADDITIONAL BOOKS

Anderson, William M. *Teaching Asian Musics in Elementary and Secondary Schools.* MI: The Leland Press, 1975 (Distributed only by World Music Press). An introduction to the musics of India and Indonesia. Companion tape. Cultural, historic background, musical examples of vocal and instrumental music, adapting classroom instruments to make a gamelan.

Buchner, Alexander. *Folk Music Instruments.* NY: Crown Publishers, Inc., 1972. Large photographs of instruments of many countries are accompanied by an informative text.

Danielou, Alain. *The Ragas of Northern Indian Music.* London: Barrie and Rockliff, the Cresset Press, 1968. A comprehensive treatment of North Indian music; many illustrations.

Films for Anthropological Teaching, 5th. ed. Washington: American Anthropological Assoc., 1972. A catalog of annotated films, some of which are valuable for their musical emphasis.

Haywood, Charles. *A Bibliography of North American Folklore and Folksong,* 2nd revised ed. NY: Dover Publications, 1951, 1961. (Two volumes.) Vol. II concerns the American Indians North of Mexico, including the Eskimos. Very comprehensive.

Hood, Mantle. *The Ethnomusicologist.* New ed. Kent, OH: The Kent State Univ. Press, 1982. If you are at all curious about the field of ethnomusicology, this book covers all aspects. Records are included.

_____. "Music, the Unknown" in Harrison, Hood, and Palisca, *Musicology.* Englewood Cliffs, NJ: Prentice-Hall, Inc., 1963. A provocative monograph that places the music of other cultures in proper perspective.

ISME Yearbook. Vol. X-1983: *Pop and Folk Music: Stock-taking of New Trends.* Jack Dobbs, Ed. Papers of the International Society for Music Education Seminar at Trento, Italy, July, 1982.

Kishibe, Shigeo. *The Traditional Music of Japan.* Tokyo: Japan Cultural Society, 1969. An informative history of Japanese music told in a concise form. Many excellent photographs, music examples.

Krishnaswami, S. *Musical Instruments of India.* New Delhi: Publications Division, Ministry of Information and Broadcasting, Government of India, 1963. Good survey with photographs of instruments used in both north and south India.

Malm, William P. *Japanese Music and Musical Instruments.* Rutland, VT: Charles E. Tuttle Co., 1959. Standard work. Comprehensive and exhaustive study of the history and development of the music and instruments.

_____. *Music Cultures of the Pacific, the Near East, and Asia.* 2nd edition. Englewood Cliffs, NJ: Prentice-Hall, Inc., 1977. Survey.

May, Elizabeth, ed. *Musics of Many Cultures: An Introduction.* Berkeley: Univ. of CA Press, 1980. Beautifully produced book of 20 essays by 19 contributors, all authorities; numerous photos.

McAllester, David P. *Readings in Ethnomusicology.* NY: Johnson Reprint Corp., 1971. Carefully selected collection of scholarly monographs representative of the diversities in the field of ethnomusicology.

221

Merriam, Alan P. *The Anthropology of Music.* Evanston, IL:Northwestern Univ. Press, 1964. Emphasis is placed on music as part of culture with music-making a behavioral entity. Includes examples from diverse cultures.

Music in our Schools: A Search for Improvement. Washington, D.C.: U.S. Dept. of Health, Education and Welfare, 1964. The Report of the Yale Seminar on Music Education, this slender volume has had tremendous impact on trends in public school music in the U.S. All music teachers should read and re-read this.

Nettl, Bruno. *Folk and Traditional Music of the Western Continents. - 2nd. ed.* EnglewoodCliffs, N.J.:Prentice-Hall, Inc.,1973. Survey of music of the American continent, Europe and black Africa.

_____. *The Study of Ethnomusicology: Twenty-nine Issues and Concepts.* Urbana: Univ. of IL Press, 1983. Thorough discussion of current trends in the field of ethnomusicology.

The New Grove Dictionary of Music and Musicians. Ed. by Stanley Sadie. London: Macmillan Publishers Otd., 1980. A completely new edition which incorporates extensive coverage of non-Western musics.

The New Harvard Dictionary of Music. Ed. by Don Michael Randel. Cambridge, MA: The Belknap Press of Harvard Univ. Press, 1986. An entirely new edition of the one-volume classic; incorporates wide coverage of musics of other cultures.

Pantaleoni, Hewitt. *On the Nature of Music.* Oneonta, NY: Welkin Books, 1985. A wide-ranging look at music—eastern, western and in-between.

Reck, David. *Music of the Whole Earth.* NY: Charles Scribner's Songs, 1977. A refreshingly different view of the phenomena of music-making worldwide.

Sachs, Curt. *The History of Musical Instruments.* NY: W.W. Norton Co., 1940. One of the landmark books in music literature. Many photographs and drawings of instruments from all over the world; comprehensive.

Shankar, Ravi. *My Music, My Life.* NY: Simon and Schuster, 1968. A fascinating account of Indian music as told by a leading performer.

Shehan, Patricia and Karl Signell. *Sounds of the World - Southeast Asia.* Reston, VA: MENC, 1986. Twenty-page booklet for teachers with 3 cassette tapes on Lao, Hmong and Vietnamese music.

Southern, Eileen. *Biographical Dictionary of Afro-American and African Musicians.* Westport, CT: Greenwood Press, 1982. Useful identification of black musicians.

Thomas, Edith Lovell. *The Whole World Singing.* NY: Friendship Press, 1957. Collection of songs from around the world; good for classroom use.

Titon, Jeff Todd, Gen. ed. *Worlds of Music: An Introduction to the Music of the World's Peoples.* NY: Schirmer Books, 1984. An excellent introductory text; recording available.

Waring, Dennis. *Making Folk Instruments in Wood.* NY: Sterling Publishers, 1985. A guide to making very simple to very complex instruments of all sorts. Clear directions, excellent variety.

Wellesz, Egon, ed. Ancient and Oriental Music (New Oxford History of Music: Vol. I). London: Oxford Univ. Press, 1957. An excellent addition to a school library. Many music examples and photographs.

SELECTED LIST OF PERIODICALS

African Arts
African Studies Center
University of Calif.-Los Angeles
(Published quarterly; $22 per year)

African Music
Journal of the African Music Society
Publications Secretary
Internation Library of African Music
Rhodes University
Grahamstown 6140 South Africa

Asian Music
The Society for Asian Music
50 Washington Square South
New York, NY 10012

Billboard Magazine
One Astor Plaza
1515 Broadway
New York, NY 10036 (Pub. weekly)

The Black Perspective in Music
The Foundation for Research in the
    Afro-American Creative Arts, Inc.
P.O. Box 149
Cambria Heights
New York, NY 11411

Black Sounds
7715 Sunset Blvd., 2nd. Floor
Los Angeles, CA 90046 (quarterly)

BMI
The Many Worlds of Music
BMI Public Relations Dept.
40 W. 57th St.
New York, NY 10019

Chinese Music
Chinese Music Society of No. America
2329 Charmingfare,
Woodridge, IL 60517-2910

Downbeat
222 W. Adams St.
Chicago, ILL 60606 (biweekly)

Ethnomusicology
Published by the Society for Eth
            nomusicology, Inc.
University of Michigan
Ann Arbor, MI 48109

Fresh! (The Main Motion in Rock and Video)
Ashley Communications, Inc.
P.O. Box 91878
Los Angeles, CA 90009 (monthly)

Jazztimes
8055-13th St.
Silver Spring, MD 20910 (monthly)

Journal of the International Folk Music Council
Danish Folklore Archives
Birketinget 6, 2300 Copenhagen S
Denmark

Music Educators Journal
1902 Association Dr.
Reston, VA 22091
(69, May 1983-"Multicultural Imperative" Issue)(73, Nov. 1986-"Everyday Music in a Chinese Province")

Popular Music and Society
Editor, Sociology Dept.
Bowling Green State Univ.
Bowling Green, OH 43403(quarterly)

Rag Time Magazine   *Sing Out!*
The Maple Leaf Club   The Folk Song Magazine
5560 W. 62nd. St.   Box 1071
Los Angeles, CA 90056   Easton, PA 18042
"America's Only Ragtime Organiza-
   tion"

SELECTED LIST OF FILM DISTRIBUTORS

Academy Films   Columbia Broadcasting System
748 N. Seward St.   383 Madison Ave.
Hollywood, CA 90038   New York, NY 10017

Harold C. Ambrosch Productions   Communications Group West
Box 3   6430 Sunset Blvd. 605
Rancho Mirage, CA 92270   Hollywood, CA 90028

American Telephone and Telegraph Contemporary Films, Inc.
Information Dept.   267 West 25th St.
195 Broadway   New York, NY 10001
New York, NY 10007
                                 Coronet Instructional Media
Association Films   65 East South Water St.
600 Madison Ave.   Chicago, ILL 60601
New York, NY 10022
                                 Dance Films, Inc.
Avalon Daggett Productions   130 West 57th St.
P.O. Box 14656   New York, NY 10019
Baton Rouge, LA
                                 Encyclopedia Britannica Ed. Corp.
BFA Educational Media   425 N. Michigan Ave.
2211 Michigan Ave.   Chicago, ILL 60611
Santa Monica, CA 90404
                                 Filmfair Communications
Brandon Films, Inc.   10900 Ventura Blvd.
200 West 57th St.   Studio City, CA 91604
New York, NY 10019
                                 Grove Press-Cinema 16 Film Library
Carousel Films, Inc.   80 University Pl.
1501 Broadway   New York, NY 10003
New York, NY 10036
                                 King Screen Productions
CCM Films, Inc.   A Division of King Broadcasting Co.
866 Third Ave.   320 Aurora Ave. N.
New York, NY 10022   Seattle, WA 98109

Churchill Films   Learning Corp. of America
662 North Robertson Blvd.   711 Fifth Ave.
Los Angeles, CA 90069   New York, NY 10022

McGraw-Hill Textfilms
330 W. 42nd. St.
New York, NY 10036

McGraw-Hill University Films
1221 Ave. of the Americas
New York, NY 10020

National Film Board of Canada
1251 Ave. of the Americas
New York, NY 10020

National Science Foundation
1951 Constitution Ave. N.W.
Washington, D.C. 20550

Original Music
R.D.1 Box 190
Lasher Rd.
Tivoli, NY 12583 (Videocassettes)

Phoenix Films
743 Alexander Rd.
Princeton, NJ 08540

Radim Films
220 W. 42 St.
New York, NY 10036

Rounder Distribution
One Camp St.
Cambridge, MA 02140 (Videocassettes, recordings; books)

Schloat Productions
150 White Plains Rd.
Tarrytown, NY 10591

Time-Life Films, Inc.
16 MM Dept.
43 W. 16th St.
New York, NY 10011

University of Indiana
Audio- Visual Center
Bloomington, IN 47401

The University of Washington Press
Seattle, WA 98105

SELECTED LIST OF RECORD MANUFACTURERS

Atlantic Recording Corp.
1841 Broadway
New York, NY 10023

AVCO Records Corp.
1301 Ave. of the Americas
New York, NY 10019

Brunswick Record Corp
888 Seventh Ave.
New York, NY 10019
(Owns BRC, Brunswick, Dakar)

Budda-Kama Sutra Records, Inc.
810 Seventh Ave.
New York, NY 10019

Canyon Records
(Native American)
4143 North 16th St.
Phoenix, AZ 85016

Capitol Records, Inc.
1750 N. Vine St.
Hollywood, CA 90028

Caytronics Corp. (The Latin Music
Co.)
240 Madison Ave.
New York, NY 10016
(Owns Caytronics, Caliente, Arcano,
Carino, etc.)

CBS Records (and CBS Int'l)
51 W. 52nd St.
New York, NY 10019

Chess/Janus Records
1301 Ave. of the Americas
New York, NY 10019

Elektra Records Co.
15 Columbus Circle
New York, NY 10023

Everest Record Group
10920 Wilshire Blvd.
Los Angeles, CA 90024
(Owns Archive of Folk and Jazz
Music, Archive of Gospel Music etc.)

Famous Music Corp
1 Gulf & Western Plaza
New York, NY 10023
(Owns Paramount, Dot, Blue Thumb)

Fania Records
888 Seventh Ave.
New York, NY 10019
(Owns Vaya-Cotique, Inc-International-Exitos, etc.)

Fantasy Records
10 and Parker Streets
Berkeley, CA 94710

Flying Dutchman Productions
1841 Broadway
New York, NY 10023

Folkways Records
632 Broadway
New York, NY 10012

Indian House Records
(Native American)
Box 472
Taos, NM 87571

International Record Industries, Inc.
PO Box 593
Radio City Station
New York, NY 10019
(Owns Baerenreiter UNESCO
Collection, Ocora, Tikva, Afrotone)

Jazz Composer's Orchestra Assn. Inc.
(JCOA)
6 W. 95th St.
New York, NY 10025

Jazzology-GHB Records
2001 Suttle Ave.
Charlotte, NY 28208

Karma, Inc. 2639 Walnut Hill Lane
Dallas, TX 75229

Light Records
Division of Lexicon Music, Inc.
Waco, TX

Lyrichord Discs, Inc.
141 Perry St.
New York, NY 10014

MCA Records Inc.
100 Universal City Plaza
Universal City, CA 91608
(Owns MCA, Decca, etc.)

Met Richmond Latin Record Sales Inc.
1637 Utica Ave.
Brooklyn, NY 11234

Metromedia Records Inc.
1700 Broadway
New York, NY 10019

MGM Records Inc.
7165 Sunset Blvd.
Los Angeles, CA 90046
(Owns MGM Verve, etc.)

Motown Record Corp.
6464 Sunset Blvd.
Hollywood, CA 90028
(Owns Motown, Rare Earth, Soul,
Tamla, etc.)

Music of the World
PO Box 258
Brooklyn, NY 11209

New World Records
(Recorded Anthology of American
Music, Inc.)
3 East 54 St.
New York, NY 10022

Nonesuch Records
1855 Broadway
New York, NY 10023

Onyx International Records
365 Great Circle Rd.
Nashville, TN 37228

Ovation Records
1249 Waukegan Rd.
Glenview, ILL 60025
(Owns Black Jazz, Ovation)

Pan American Records Inc.
3751 W. 26
Chicago, ILL 60623

Phonogram, Inc.
1 IBM Plaza
Chicago, ILL 60611
(Owns Mercury, Philips, etc.)

Polydor, Inc.
1700 Broadway
New Ylork, NY 10019
(Owns Polydor, Archive, Deutsche
Gramophon, etc.)

RCA Records
1133 Avenue of the Americas
New York, NY 10036
(Owns Victor, Red Seal, Camden,)

Record Club of America
Box 517
Manchester, PA 17345

Request Records
66 Memorial Highway
New Rochelle, NY 10801
(Specializing in international titles)

Roulette Records Inc.
17 W. 60 St.
New York, NY 10023
(Owns Roulette, Tico, Alegre, etc.)

Rounder Records
One Camp St.
Cambridge MA 02140

Scholastic Audio-Visual
50 W. 44 St.
New York, NY 10036

Shanachie
Dalebrook Park
Ho-Ho-Kus, NJ 07423

Sleeping Bag Records
1974 Broadway
New York, NY 10023

Stax Records Inc.
98 N. Avalon Ave.
Memphis, TN 38104

Tara International, Inc.
1370 Avenue of the Americas
New York, NY 10019
(Owns Mega Records, Metromedia)

Creed Taylor Inc.
1 Rockefeller Plaza
New York, NY 10020
(Owns CTI, Kudu, Salvation)

United Artists Records, Inc.
6920 Sunset Blvd.
Los Angeles, CA 90028
(Owns United Artists, Blue Note, UA
Latino, etc.)

Vanguard Recording Society, Inc.
71 W. 23 St.
New York, NY 10010
(Owns Vanguard, Bach Guild, etc.)

Vox Productions, Inc.
211 E. 43 St.
New York, NY 10017
(Owns Vox, Candide, Musical
Traditions of the World, Turnabout)

Warner Brothers Records, Inc.
4000 Warner Blvd.
Burbank, CA 91505
(Owns Warner Bros., Reprise, etc.)

ADDITIONAL RESOURCES

Airlines

American Folklife Center, Alan Jabbour, Head
Library of Congress
Washington, DC 20540

Anthology Record and Tape Company
135 West 41st Street
New York, NY 10036
(Distributor of Oriental and African recordings)

Archive of Folk Culture
Joseph Hickerson, Head
Library of Congress
Washington, DC 20540

(Send for: *A Brief List of 16mm Sound Motion Picture Films on Folk Music and Folk Dance with Rental Distributors* and Catalog of Folk Recordings selected from the Archive of Folk Song.)The Archive will also send, on request, selected bibliographies in special areas such as Jewish Music, Latin American Music, etc.

Arhoolie Records
10341 San Pablo Ave.
El Cerrito, CA 94530
(Distributor of blues classics, ethnic, folkloric and old timey)

Asch Mankind Record Series
632 Broadway
New York, NY 10012

Audio Research Services, Inc.
739 Boylston St.
Boston, MA 02116
(Stocks Barenreiter, UNESCO and similar labels.)

Chambers of Commerce
Consulates

Embassies

Ethnoproductions
Dept. of Music
Univ. of Calif.
Los Angeles, CA 90024 (Excellent recordings with comprehensive notes; send for catalog)

Films on Traditional Music and Dance: A First International Catalogue. Paris: UNESCO, 1970. Compiled by the International Folk Music Council, London. Edited by Peter Kennedy.

Global Perspectives in Education
45 John St. Suite 1200
New York, NY 10038
(Many publications on implementing multicultural programs of all sorts; book reviews; information about workshops; curriculum development; resource lists)

Modern Talking Picture Service, Inc.
2323 New Hyde Park Rd.
new Hyde Park, NY 11040 (Free loan films; send for catalog)

Schwann record catalogue; International Folk and Pop Music editions

The Society for Asian Music
112 East 64th St.
New York, NY 10021 (Publishes *Asian Music*)

The World Music Institute
155 West 72 St. Suite 706
New York, NY 10023
(Sponsors ethnic music Festivals, concerts by international musicians; mail order service for booklets and recordings of the music of Africa, Asia, the Middle East, Europe and the Americas; nonprofit organization with memberships)

Index

Acculturation, 146, 153, 157, 185, 195, 208
Acoma, 130, 133
Adderley, Julian "Cannonball," 94
Aerophone, 42, 43, 45, 54
Aesthetic, 17, 19, 22, 35, 36, 83, 88, 111
African Dances and Games, 72
Afro-soul, 44, 61, 62
Agbe, 51
Aguinaldo, 208, 209, 210, 211, 212
Alabanza, 195, 196
Aleichem, Sholom, 154
Alghaita, 44, 55, 56, 57
American Indian Music for the Classroom, 137
American Indian Sings, The, 121, 130
Ancient music, 144
Apache, 131, 133
Apache fiddle, 122, 124, 131, 133
Arabic lute, 151 (*see also: Ud*)
Arabic music, 145
Arapaho, 128
Arawak Indians, 208 (*see also:* Borinquen Indians)
Areitos, 208
Armstrong, Louis, 78, 90, 96, 97
Arts and Crafts of Hawaii, 173
Ashantihene, 46
Ashkenazic, 147, 149, 154, 156, 158
Aston, Peter, 22
A Treasury of Jewish Folksong, 155
Atumpan, 44, 46, 48
Aztec, 192, 193, 194

Babylonia, 145
Ballard, Louis, 121, 122, 123, 137
Balona, 197 (*see also: Valona*)
Barnes, Nellie, 121
Basie, Count, 78, 88, 91, 92, 98
Bata batteries, 46, 49
Bear Dance, 123
Beatles, The, 104
Bebey, Francis, 63
Bebop, 92, 93, 110, 111
Behague, Gerard, 197
Beiderbecke, Bix, 97
Bella Coola, 134
Bells, 40, 41, 42, 50, 55, 60, 61, 65, 193, 208
Bennett, Lerone, 77
Berger, Henry, 178

Berk, Fred, 158
Bible, The, 144
Black church music, 105, 106
Blessingway, 131
Blue notes, 87, 88, 90, 101
Blues, 77, 79, 87, 88, 89, 91, 95, 104, 111
characteristics of, 87
Blum, Odette, 72
Bogongo, 59
Bomba, 208, 209, 210, 212, 213
Boogie-woogie, 93, 100, 102, 104, 110
Bop, 92, 93, 94, 99, 100
Borinquen Indians, 208 (*see also:* Arawak Indians)
Brown, James, 78, 79, 80
Brown, Ruth, 104
Buffalo Dance, 123, 128
Butler, Jerry, 80

Calabash, 44, 58, 208
Call-and-response, 41, 56, 60, 64, 83, 84, 89, 91, 97, 98, 208, 209, 212, 214, 215, 216
Calypso, 213
Cameroons, 62
Cancion, 195, 197, 199
Cantillation, 146, 147, 148, 149 (*see also:* Liturgical song *and* Chant)
Cantor, 147, 149
Cayuga, 125
Ceremonials, 122, 123, 125, 127, 128, 130, 131, 132, 134, 136, 138
Chant, 146, 147, 148, 149, 150 (*see also:* Liturgical song *and* Cantillation)
Charles, Ray, 89
Chase, Gilbert, 84, 91, 93
Cherokee, 120, 125
Cheyenne, 128
Chibudu, 52
Chickasaw, 125
Chi-Lites, 106
Chippewa, 128
Chock, Yona Nahenahe, 177
Choctaw, 125
Chopi, 51
Chordophone, 42, 43, 57
Cleveland, James, 106, 107
Coasters, The, 104
Coleman, Ornette, 94, 103
Coltrane, John, 94, 95, 102, 103, 111
Comanche, 128

231

If you have enjoyed *Teaching the Music of Six Different Cultures* you will enjoy our other in-depth yet accessible book-and-tape sets of music from around the world. Most take a long look at one culture in particular, include lots of photos, musical transcriptions, cultural background information and a companion tape of every song or piece included in the book. The companion tapes feature performances by musicians from the culture highlighted in almost all cases. All are appropriate for all grade levels and Introduction to World Music courses.

Silent Temples, Songful Hearts: Traditional Music of Cambodia by Sam-Ang Sam and Patricia Shehan Campbell (American Folklife Center Award Winner)

From Rice Paddies and Temple Yards: Traditional Music of Vietnam by Phong Nguyen and Patrician Shehan Campbell (American Folklife Center Award Winner)

Let Your Voice Be Heard! Songs from Ghana and Zimbabwe by Abraham Kobina Adzenyah, Dumisani Maraire and Judith Cook Tucker

La-Li-Luo Dance Songs of the Chuxiong Yi, Yunnan Province, China by Alan Thrasher (Not appropriate for the lower grades.)

Los Mariachis! An Introduction to the Mariachi Tradition of Mexico by Patricia Harpole and Mark Fogelquist (director of El Maricahi Uclatlan)

Songs and Stories from Uganda by Moses Serwadda, illustrated by Leo and Diane Dillon

Moving Within the Circle: Contemporary Native American Songs and Dances (Complete set includes book/audio tape/ color slides) by Bryan Burton

The Lion's Roar: Chinese Luogu Percussion Ensembles (Complete Set includes book, audio tape, color slides) by Han Kuo-Huang and Patricia Shehan Campbell

World Music: A Source Book for Teaching by Lynne Jessup (an annotated bibliography).
New titles always in preparation!
Send for our catalog or order from your favorite dealer.
World Music Press PO Box 2565 Danbury CT 06813-2565